THE FIRST HALF

THE FIRST HALF

Gabby Logan

PIATKUS

PIATKUS

First published in Great Britain in 2022 by Piatkus

1 3 5 7 9 10 8 6 4 2

A CIP catalogue record for this book
is available from the British Library.

ISBN 978-0-349-43307-3

Typeset in Bembo by M Rules
Printed and bound in Great Britain by
Clays Ltd, Elcograf S.p.A

Papers used by Piatkus are from well-managed forests
and other responsible sources.

www.littlebrown.co.uk

For Reuben and Lois

Contents

Introduction

When I was very little, I'd lie in bed at night and try to imagine what the edge of the universe looked like. My stomach knotted with anxiety as my eight-year-old brain tried to comprehend infinity, palms sweating as I willed myself to picture a final frontier, an ending to the universe.

It wasn't just the size of the universe and its infinity that troubled me; it was also how many of us there were on Earth. I wasn't bothered about overpopulation back then; rather, as a fairly normal, borderline narcissistic child, I wanted to know *Why do I matter? Why was I born?* I asked the best and the biggest questions because I had time to think and space in my head – no subject was off limits.

As I got older, I lost that time for pondering life's big questions. The ephemera of daily life – the career, the mortgage, the marriage, the family – is all materially cosy, but doesn't really lend itself to lying in bed for hours thinking about black holes and whether a star thousands of light years away has just died.

In my adult life, the closest thing I have experienced to a return to that childish freedom to think about anything I wanted happened in March 2020, when the world experienced a global pandemic and we were forced, as a planet, to reset.

It took me a couple of weeks to stop panicking that I would never work again before I decided to make the most of the downtime and enjoy the freedom it gave me.

Time was abundant, and so were my thoughts. For the first time, I had the chance to think about how the child who had obsessed over the concept of infinity had ended up as the adult version of me, a woman who dropped her physics GCSE at the first chance and now talked about sport on telly for a living.

There was no easy answer, no clear journey that had taken that young girl to the adult me, and it made me realise that it is the individual events in all our lives that can change their trajectories. All of us have decisions to make every day that can change the direction in which our lives are travelling; some are obviously ginormous, like whether to commit to a twenty-five-year mortgage. Others are more subtle, more *Sliding Doors*, but they are all turning points that can alter the course of our lives and take us to places we may not have expected.

I was curious about the level of consciousness we have when we are at a crossroads and there is a turning point being offered.

What, for example, was the reason I walked into a bar I had never been in before, against my gut instincts, at the request of a persuasive girlfriend at 2am? Within five minutes of arriving, I met the man who would become my husband (and still is). Turns out my gut was wrong; it did seem like my destiny was calling that night. But I had to be ready to love and to be loved, and I think the person I had been a year before might have missed that moment. What had life taught me that led me to be in that position that night?

When I sat down to write this book, I was really not keen on the idea of writing a biography that charted my life in a regular, linear fashion. Largely because I sincerely thought that nobody would be that interested in how well I did in my maths GCSE (C) or what my first dog was called (Sadie). But by gathering my turning points together, I found a way of telling the story of the events that have shaped me and brought me to where I am today – a story of family, love, loss, determination, career highs and lows, and the wonderful world of sport, which has always been at the centre of my life, even though its purpose for me wasn't always to be the best at something and win medals.

I am fully aware that, on the surface, 'sport' can be a turn-off for some. I remember a well-known TV presenter coming up to me at a drinks party in the late nineties, when my career was just starting, to tell me that she hated football. Like I was the sports gate keeper.

Football has had some terrible moments in recent history, and it can bring out the worst in people and society, but it can also be an incredibly powerful force in bringing challenging conversations to the front of the news agenda, as well as delivering moments of enormous national joy and coming together. But rest assured, this book is no more about football than the award-winning TV show *Ted Lasso* is.

And when I say sport, I don't mean the nuts and bolts of playing it. For me, it was always about community and self-expression. It just happened to be the 'thing' my family did; it could just as easily have been music or art or farming. The opportunities that came to me as a child were as a direct result of my dad's sporting success and hard work (he always said he wasn't the most talented player, just one of the hardest working). And the life lessons sport taught me were integral to who I later became.

A lot of this sounds quite deep, and that is not a quality that is associated with me very often, if ever. I promise that you will not get to the end of this book and find me telling you why we are all here. I have no idea. There are turning points in this book that are extraordinarily meaningful, but there is also a lot of nonsense and frivolity; like the time I tried to persuade my parents to let me move to Florida at nine years old so I could become a tennis player, or the time I accidentally became a Rose of Tralee, or how I almost became a Gladiator when I was eighteen.

So, if you have only seen me doing 'straight' sport, you might not necessarily recognise me at times over the next few hundred pages. To a certain extent, we all have a work face and a real-life face, and this book is about the real me.

My work face now is a lot older than the one that started in local radio in 1992, and the year this book is published will mark thirty years in the industry for me. Nobody is more surprised than me that I am still doing what I love; my first TV boss told me straight up that I'd be finished at twenty-eight years old on his channel. Thankfully, the half century, which I am fast approaching, is no longer a glass ceiling for women in the media to smash – but there is always work to be done.

Considering my age, you might think the title of this book is a bit optimistic. The Economic and Social Research Council suggest middle age is anything between thirty-eight and fifty-six years old. I know this because I started a podcast called *Midpoint* a couple of years ago, where I interview famous people who are in this demographic. Nobody likes being called middle-aged – it's historically synonymous with beige, elasticated waistbands and barge holidays in Norfolk (nothing wrong with Norfolk, by the way). I've had four relatives who lived to be one hundred years old, so if the (metaphorical) whistle has blown and I am trudging into the dressing room, consider this book as a half-time talk, covering what went wrong, what worked well and how I might change things in the second half.

1

One Monday in May

25 May 1992

I was asked to be a contestant on the very first series of the TV show *Gladiators*. I'm not showing off. Such an invitation might imply some sort of physical prowess, or suggest that I had seriously defined muscles. I had neither. Nutritionally, I was bankrupt, living on a low-cost diet of high-sugar cereals for breakfast and lunch, drinking Tia Maria-infused milk from a mug at night, along with a few scoops of coffee-flavoured Häagen-Dazs ice cream to wash it all down. I don't recall drinking water nor eating fresh vegetables for the best part of a year. It was a 'gap year' from formal education, but it was turning into a 'filling-out year' when it came to my phy-sique. I was nowhere near the shape of a human being who was about to trouble Jet on the Swingshot – not that anyone knew who Jet was yet. (If you are under the age of thirty, you still won't know who Jet is; in fact, you will probably be confused by quite a few of the cultural references in the early part of this book. Stay with me, though; you've invested in the book now.)

I'll concede I had once been an international rhythmic gymnast, which sounds more impressive than it is. I'd retired the previous summer because of sciatica. Sciatica turned out to be fairly useful fifteen years later, as by comparison it made childbirth seem quite doable, but as an eighteen-year-old, it was hideous. I struggled to walk in the morning and popped pills to get me through the day. The only way to deal with it was to stop doing the thing I loved: bending over backwards.

The *Gladiators* TV 'thing' had come out of the blue. I'd arrived home on a dark February afternoon from one of the four disappointing jobs I was working during my gap year, to find an answerphone message asking me to meet Nigel Lythgoe. Nigel, it transpired, was Head of Light Entertainment for London Weekend Television, and he wanted me to go to his offices at Gabriel's Wharf on the Southbank of the River Thames to discuss a new TV show he was producing. I liked answerphones; the red flashing light invariably indicated a message from my Nana Sheila wanting to know what I would like for Christmas (usually in June), but I always clung on to the possibility that the red light was a flashing beacon of good fortune and that I was about to hear life-changing news. It's sad that we don't have answerphones flashing when we arrive home now – I miss them. It was a symbol of patience, of a time when we had to wait for things, when we didn't expect everything to happen *right now*. On that dank day, the red light delivered: I got my life-changing call, and I duly booked myself in for a meeting with Nigel.

'The British Gymnastics Association have suggested you would be a good person to audition for my new Saturday night ITV show, *Gladiators*,' Nigel said charmingly, swivelling on his soft grey leather chair. I liked Nigel, with his open-neck silky blue shirt and his expensive blond wavy bouffant: there was a 1970s vibe about him – in a non-lascivious way. (Years later, we'd learn that TV in the 1970s was mainly fronted by people who *were* lascivious.) If Nigel Lythgoe is ringing a bell, you may have watched *Pop Idol* in the noughties, where Nigel was the other man on the panel along with Simon Cowell. After that, he conquered the USA with a dance show hosted by Cat Deeley. It's safe to say that Nigel knew his TV onions. On the other hand, I knew nothing about TV.

My reply should have been: '*Gladiators*? Well, I'm afraid you're barking up the wrong tree, Nigel. I am one of the bendy rhythmic gymnasts – more ballerina than body builder. I would not make a good Gladiator. Goodbye – and best of luck with the show and your fabulous hair.' Instead, I heard myself say: 'That sounds interesting, Nigel. Tell me more about the process of how you are selecting the Gladiators.' I puffed out my chest and flexed my tiny biceps, with all the audacity and energy of a desperate youth.

I wasn't desperate to be famous for fame's sake; I was looking for something exciting to do, to give my gap year purpose, and leave me with a good conversation piece for Freshers' Week. Some cash would be nice, too. I was nearing the end of the world's worst year out, flogging my dead-end jobs to pay my share of someone else's mortgage and achieving but a tiny fraction of the international travel I had mapped out twelve months earlier.

I was a long way from the girl who'd juggled four A levels with thirty-five hours a week of rhythmic gymnastics training, existing on mono diets of courgettes, oranges or cauliflower. I'd pick a food and then stick to it for weeks, eating very little else. I had willpower in those days, well that was my take on it, a medically trained person might say I was walking dangerously close to the edge of an eating disorder.

Recognising these physical limitations, I forced myself to the local council gym for a crash course in muscle building. Council gyms in the 1990s were a fitness pay-as-you-go offering: no tuition, no coaches, and no long-term commitment; you could give yourself a hernia for £1.75 a time. Cleaning the machinery was apparently optional, and most gyms smelled of stale male sweat, like the old blue gym mat you once dragged out into the hall for PE when you did it in your pants. Filming for this new ITV show *Gladiators* was due to begin at the National Indoor Arena in Birmingham in just a few weeks; the mother of all physical makeovers had begun. Progress was slow – there's a limit to how far being an autodidact can take one in the world of power lifting.

At the *Gladiators* audition, even though I lacked the strength needed to pull myself up a rope hanging from a large oak tree, the producers liked me enough – or they were desperate enough – to keep me involved. I might not have had the physical prowess to be given my own Lycra onesie costume and a name like 'Ice Queen' or 'Boudicca', but I was asked to appear on the show as a contestant. With hindsight, if I was anything to go by, it would seem the producers were aiming for the Gladiators to win all their battles against the public.

At this point, I was living with a twenty-eight-year-old Olympian who was going through a divorce. Although neither his age nor the divorce situation fill me with pride, the Olympian bit is quite impressive. When I arrived home from training at the gym that Monday evening, Gary, the Olympian, was in our tiny postage stamp of a garden, stoking up the £5.99 barbecue we'd bought at a petrol station. So small was this garden that Gary once used kitchen scissors to cut the grass. It was a bog-standard London two-up, two-down terrace house, split into flats. Gary had purchased the two-down part a few years before I came into his life and decorated it in chintzy material. Quite rightly, it was his pride and joy, closely followed by his black Golf convertible and his lemon-coloured cashmere Kenzo blazer.

The neighbours from the two-up were joining us for some burgers, because they didn't have a postage-stamp garden of their own to sit out in on this balmy bank holiday evening. It was Gary's idea that we should entertain, like a proper couple, but ours was a relationship that was destined to fail. (Not because I didn't like entertaining, although I have met a woman since who said that 'not hosting enough dinner parties' was number three on her husband's list of ten reasons why he was divorcing her. He actually wrote out a list! He also cited her inability to ski at number seven. You can read into that whatever you like: I read that he was an arse and she's well rid.)

The windows and patio doors of our flat were flung wide open, and it seemed that everyone on our street had had the same idea as us that evening, so the air was filled with the chatter of dozens more neighbours and their kids playing outside and the smells of their burning coals wafting in. The endorphins of my workout were flowing through my veins, Jazzy Jeff and the Fresh Prince's 'Summertime' was blasting out of the stereo, I was four months away from going to Durham University to read Law – tonight, my life didn't seem so bad after all.

I was about to turn on the shower when the telephone rang. We had two landlines, as was the norm in pre-mobile phone days, even in a miniscule flat like this. The kitchen was en suite to the bathroom; you could sit on the toilet and stir a pan of soup at the same time if your ladle was long enough. And yet we had two landlines – chatting was very important in the last century.

'Hello,' I answered the phone sweetly. Not the 'Hello?' we

utter now when the landline rings, the suspicious *'Who the hell is ringing me on my landline at this time of day?!'* – no matter what time of day it is. No, this was the friendly, hopeful 'hello' of the early nineties.

'Gabby.' It was my mum's voice. 'Daniel is dead.'

Daniel, my fifteen-year-old brother, was fit and healthy and gorgeous, six feet tall and full to the brim of life and love. We'd gone for a run together on Wimbledon Common a few weeks before; after the first kilometre, to highlight my lack of cardio fitness, he had run the remaining four kilometres mostly backwards. He didn't suffer from coughs or colds; he never had a day off school. He was a footballer of huge repute. He'd signed for Leeds United, who had just won the League, and he'd been scouted by Wales. He was due to start his pro-fessional footballing life in the middle of June. Those who knew about such things said he was destined for a great career.

My head was utterly scrambled. I couldn't hear what Mum was saying. She was sobbing too loudly – or maybe that was me.

My mind fumbled for an explanation. I pictured him in a car with some boys, one of them losing control. I could visualise the exact road in Leeds – next to Roundhay Park – where the terrible accident would have taken place. They were going too fast round a bend, it was a bank holiday Monday, the driver had only just passed his test. That's what young boys do, they make reckless decisions. But Daniel had never been in trouble: he was a sportsman, never hung with the wrong people, had never taken a drag on a cigarette, nor entertained those who did. Whose car was it? Why did he have to make this horrendous choice now, when his life was so incredible, with so many opportunities laid out before him? I wondered if he had died at the scene. Had he been cut from the wreckage?

The sound of my mum's voice interrupted my thoughts: 'He collapsed in the garden, playing football with Jordan and Daddy,' she told me.

There was no terrible accident.

He dropped down dead in his own garden.

I imagined an old man who had lived his wonderful life to the full, in his shed, smoking a pipe and sipping his tea, listening to the radio, having a rest before he did some pruning – and then the next thing the neighbours are banging on his door because they hadn't seen him for a couple of days. *That's* how people die in their garden.

'You don't die in the garden at fifteen years old when you are fit and well! What do you mean? How?'

And then she did her best to explain what she thought had happened. Mum and Dad were going out for dinner – they were always prolific socialisers, they loved going out for dinner. It's only in the last few years she has stopped sounding disappointed when she calls me at 7pm on a Saturday night and I am in the house, hunkering down in my pyjamas with the kids, getting ready to watch a movie.

Mum had made the boys lasagne and was clearing up while Dad, Daniel and my little brother Jordan, who was six years old, had a kickabout in the garden. Post-dinner sport and outdoor games were a consistent feature of our childhood. My sister and I were no longer living at home, but the tradition continued with our brothers. When we lived in Vancouver, Canada, our house had been opposite a running track, and after dinner we'd have full-blown races, complete with staggered starts and disqualifications if you left your lane.

Dad had kicked the ball a little too hard, Mum told me, and Daniel went over to the longer grass to fetch it. He bent as if to pick it up, then stumbled and fell over, face-down. Dad wandered over, expecting to be pranked, to see his beloved boy turn and laugh at him for being overly concerned.

They had a perfect relationship; I only truly understand how perfect now because I have a boy of the same age. You can love the bones of your fifteen-year-old boy, but don't expect to ever really understand their moods or why they go to bed as one person but rise for breakfast the next day as another. Not Daniel, though; he rode through his teenage years with charm, joy and humour.

It is easy to deify the dead, but I am only telling you what everyone who knew him would say. That bank holiday Monday, he and Dad had played eighteen holes of golf together in the morning, then watched more golf on TV in the afternoon. They adored each other's company.

But Daniel didn't turn when Dad approached him. So Dad rolled him over, and saw his eyes were vacant, his pulse gone, his body limp. Dad screamed for help.

Jordan, six-year-old Jordan, ran to the house, calling for Mum, who ran outside. Dad desperately told her to call an ambulance. She dialled 999, then she called our neighbour, too; he'd worked on oil rigs all his life and had advanced first aid. She wasn't panicking, because healthy fifteen-year-old boys don't die in their gardens playing football. It was heatstroke, she'd decided. Temperatures had been in the mid-twenties that day. He was dehydrated.

The neighbour, Maurice, appeared immediately, and he tried hard, he tried so hard to get Daniel's heart going again, to make him breathe. Then, after what seemed like ages to everyone, but probably wasn't more than fifteen minutes, the paramedics arrived.

Dad went in the ambulance with Daniel. Mum drove behind with Jordan. Dad was praying, willing Daniel to breathe. 'God, bring my son back to life. Open your eyes, son, say something to me. We need to play football again. We need to watch golf and go to matches. We have so much to do. You have so much to do.'

The ambulance went around a bend at speed, and one of Daniel's arms flew out and landed in our father's lap. Dad took his hand and caressed it, held it tightly to his face. The hand was lifeless. He said later that was the moment he knew.

The professionals rushed Daniel into theatre and Dad hoped for a miracle outside. The family waiting for news was swelling in numbers; Mum had rung her sister and our grandma to come down to the hospital, bringing other family members with them. Daniel had heatstroke, she told them from her car phone as she followed the ambulance through the streets of Leeds.

I was 200 miles away in Southfields, London, finishing my gym session, totally oblivious to the mayhem and tragedy that was unfolding for my family.

There was a familiar face waiting for them when they arrived at St James's Hospital: Dr Adams was on duty. He had been the doctor for Leeds United when my dad was playing there in the 1970s. He was the doctor who had delivered me into the world at my parents' first home on 24 April 1973.

Dr Adams came out of theatre after thirty minutes of trying to bring Daniel back to life.

'I am so sorry,' he said.

Once those words are uttered, does anyone hear or remember what comes next?

My parents went in to see Daniel, to kiss him and tell him over and over that they loved him. There was a tiny drop of blood on his face; his torso had been cut in an attempt to get his heart going, and the blood had flicked off the scalpel. Aside from that, his beautiful face was still perfect, unblemished.

They drove home without their son. They went straight to his bedroom. He had made his bed perfectly that morning, which was unusual. For some reason, he had left his wallet, with a National Insurance card and a playing card in it, on his bed. They didn't even know he used a wallet. It was an unfamiliar scene, and the room stayed that way for a couple of years. His clothes remained in the wardrobe, ready to be smelled and caressed, and his bed became a place of refuge for anyone who needed to curl into a ball and cry in the middle of the day.

'It was a huge heart attack, we think.'

That was the best explanation they had on that very first night. Back then, there was no internet full of information and case studies where they could conduct an amateur search for possible causes or similar cases.

In the months after, because of the high-profile nature of his death, we received thousands of letters from families who had been affected – often with more than one child dying – from what we later found out was hypertrophic cardiomyopathy, sometimes called sudden death syndrome.

My sister Louise, eleven months younger than me, was in Tokyo modelling. Her return was the first of many questions and puzzles to unravel. What should we do? Get her home on false pretences so she didn't have to make a wretched thirteen-hour flight alone with this awful news, or tell her the truth while she was still in Japan?

We told her the truth, which was the right decision. When she landed at Heathrow Airport, every newspaper had Daniel's face on its front page. Dad was the manager of the Welsh football team, so it was a story of national 'interest'. I have often thought about what that flight must have been like for her. Imagine travelling thirteen hours, at 35,000 feet, with only the news of your brother's death to keep your mind occupied.

Gary didn't know what to say – nobody does, and you'll never get it right. Thankfully, he had a decent record collection, and he quickly found the Elton John vinyl album with the song 'Daniel'. That evening, we played it over and over and over. It soothed me, and, convinced that Elton was singing to our family, I eventually found sleep. Imagining our Daniel leaving on a plane, flying so high that I couldn't see him. Elton had apparently been told that Daniel had been named after this song, and later sent flowers to our family, along with a beautiful note. Some idiot stole the note from his grave, assuming Elton had penned It himself, and not a florist called Julie in a Leeds branch of Interflora.

The first morning – and many more after that – were repetitively, dismally awful. I would open my eyes and, for one brief millisecond, life was normal and full of hope and possibility, and then the thud of my new reality would hit me, like a boulder landing on my broken heart. I would lie there for minutes, sometimes hours, unable to move, because I knew when I did get out of bed, it would be real; I would see my bloodshot eyes and sallow, lifeless face in the mirror.

Brushing my teeth and getting into the shower – simple, mundane tasks – required Herculean effort. All of my movements were heavy and leaden, as if my bodyweight had doubled overnight. Death weighs you down.

That first day, I dialled the number of my family home.

'Hello.'

'Mum, it's me. Are you OK?'

She isn't OK. It's 8am, the morning after her world was shattered.

'No, I didn't sleep at all. I waited until 7am, and then I rang Val Lumsden and told her Daniel had died.'

Jimmy Lumsden, Val's husband, had played football with my dad, and their teenage son had died over a year before.

Mum had seen Val in restaurants over that time with friends, and assumed that Val must know something, that she would have a secret, a trick about coping with grief, that she could share with Mum.

Val dashed round as soon as Mum called, but she had no 'trick' to bring. As she walked in the door, she said, 'Christine your life has changed now, and it won't be the same again.'

Val was right. Nothing was ever the same again.

There is before Daniel died and after. I am sorry we had to start all of this on such a sad day, but 25 May 1992 really did change everything.

You might now be thinking that this is not the book you were expecting from that smiley blonde woman who presents the sport on the telly. But when I started to think about the important moments in my life that have brought me to where I am today, I instinctively wrote about the day Daniel died, and I realised quickly how monumentally important that moment was to my life; how embedded it is, as if it has seeped into my DNA.

We can never really know who we'd be without the very big stuff that shapes us. At nineteen, I wasn't a fully formed person, and it's clear what happened to my family, and the way I responded to Daniel's death, was transformative.

While I'd always been an independent and determined child, Daniel's death made me fearless. I wasn't worried about failing or looking a fool, because, well – what could hurt me as much as his death had?

I became a young woman on a mission, in a hurry to achieve something, to have something, that would make the pain of his death worthwhile.

2

LA Olympics

S port has always been at the centre of my life. It has given me life lessons, introduced me to spectacular people and brought me complete and utter joy – as well as frustration and tears.

It's been woven through my life even when I didn't feel I had a place in sport anymore. When I tried to climb away, it came back at me again with another lesson. Then I married a sportsman and had sporty kids, so I am resigned to the fact that it is probably with me forever – and it carries on being a brilliant teacher.

But where did this lifelong love affair with sport begin? Was it a result of growing up as the daughter of a footballer, with sporty siblings and a competitive mindset built in to the very structure of my childhood? All of this will have played a strong part in my passion for sport, I'm sure, but in fact, the moment it all really started for me was in the rather unglamourous setting of a hotel in Slough during the summer of 1984. Let me explain.

I was eleven years old and, looking at photographic evidence of that period, I appear to have been on rations. Did we have some kind of national food shortage? I must have been in the middle of a growth spurt: my legs look like a baby giraffe's, and yet my nose has not taken on its teenage proboscis-like quality; it's still fairly cute. Nobody in my family ended up with a cute nose, except my sister Louise, but she also tans well and has straight, manageable dark hair, unlike my own unruly mousy, wire-like straw. The theory often offered to explain Louise's appearance is that my mum fancied David Essex (the swarthy 1970s pop star) so passionately while pregnant with my sister that she birthed a child who looked like him. I don't subscribe to this theory, because my own son does not resemble Denzel Washington.

Anyway, none of my trousers reached my ankles during this period – and not in a chic French way. As the oldest child and grandchild, I had no hand-me-down clothing. (That changed when I was fifteen years old, and my mum's stylish septuagenarian Jewish friend, Carole Rakusen, gifted me a collection of 1970s couture Courrege, which, looking back required a lot of courage to wear in Leeds in 1989. But that was still a few years away.)

To complete the sartorial mess of my appearance, in a fit of liberal parenting, Mum had allowed me to buy and use one of the most dangerous products available to teenagers in the 1980s. Not heroin, although it was having a comeback. No, the product was Sun In, and it was singlehandedly responsible for transforming the hair of a generation of mousy girls and boys into an identikit shade of strawberry blond (or ginger). It promised to lighten, to lift your natural colour, but what it did, with the over-vigorous application of an enthusiastic teen's hand, was swamp the hair with hydrogen peroxide so that absolutely nothing natural of your original hair was left. The texture went from silky and healthy to frazzled. I gather they've changed the formulation since those days, but at the time the only saving grace was that we all had the same hair, so shame was minimised. That, and the fact we had no social media, so none of us shared photos and commented on them. If you wanted to insult someone, you did it to their face, in the playground or on the bus. Simple times.

It was with this new luminous orange frizz and lanky frame that I was about to hit London town, the destination for our family summer holiday of 1984. We seemed to have stopped going on regular family holidays in around 1982. Prior to this, we'd get on planes: we travelled to America before it became a package holiday destination and stayed with Great Aunty Lily, who was the housekeeper for a wealthy family on Long Island. Her husband, a small, Scottish, bagpipe-playing man called Stewart, was the gardener.

We also spent a few idyllic weeks in a stunning villa on the Caribbean Island of Montserrat (before its volcano exploded). On that trip, I saved Daniel from drowning. After noticing he was face-down in the pool, I jumped in and swam him to the side, where an adult appeared to take over the rescue. I was given a lot of positive feedback for my heroism and enjoyed the attention so much that I pushed him into the pool the following day so I could save him again. The attention wasn't so positive the second time.

After all this exotic travel in our early years, things changed, and instead of flights, we went on the road with Mum. The hours spent on the UK's motorways allowed us to invent some interesting car games, none of which I have been able to format into lucrative TV shows as yet.

It usually went like this: somewhere on the M5, I would announce to the other two what would happen next.

'We're going to play "the baby-wipe challenge". How many junctions can you keep a baby wipe in your mouth for?'

'What does the winner get?' Daniel asks.

'When we get to the next Little Chef, you get an extra lollipop – the ones on the counter.'

'They're free,' he replies.

I ignore him.

'OK, let's go.' We each pop one fresh baby wipe into our mouths.

Within a few seconds, I surreptitiously remove the baby wipe. Louise spots my skulduggery and copies me.

I keep my mouth shut and start to feign sickness after we pass the first junction.

Daniel isn't feigning. He looks a bit green.

We pass another junction.

We're too quiet for Mum's liking.

'What's going on back there?' she shouts.

'It's the baby-wipe challenge,' I say, without opening my mouth. It comes out as: 'MMMMmmmmMMMMMMMM MMmmmmmmMMM'.

'What? What's wrong with Dan?' Mum is getting irate.

'MMMMMmmmmmmMMMMMMMMMmmmmmmmMM MMMMM,' I reply.

'Whatever you are doing Gabrielle, stop it now and speak properly – or we won't be stopping at the Little Chef for lunch.'

I take a big, dramatic sigh, and remove the non-existent baby wipe, disposing of it where I had put the real baby wipe.

'Sorry guys, the game's over. No winner.'

Daniel responds by throwing up his breakfast on a travel rug.

Half an hour later, we all enter a Little Chef close to Cirencester, smelling of sick.

*

This might be a good time to introduce you to the cast of characters that appears in so many of the events in this book.

My dad, Terry Yorath, was an international footballer for Wales who signed for Leeds United from Cardiff as a fifteen-year-old. He lived in 'digs' when he arrived there, 260 miles from home, and from his stories, the old-school footballers' digs sound a lot like living in a foster home. He was a handsome lad, all long blond wavy locks and big blue eyes.

My mum, Christine, was tall and striking, with grey-blue eyes and dark hair. A Leeds lass born and bred, she was the eldest daughter of Fred and Sheila Kay, who were the epitome of the hard-working working class. My mum's first cot was the bottom drawer of a chest of drawers, and their house had no bathroom and a toilet in the yard, but they were grafters.

Grandad Fred was a charming bookmaker with a fantastic head of grey hair and an eye for a nice suit. He was debonair and a much-trusted and loved bookie, which is why he didn't make much money, Mum said. He was also almost thirty years older than his wife. Nana Sheila was a graceful beauty who ran her own greasy spoon café, if that isn't a massive oxymoron. 'Sheila's Café' was right opposite Elland Road, where Leeds United play football.

Nana Sheila woke at 4.45am, six days a week. Like all the women in our family, she was a grafter. Starting at 5.30am, she would cook breakfasts for footballers, businessmen, lorry drivers and a whole host of eclectic loyal customers. In the holidays, I occasionally worked for her, washing floors, shelling eggs and clearing tables. I regret that neither of my teenagers has shelled eggs at 6am, washed a concrete step with boiling water or served a grumpy trucker a cup of tea; there are some life skills that take you places conjugating verbs just can't. Not that my kids can conjugate verbs either. (I realise that in the order of this book, I haven't given birth yet, but rest assured I do have kids one day – and they have never washed a concrete step at 6am.)

Dad met my mum at a youth club when she was fifteen and he was sixteen. Dad, ever the charmer, had asked my mum if he could drop off some trousers at her mum's café so she could iron them for him. She declined, which I am proud of, and it took him another year or so to win her round, spurred on by his realisation that she had better legs than his current girlfriend. They were engaged at seventeen, on the night of the *Eurovision Song Contest* (which I have just found out was won by Sandie Shaw singing 'Puppet on a String').

My parents got married just before my mum's twenty-first birthday and had three of us kids very young, starting with me when they were twenty-two, Louise when they were twenty-three, and Daniel when they were twenty-six years old. This might explain why they then took a ten-year break before they had Jordan in 1986.

Dad was earning more as a footballer in his twenties than anyone in his family had ever dreamed of, and I would say he was heavily influenced by my mum's family. He was very close to her brother Nigel, and loved my Grandad Fred. Our childhood was punctuated by regular big family gatherings, weddings, christenings and religious occasions. There was always drink, chatter and music – and cigar smoke, if Grandad Fred was around.

Dad didn't grace all of our childhood holidays, because he was always working, which is the norm with footballers, and especially football managers, who work even harder and longer days. Footballers are never available to go on holiday when the rest of their family are; they start pre-season training long before schools break up for the summer, and then they work non-stop until the following May.

They train every day in that time, including Christmas

Day. If they are international players, they will have a World Cup or a European Championship or a tour, and then they get a couple of weeks off sometime around the beginning of July before it all starts again.

If my dad was playing at the top of his game now, the chances are we wouldn't have loaded up a silver Ford Cortina Estate and headed down the M1 to the Holiday Inn Slough (or London, as I liked to call it). If Dad was playing now, we'd have jumped on a silver private jet and headed off to our Majorcan finca for a few days. But would we have been grounded, well-balanced children? Who knows, but I would like to have given it a try.

It wasn't until the invention of Sky TV that the big money really started rolling in for footballers, so back in the early eighties, my dad probably earned about the same as a GP. Which was a nice salary for a lad who'd left school at fifteen, but certainly not rock-star money. Also, a GP works until they are sixty-five, while my dad's playing career ended when he was thirty-five – and with it, the salary. He sometimes forgot to put enough money aside for his tax, and didn't bother with any extra pensions or investments, so we didn't have the private education, second home or fleet of fast cars that most people associate with being the child of a profes-sional footballer.

The perks of his job were mainly free tickets to football matches and a certain amount of notoriety, which wasn't always positive. Our childhood was great because we were loved and safe, but its lack of opulence might disappoint some who think football has always had its pitch paved in gold.

Back to this holiday to London (Slough): the two main items on Mum's agenda seemed to be a visit to Windsor Castle and a shopping trip to Oxford Street. To me, Oxford Street has never been anything more than a bigger version of every high street in the land. Even back then, when you couldn't press a button on a computer to bring you stuff in a white van immediately from Amazon, and physical in-store shopping was still a thriving money-maker, I didn't get the allure of Oxford Street.

But my mum loved it almost as much as she loved the Bull Ring in Birmingham, Rackham's in Coventry or Schofields in Leeds; she was, and still is, a big fan of shopping. Sometimes, if Dad was playing football away at the weekend, we would spend seven hours in whatever town centre we lived in, and my siblings and I conducted much of it lying on the floor of various ladies' changing rooms, asking 'How long now?'

When I want to relay to my children how lucky they are in life, I have been heard to say, 'For god's sake, I don't even take you shopping on a Saturday afternoon.' Our generation, the generation who were dragged out shopping on Saturday afternoons, went on to invent the iPhone, so maybe it is good to experience genuine boredom from time to time.

For me, though, the most important, life-changing part of this holiday wasn't the visit to Windsor Castle or the giant Marks and Spencer: it was the time we'd spend in the hotel.

On 28 July 1984 the President of the United States, Ronald Reagan, opened the twenty-third Summer Olympics in Los Angeles. For the first time in Olympic history, my sport, rhythmic gymnastics, was included in the programme, and one of Great Britain's two gymnasts was from my club, City of Leeds. I had a personal connection to the biggest show on earth in the shape of Lorraine Priest.

Lorraine Priest was eighteen years old. When you're only eleven, that may as well be twenty-six. She was a grown-up: she drove a car and was heading off to Loughborough University after the Olympics to study Sports Science. That sentence is loaded with things I had no clue about at the time. First of all, where – and what – was Loughborough? Secondly, there was a science about sport? Finally, nobody in my family had ever been to university, so Lorraine was about as exotic a creature as you could imagine. Only she wasn't; she was average height, with short dark hair with a strong Leeds accent, and she went to a fairly standard state school in the city. She was a very normal girl, doing extraordinary things.

Rhythmic gymnastics was never on TV, and now that I work in TV, I understand why. As beautiful as it is, it's not exactly a mass-participation sport. Back then, though, I was convinced it was a conspiracy against us. I had come to rhythmic gymnastics by accident. My real passion was tennis, but we'd moved to Leeds and there were no public indoor tennis courts, and it was winter. So I followed Louise to the City of Leeds Gymnastics Club, which had one of the most respected judges in the world as its head coach, Anne Talintyre. I had done a bit of gymnastics in the past, but at Leeds I found rhythmic and I fell in love.

I knew I'd be lucky to catch Lorraine on telly, so I'd record or watch every minute of the BBC's coverage I possibly could. BBC's *Breakfast Time* with Frank Bough started the day, then Bob Wilson took over at 9am. David Icke had a lunchtime show, and then *Olympic Grandstand* rounded up the best of the action at 6pm with the master himself, Mr Des Lynam.

Four middle-class, middle-aged white men presenting the entire coverage – it's a wonder I ever thought this might be a career for me, but we shall get to that at a later stage.

Meanwhile, in the Holiday Inn Slough, the magic began to happen, for it was there I woke up to the beauty of all sport. I was transfixed. What started as a relentless search for Lorraine's hoop routine fast became a love of the entire Olympic circus:

Carl Lewis, Tessa Sanderson, Daley Thompson, Mary Lou
Retton, Greg Louganis; the personalities, the back stories,
the VT montages, the Des Lynam one-liners – I was smitten.
I wanted to soak up every minute. And what's more, I had
discovered a new ambition: I wanted to go to an Olympic
Games. (To be clear, I didn't just want a ticket to the women's
ten-metre platform diving final; I wanted to represent Great
Britain in rhythmic gymnastics at an Olympics.)

One evening, while waiting for Mum's rollers to set (she
has worn rollers almost every day since 1965; I am amazed
she still has such good hair – or any at all), I managed to
catch some of the rhythmic on the telly. It included a routine by Jacquie Leavy, another British gymnast, who was
from Coventry.

We had moved from Coventry to Leeds just the year
before, and we knew Jacquie from our days at the Coventry
Gymnastics Club. To me, this was fate, a sign that my new
dream was not an impossible one. Jacquie and I would
cross paths again much later in life, as she was a reporter at
Sky Sports when I started my TV career there. Jacquie and
Lorraine were pioneers of Olympic rhythmic gymnastics
in the UK, and were probably my first sporting heroes. But
when I am asked that exact question in interviews, I usually
say the Spurs and England footballing genius Glen Hoddle,
because saying 'Jacquie and Lorraine' sounds like I am pro-
moting a hairdressing salon in Luton.

When I say I recorded as much of the BBC's Olympic
coverage as I could, this doesn't mean I pressed a red button
on my Sky remote. No, I had my very own VHS tape, which
might at different times have contained the end of the javelin
final, five minutes of *Top of the Pops*, followed by some swimming and then maybe ten minutes of *Whicker's World*; it was
like a montage of its time. The highlight of my packed VHS

was an athletics montage that was cut to the Spandau Ballet track 'Gold'; it was an iconic piece of telly. During the cold, dark winter months when coming home from school and eating salt and vinegar Monster Munch in front of *Grange Hill* felt like a better option than heading out to training, I'd pop the tape on, and after just the opening blasts of 'Gold', I would be in my leotard and out the door. It was nectar to an aching teenage soul.

Choosing to be a rhythmic gymnast was never a career move. You can't cherry-pick your passion, of course, but if you could, you probably wouldn't choose a sport that had zero future earning possibilities, barely registered on the nation's consciousness, took up about thirty hours of your week, and meant that at the most vulnerable point in your young life, namely puberty, you lived in a leotard.

My dad could never quite get his head round why my sister and I spent so many hours after school slogging away at a sport that could never become a career. His own life had been elevated by sport; it had given him opportunities and a material life he could never have dreamed of. So to him, just doing a sport for its own sake seemed a bit bizarre. That's not to say he wasn't proud. I am sure, in his own quiet way, he was.

But let's not forget women's football was banned for fifty years by the FA until 1971, so playing football professionally was not an option for me and Louise. Golf and tennis seemed to be the only sports women made a living from in the mid-eighties. We were certainly much more comfortable as a family than my dad's had been, so we didn't need to look at sport as a potential income stream – and I truly believe that children shouldn't look at sport as a potential future salary or a profession. It must always start out as fun, because for the vast majority of kids, it is never going to be a job. If you have a great time with your pals and you enjoy sport, then that is enough: you will be fit and healthy, and have great habits for life.

That summer, the Olympics of 1984 opened my eyes and fuelled my passion for all sport. Sport became a channel for my competitive spirit. What I really loved about it was the harder you worked, the more you achieved. This sort of tangible progress really appealed to my inner meritocrat.

   If you had told me then that thirty years later, I would be one of the hosts of the London Olympics on the BBC, and that we would use the track 'Gold' to close our show one night, I'd have thought you'd lost your mind. Not at the suggestion that London would one day host an Olympics, but at the idea that I would ever present sports for the BBC. For one thing, I had a Leeds accent. For another, I was a girl.

3

Vancouver

When people ask me where I am from, I say Leeds, a city I absolutely love, but at the time of writing, only twenty per cent of my life was spent there. I was born there, moved away, and then returned there for senior school. Moving house and even country was never a problem to us as kids; it's what footballers' families do — often to and from places you would never normally aspire to live. (In 1980, however, when my dad was transferred from Coventry to Tottenham Hotspur, my mum decided, much to my annoyance, that we would not be moving to London. We would stay in Coventry, because by the time she found a house they could afford in London with a garden, they were actually in north Hertfordshire. If my parents had bought a house in Notting Hill in 1980 for £100,000 — which was the not inconsiderable budget they were working with — it would be worth about £35,000,000 now, but back then we all looked at houses as homes, not investments or pension pots.)

When I was eight, Dad was transferred from Tottenham Hotspur to the Vancouver Whitecaps. This was not a move to further his career, but one to further the family bank account. He was one of a few – usually retirement-age – players crossing the Atlantic for one last hurrah. In today's footballing landscape, it would be the equivalent of going to play in China or Qatar.

Pele had joined the New York Cosmos at around this time, and George Best had headed off to the Los Angeles Aztecs and later the San Jose Earthquakes. We might have stayed in Coventry over London, but my mum wasn't daft – she wasn't going to miss out on *this* relocation. Credit where credit is due: Coventry to Vancouver is one hell of a trade-up. Don't get me wrong, I loved Coventry, and I was very happy there, but have you ever been to Vancouver? If Vancouver was one of the original supermodels, it would be Christy Turlington: stunningly perfect, healthy and uncontroversial. The one you'd probably want to have kids with.

Dad moved out to Canada in the winter to start playing, but we had to finish school and try to sell the house, so the intention was to move in the summer when school was out. Footballers' families often follow a few months behind the breadwinner, especially in those days, when a footballer could be transferred at any time of the year rather than within two short windows, which meant in theory you could be playing for Coventry on a Tuesday and Brighton on a Wednesday.

Being a footballer is not a nine-to-five job, and of course footballers work every weekend, but when he was playing in Coventry, we had still seen quite a bit of Dad. He'd finish work before 2pm most days, so we were used to having him pick us up from school. He rarely got out of the car, because the other thing about being a footballer and living in the city in which you play, is that everyone supports that club. If they'd lost at the weekend, he'd have to keep his head down; if they'd won, he might get out of the car to receive some plaudits and sign an autograph.

One day, he picked us up from school in his cream Austin Princess and, as we piled into the car, he pointed to the foot-well of the front passenger seat.

The carpet was brown, and it was hard to make out at first what he was pointing to, until we spotted a pair of sparkly eyes staring back at us. They belonged to the cutest brown shaggy-haired puppy. Sadie, our beloved first dog, a chocolate brown standard poodle, had recently died. There is no greater thing a parent can bring to a school pick-up than a new puppy. With hindsight, I can't believe my mum let him have such an enormous parenting win.

So, although Dad had to spend weeks away in the summers with Wales, and despite the fact that he worked every Saturday, he could turn up at school at 3.30pm with a puppy every now and again. (The addendum to this particular story is that the puppy in question, which was named Clara, turned out to be a bit nuts and had to go back to her original home in Gloucestershire.)

When you are in primary school, nobody really cares what your parents do for a job. But everyone at St Thomas More school knew who my dad was. There was a set of twins who were quite good at football and fairly obsessed with Coventry City, and they would often give me grief about Dad, saying he was rubbish and that he should be transferred. The odd bit of stick was normal, but this was going on and on, and I'd had enough.

It was getting to me, so I finally told Dad that it was upsetting me. I had resisted, because I was aware that in doing so I was pointing out that they had said his playing was crap. Dad pondered what to do. Eventually, he had an idea.

'You go and ask them what their dad does for a living,' he said, with a look of indignation.

'Why?' I asked.

'Because you can tell them that whatever rubbish job it is, I'm sure he'd rather be a footballer.'

He was probably correct, but I thought this was quite an arrogant and risky retort. Besides, what if their dad was in fact the head of the United Nations? Unlikely he'd live in Coventry, I suppose, but the Pope came to visit in 1982, so anything was possible. So I said nothing – even at that young age, I could see this might be a problematic route to go down.

The twins carried on being horrible about Dad until he finally had a good game. Coventry won, and they shut up.

So although I didn't get grief for his footballing prowess from my classmates anymore, the six months Dad was living in Vancouver without us was tough.

Daniel was almost five years old at this point, and my sister and I were seven and eight. I have always been proud of my role as the leader of the pack, and even then I took the responsibility seriously. Dad would often have little pep talks with me on the phone, reminding me of how tough it was for Mum, and asking me to set a good example for the other two.

Because of the time difference, we had our longest chats in the morning before I went off to school. One day, Mum called me up to her room and said Dad wanted to speak to me with some urgency.

'Gabby, I have a really important job for you to do,' he said. 'I want you to go to my bedside cabinet and take some money, about five pounds, and go to the corner shop on your bike and get Mother's Day cards for Mummy from the three of you. It's this Sunday.'

'OK Daddy, I will. Have a good day,' I lied.

I knew it wasn't Mother's Day that Sunday, as we had already celebrated it a few weeks before. I now know that the Mother's Day in North America is a few weeks later than ours, but I didn't at the time. For some reason, that conversation floored me. I said goodbye, got off the phone and burst into tears.

My poor Daddy, he hasn't got a clue, I thought. I didn't have the heart to tell him he was wrong. I imagined him sitting in his Vancouver hotel, just being wrong about stuff because he didn't have us to correct him, didn't have my mum to tell him what to do.

Mum heard me crying and I couldn't tell her why. 'I have terrible tummy ache,' I fibbed.

'Well, you can't go to school if you're in that much pain,' she said.

'No, I'm OK.' I wept even harder now, unable to catch my breath. 'I *have* to go to school,' I begged. It was not unusual for me to be desperate to go to school. But in spite of my protestations, she wasn't convinced and kept me at home.

I wasn't really sick, of course, so I had to pretend my tummy hurt, and lie in my bed, eating dry toast and sipping water, all so I could preserve my dad's integrity. I'm not sure why that incident is etched in my mind so firmly. Possibly it's because that day, I realised that my parents weren't perfect, they didn't know everything and maybe, at eight years old, I wasn't quite ready for that truth.

We arrived en masse in Vancouver in the summer of 1981. I can remember exactly what we wore for this seminal journey: Mum had bought us matching OshKosh B'Gosh denim dungarees, and we had Kickers shoes on in different colours (red for me, blue for Daniel and green for Louise), with a T-shirt to match the shoes under the dungarees. Mum was insistent that when Daddy met us at the airport at the other end (after a ten-hour flight) we would all look smart. She was also of the school of thought that if you dressed to impress when arriving at the airport, you might get an upgrade. It never worked. I now know why – who in their right mind would upgrade three kids under nine? But you have to take your hat off to her optimism.

In the 1980s, North America was exotic. The road signs, restaurants, fashion, petrol stations and even the way the towns were built was truly different to the UK. I have been lucky enough to travel the world for work and we're now so globalised that a shopping mall in Rio is as familiar as one in Sheffield; these days, there's an unsatisfying homogeneity about the planet's biggest cities. But in 1981, Canada felt forward-thinking and futuristic.

Now, if my kids want a bag of Hershey's Kisses after school, they don't even need to leave our small local town in Buckinghamshire, let alone the country. In the 1980s, if you wanted American chocolate, you had to go to America; there wasn't a special aisle next to the gluten-free section at Sainsbury's.

We started our new adventure in a motel, a proper one where the door to the room opened on to the street. I was always the first awake, so, to avoid waking the rest of the family, I'd get dressed in the dark and sneak out to the 7Eleven at the end of the road, where I'd buy a Dr Pepper and some watermelon bubble gum. Just thinking about it now is making my mouth water. After a few weeks of this idyllic situation, eating out every night and never really having to put our clothes away, our new home was ready to move into. My parents had decided to rent out our house back in England,

and in turn we would rent rather than buy in Vancouver. This turned out to be lucky, because a year later, when we were getting ready to return to the UK, there was a massive property crash in Vancouver. If we'd bought a house there in the summer of 1981, we'd all still be living in Vancouver right now, trying to pay it off.

It had been left to Dad to find our home. This was a monumental gamble. My mum is now a property developer and interior designer, and she is fastidious about houses. Home design has been her life's passion. Even then, when she wasn't making her living from property, she didn't buy *Vogue* or *Good Housekeeping*; she bought *Architectural Digest*. At the time, the magazine was so rare she had to order it especially through WHSmith, who imported it from the US just for her. She had her own drawer in a filing cabinet at the back of the shop, where once a month a new edition would arrive for which she had paid a small fortune.

And yet, and yet, she let Dad choose a family home, on his own.

He drove us to West Vancouver, into the salubrious British Properties, named because the Guinness family (of Ireland, of course, but hey, let's not worry about technicalities) had bought 4,000 acres of land and started building mega houses there in the 1930s. How posh was it? Some of the roads were heated so that when it snowed, the residents could get out safely in the depths of winter, probably just to go skiing. Winding up the side of the mountain, with the houses getting bigger and better, we finally reached our new road, Elvedon Row.

The higher up you were, the better the view, and by now we were oxygen-mask high. Halfway along Elvedon Row stood number 905, a large, dramatic, white Spanish-style house with lots of glass and a flat roof. As we turned into its incredibly steep drive, the three of us kids in the back of the car quietly assumed that Dad had robbed a bank. Dad had the look of a very chuffed man, a man who had made his wife and family happy and surpassed their very low expectations.

We raced up the steps of the house to its impressive dark brown double front door with silver handles and knockers. Once inside we ran around its vast rooms, bagged our bedrooms, found a basement that was about the size of our whole house in Coventry, and took in the breathtaking views of the Lion Gate Bridge and the Pacific Ocean. It was insanely beautiful. *We must be wealthy in Canada,* I thought to myself.

You are now expecting me to tell you that it was the wrong house; that somehow the agent had given us the wrong keys. Well, it's almost worse than that. You see, my dad had signed the contract for the house for twelve months, only he had misunderstood the rent. To cut a long story short, what he thought he was paying for a year turned out to be the monthly rent. He was already at the upper end of the budget so times it by twelve and you can see it was quite a big accounting error. In effect, it meant that once food, utilities and other expenses had been covered, my parents would return to England with nothing much but memories, rather than the large nest egg they had planned on.

I love the gung-ho-ness of how they lived their lives though. They were thirty-two years old with three young kids, spending most of their income living in a beautiful house, in a strange country. We even went to a fee-paying school; it was the only way to get a Catholic education in Vancouver. You'd have thought religion might take a back seat after the rent cock-up, but Dad was a recent convert to the ways of the Lord.

He had converted to Catholicism in secret to be like the

rest of the family. I don't mean that we were secret Catholics, I mean he hadn't told us he was converting. He pretended he was going for a mid-week pint with Monsignor Gavin at St Thomas More. Gavin was a former Irish rugby international, so he and my dad always got on well, chatting about sport. But there was no pint, no chat about sport. Dad was learning the catechumen, getting ready to be baptised.

Church was important. We went every Sunday in Coventry and probably received Communion once a week at school. My Catholic God was not the dark, brooding, guilt-inducing God I have read about and seen in films since, the one many other Catholics experienced at school. The one we worshipped didn't seem so judgemental. He was jolly and colourful, and the hymns we sang were more like folk songs.

We didn't have scary-looking nuns educating us. Even the church building itself (this being Coventry, which was bombed to bits in the Second World War) had been erected in the 1960s, and could easily be mistaken for a council leisure centre from the outside. I think church for our family was about community as much as Communion.

As for the doctrine, we had a set of rules that we tried to live by, and if we didn't manage it, we could confess on a Saturday morning. Most of the rules seemed fairly sensible: not stealing and not swearing and being good to other people are fairly difficult to argue against. It seems to me that most religions are generally OK, until people start getting extreme about them.

In Vancouver, I remember my parents seeming more in love, kissing and holding hands and arguing less. Dad was keen to please Mum. Perhaps when you are thrown together in a new country and there are none of the safety nets of home, you dig in and work as a team.

Back in Coventry, it felt like there had been a lot of dis-agreements and a bit of late-night arguing before we'd left. Never decipherable enough for me to tell you exactly what it was about, but in a tone and at a volume that was worrying for an eight-year-old lying in her bed. Every disagreement sounds like the end of a relationship to a small child.

Vancouver was healthier for everyone.

When it came to watching football, while we didn't get to go to White Hart Lane to see Dad playing for Spurs very often, we had started to occasionally watch his games in Coventry. Highfield Road was a classic old English city-centre football ground, surrounded by terraced houses where the actual fans who went to the games lived. This is something of an alien concept to Premier League fans now.

It was all Bovril, crisps and noisy chants, and the crowd was mostly male. It was fun, if not exactly glamorous. I enjoyed seeing the police horses controlling the crowds on the way in, and loved the excitement when a goal was almost scored, then the unbridled joy if one actually went in. Men, mainly men, going crazy and hugging each other in a way they just wouldn't outside the sanctuary of this ground.

In Vancouver, attending a football match was very dif-ferent. It was modelled on American franchise sport, and families and women were welcome. 'Celebration' by Kool and the Gang rang out when there was a goal, and occa-sionally a live band played at half-time if the queue for the hotdogs was too tedious to bear.

'We are going to have a great night tonight,' a woman's voice promised over the tannoy. 'Someone is going home a little bit more sparkly. Under your seats, there is a number.'

Everyone stood up and the sound of seats smacking back into their upright position rang through the air.

'Have you found a number? Take a close look at it, because ... number 3,498, you are going home with a one-carat diamond. Oh yeah!'

Cue fireworks and more music. They were literally buying fans. It had the feel of a testimonial match, every single week.

The league took place over the summer months, along with a five-a-side indoor league over the winter, so that football didn't have to compete with NFL or ice hockey, which were by far the bigger sports. As it was a North American League, away fixtures could be three time zones and seven hours away. Games were bunched together, for example three matches against Tampa, Jacksonville and New York over the space of two weeks. It meant Dad would go away in large chunks, and, as usual, Mum would just get on with it, bringing us up and keeping us fed, watered and loved in a new country. We were in this adventure together.

She had incredible resilience and was fairly courageous in the way she attacked new projects. All of these moves were packaged as wonderful opportunities by her and as a result, we never feared the change.

Sport was plentiful, weaving into life in a way that just wasn't as apparent back in England in 1981. Local recreation centres offered a range of activities from curling to rock climbing for as little as fifty cents, which even then was criminally cheap. We could do a different sport every day; we learned to ice skate, and did gymnastics, athletics, judo and ice hockey. For me, there was also tennis.

I often played with my best mate from school, Maureen Clay. Maureen had a classic 1980s bowl haircut, and lots of cute, perfectly placed freckles. Her nickname was Pud. Everyone called her Pud, even the teachers.

Early on in our friendship, in a desperate attempt to be more like her and therefore more likeable, I told her my

nickname back in England had been Cheesy. What kind
of fool would want Cheesy to follow her as a nickname
4,000 miles across the world, even if it was a genuine one?
Unsurprisingly, it didn't stick. I was able to invent a back story
to suit my audience, though, and I played on my Englishness.
It was 'cute', according to the older kids at St Anthony's. I
adopted an RP accent and pretended I was missing Earl Grey
tea and digestives. I would happily repeat phrases that were
thrown at me for merriment.

'Fish and Chips.'

'Lady Diana.'

'London Bridge.'

'Brexit.' Only joking.

After a few weeks, though, the pendulum had swung the
other way. I was bored of pretending to be a distant relation
to the Queen, so I dropped the accent totally and became a
Canadian. I am fairly sure my talent for mimicking accents
started at around that time. Some people have an ear for
music, others can hit a golf ball a very long way. Well, I can
pretty much do any accent on demand. I would rather be able
to play the piano, but you have to go with what you are given.

Psychologists say that when you morph your accent to
fit in with your environment, it is a sign of high emotional
intelligence, as you are making the other people feel more
comfortable by sounding like them. Other people say you
might be taking the piss, and in certain countries it would
be seen, quite rightly, as being racist. I don't recommend it,
and I rarely put on an accent these days.

The Clay family were great people to know. Maureen was
the middle child of three. Her mum, Mary-Jo, was a Canadian
who looked a bit like the tennis star Billie Jean King, and her
dad, Colin, was a property developer who'd arrived from
Johannesburg in the 1960s with 'just a dollar in my pocket'.

Mary-Jo encouraged the kids to play tennis (so perhaps she actually was modelling herself on Billie Jean). The Clays were members of an exclusive country club, and I was allowed to play there with Pud at the weekends sometimes. After the house rent debacle, it won't surprise you to learn that we were not members of any posh country clubs.

The Clays went to Hawaii at Christmas and skied at Easter, and then in the June break they'd decamp to their home in Palm Springs to play tennis. I'd won the friendship lottery with Pud in many ways.

I'd left behind a mate in Coventry who lived above her parents' fish-and-chip shop, which had its own perks but no tennis court.

One day after school, I heard my mum on the phone to Mary-Jo. 'That's very kind, but I really don't think we should let her go, she's just too young.'

'What was that about? Where am I not going?' I asked in my shiny new Vancouver accent.

'The Clays wanted you to fly down to Palm Springs during the holidays and join them for a week to play tennis with Pud.'

' . . . And you said no?' I laughed in disbelief.

'It's not safe for a nine-year-old to travel alone like that to a different country,' Mum reasoned.

'Well, I could die right now if this oven blew up because of a gas leak,' I argued, 'and I would die having never been to Palm Springs.'

As macabre and dramatic as my logic might have been, it worked. A month later, at just nine years old, I was flying on my own to Palm Springs to play tennis and hang out with my best mate. I was given a small amount of spending money and an emergency fund of fifty dollars in case there was a disaster. After twenty-four hours, I had spent the emergency fund on a cerise pink Lacoste tennis top, which might be the coolest thing I have ever owned. Anyway, what kind of a disaster would fifty dollars really help with? I had an amazing week with Maureen, playing tennis all day every day and hanging out by the pool. After forty years we recently connected on social media and Maureen still looks just like my Pud who made me fall in love with tennis.

Years later, Mum told me that when she left me on my own to get on the plane at Vancouver Airport, I didn't turn around to wave goodbye as I went through security with the chaperone the airline had supplied. To be honest, I also ditched the chaperone once we got through passport control.

I loved my family with all my heart – in fact, at this point in my life, I was going through that terrible period of crying in bed at night as you imagine some dreadful accident that might befall your parents. You must have been through that, too. I was particularly worried the Lion Gate Bridge would collapse as Dad was on his way to work. I remember getting out of bed in tears one evening, finding him and Mum snogging on the sofa, which was awkward, and asking if he could go to work via a different route in future. He explained that the journey without using the bridge would take him two hours longer and he wouldn't be able to drop us at school if he did that, so he would have to continue to use the bridge, which he assured me was very safe.

I went back to bed placated by this, and hopefully they got back to snogging on the sofa. In later life, this fascination with the Lion Gate Bridge led me to write a thesis on the great bridge builder Isambard Kingdom Brunel.

Only joking.

As I say, I adored my family, but I didn't want to be a bother. When you are the oldest, there always seems to be someone needier than you. I don't know why I was so determined to be prematurely independent, but it was probably this trait that led me to research Nick Bollettieri's tennis camp in Florida. Over the years, Bollettieri coached Jennifer Capriati, Andre Agassi, Anna Kournikova and a whole host of other tennis champions.

After the success of my week in Palm Springs, I was ready to fly the nest. I was nine years old, after all. So, after seeing a documentary about Bollettieri, I concocted a plan.

It went something like this.

'If you send me to Bollettieri's, I can train all day and do school work. The cost of staying there includes food and coaching. Within a few years, I'll be a famous tennis player and earn a lot of money, so I will pay you back quite quickly,' I pitched.

'What about us?' Mum said.

'I didn't know you wanted to be tennis players too. But they might have family rooms.'

'What about *seeing* us, you not being at home. Won't you miss us?'

'We can write to each other,' I suggested.

I think I was close to getting the plan over the line – the thought of getting rid of me for a while must have been tempting. But it was also fairly pricey, and sporting success does not come with any guarantees.

Anyway, my dad's contract with the Vancouver Whitecaps was coming to an end, so disappointingly enough, they decided I had to fly back to England with the rest of the family.

Not that flying with the family meant I actually flew *with* the family. The Air Canada planes we travelled back and forth on had four seats in the middle and two at the wings. As we were a family of five, this meant one of us always had to travel on their own.

In most families, this would typically be the dad. But my dad, in spite of captaining his country and playing in front of thousands of spectators every week, was painfully shy; he hated the company of strangers. So it was my job to suck it up and spend ten hours next to a stranger making small talk if required. This turned out to be a useful skill for the career I would eventually fall into.

Sometimes the 'spare' seat wasn't even in the same cabin. Occasionally, when I found myself waiting at the baggage carousel on my own, I suspected they had sent me on a completely different plane.

My mum had tried, in vain, to encourage my dad to be less shy. She told us a story about when, early on in their marriage, before they had kids, they were Christmas shopping in Harrogate. As they returned to the car, laden with presents, they came across a homeless man sitting by their vehicle, begging for change. He had no shoes on, it was freezing and there was sleet in the air, which would soon turn to snow. Mum was horrified and desperate to help him.

'Give him some of your trainers,' she said tearfully. Being a professional sportsman and a little bit untidy, Dad always had trainers in his car, some of them box-fresh.

'You do it,' he begged Mum. This was not within his comfort zone.

'No, go on, you do it.'

'I can't. You know I don't like things like that.' He didn't mean talking to the homeless man. He meant communicating with strangers full stop.

Eventually, he relented.

Mum watched with pride as he walked up to the man and held out the trainers, only to watch the two of them engage in conversation. My dad turned and walked back to the car, still holding the pristine Gola pumps, a few minutes later.

'How embarrassing.' Dad was bright red. 'He doesn't want them; he asked if I had any others, in a different size.'

If only the man had taken the trainers, giving my dad a more successful experience with one of his rare attempts at speaking to a stranger, then I might not have had to fly across the Atlantic on my own.

Lessons in a Leotard

England at the beginning of autumn 1982 was grey, damp and cold. There were still tenants living in the house we had left behind, so we moved into a two-bedroomed flat in a high-rise block in the centre of Coventry. We had bought this flat before we left for Vancouver as the tenants had already moved into our family house, and we'd lived there for a few months in the spring of 1981 before our Vancouver adventure. Living there in the spring was a little different to coming back to a dark cold winter when heading out to the park after school wasn't really an option.

It wasn't a great time to live in a high-rise flat in the city centre. It was a time of unrest, of rioting in various cities around the UK – remember Brixton and Toxteth? Well, the racial unrest in our area had started down the road in Birmingham because of the wrongful arrest of a young black man. Coventry had its fair share of rioting; skinheads in Doc Martens charging at young black kids and vice versa. It made for a horribly intimidating atmosphere. Coventry's place in the cultural history of this period was cemented when local band The Specials released their hit song 'Ghost Town'. I am sure you know it, but if not, google it – it's incredibly evocative.

Desolate – that was the Coventry we moved back to. We went from glorious Vancouver to a Ghost Town.

It would be hard to think of a bigger cultural reality check when moving between two cities within the English-speaking world. In the month we arrived home in the UK, Channel 4 was launched. That made a grand total of four TV channels in the UK, which was about 146 fewer than we'd had in Canada. The terrible telly, the awful food, the social division, the racial tension, the unemployment, Margaret Thatcher, Arthur Scargill – it was not a jolly time to come home.

On one particularly grey, gloomy and stressful day, when the tiny flat was getting too much for my mum to handle with her three lively kids, she was heard crying to Dad: 'You might as well have dragged me back from Vancouver to Warsaw.' Years later, I worked in Warsaw when I hosted the World Cycling Championships for the BBC, and I think my mum did the city a disservice. It's got fantastic restaurants and beautiful old squares, but you get her point. Unless I misheard and she said Walsall, which is just outside Birmingham.

I didn't actually mind being back in Coventry; it was a good way to decompress before the inevitable 'next move', because for at least a short while we'd be at our old school with familiar friends and teachers. When you are nine years old and you have already lived at seven different addresses, you feel you can move anywhere, so in my mind I suppose I always thought that I would be back in Vancouver one day. Nothing was truly permanent.

The flat was pleasant enough. It had a corridor down one

side where the two bedrooms were situated, with a bathroom in the centre, and a lounge down the other side attached to a tiny kitchen. This meant there was a natural circular route that we could run around and chase each other, with only two fully-paned glass doors to navigate along the way. A full lap of the flat was probably about ten metres.

On one occasion, when I was the chaser, I was making up the distance, getting closer to my brother Daniel on each lap. He could feel me breathing down his neck. In an attempt to stall me, he pushed the door closed behind him as he ran over the threshold. I ran at full speed towards the door, assuming it hadn't caught the latch, and that I'd only need to pushed at the glass with two hands to open it. Only it *had* caught the latch, and was firmly shut. At the speed I was running, I went straight through the glass of the door and into the lounge on the other side. I felt like the Incredible Hulk: there was glass falling from the sky, blood oozing from somewhere, a terrifying cacophony of screams and eventually tears. I still have the scars on my right hand to show for it.

Mum vacuumed up before we went to the hospital, which tells you all you need to know about her impeccable housekeeping standards.

'We'll be glad when we get back later,' she shouted over the noise of the vacuum, as I held my hand aloft, wrapped in a red-and-white tea towel.

I had been due to have my first cello lesson the next day. We had to cancel it, so I guess we'll never know if Jacqueline du Pré would still be the greatest cello player who ever lived if that door hadn't been slammed shut.

I think we do know, actually.

Even with the kind of recreational inventiveness we displayed with our chasing game, tennis is not an easy sport to practise in a small flat. But, as luck would have it, the block of flats was built on top of a car park, which had pebble-dashed pillars. The pillars served as my very own ball machine; as I hit the ball against them, the irregular pebbles would send the ball flying back to me in random directions. And only occasionally did I misjudge it and hit the ball into a tan-coloured Rover or Allegro (for younger readers, these are cars, not dogs).

There was, however, a newly built indoor tennis centre in Coventry that was relatively cheap. You didn't have to be a member to play, and there were group classes, which my mum was happy to sign me up for. It was also where my sister Louise had started doing sports acrobatics, a genre of gymnastics that involves lots of balancing on top of people, and she also tried out a bit of rhythmic gymnastics there for the first time. It all looked fun and quite graceful from my tennis lessons a few courts down, but I wasn't interested in joining in. I was still intent on becoming the next Tracy Austin.

US tennis star Tracy was cookie-cutter cute: she had bunches and ribbons and was number one in the world in 1980 at the age of eighteen. With hindsight, I now question the wearing of bunches at the age of eighteen, but she was just the kind of woman-child that young children like me loved. One day, I was a little bored as we warmed up with the classic 'frying pan' drill, so I said to the class, 'I bet Tracy Austin doesn't do this.'

The coach, who was a rather classically handsome tennis instructor, probably called Craig, all floppy blond hair and bronzed legs even in the middle of a Coventry winter, and who I probably had a crush on, said, 'Sorry, Tracy, but we need to do the basics first.'

After that, he never called me Gabby again. It was, 'Tracy can get the cones in,' and 'Tracy can demonstrate this serve,' and so on. I was secretly flattered, but pretending I was annoyed one week I made labels, like business cards, which I handed out to everyone. They said: 'My name is Gabby Yorath, not Tracy Austin'.

I clearly had no embarrassment gene, and if there is one thing that I think helps in my current profession, it is not becoming embarrassed too easily.

After a few months of unemployment, three kids sleeping in bunkbeds in a small box room, a couple of A&E visits and the odd run-in with an angry car owner whose wing mirror had tennis ball-shaped dents in it, Dad was finally offered a job.

He was to become player-coach at Bradford City, which meant the family was upping sticks again. Dad's legs were not getting any younger and he wanted to move into management, so this was a good way to ease him out of one profession and into another. Conveniently enough, Bradford is only ten miles from Leeds, which is where all of my English-based family lived. Mum was more than happy to head back to her home city.

Dad loved Leeds; he'd arrived on his own as a schoolboy from Cardiff and made his name at Leeds United in the 1970s in a team that attracted global fame and a fair amount of domestic disdain. People regularly list all the players they hated from that team to me, apropos of nothing, often including my dad. Then they back it up with 'he was so hard'.

The renowned football hard man, the Scottish international Graeme Souness, once said on Sky TV that my dad was the toughest man he'd ever played against, which filled me with a strange sense of pride. David Beckham's kids get to hear people eulogise about their father's incredible free kicks and silky skills, whereas my dad would chop you down and leave an imprint of his boot studs on you. It takes all sorts.

I heard the story of Dad's arrival at Leeds many times when

I was a child, but its poignancy fell on deaf ears. It was only as an adult and the parent of a teenage son that I was able to comprehend the enormity of the sacrifice he made and what a dreadfully lonely experience it must have been for him, leaving home and going there alone.

On the final day of a week's training and trials, the decision of who was to be offered a professional contract was due to be announced. In that era, apprentices had to wash boots, scrub floors and clean offices – anything menial that was asked of them. On that last morning, Dad was sent into the office of the management to clean. When he saw a pile of papers on the desk with the names of the boys who had been selected, it was just too tempting, so he took a peek.

To his great disappointment, he was not one of the two. He kept this to himself and waited for his fate to be sealed. But later, when the letter arrived at his parents' home, he *was* one of the chosen boys. It transpired that one of the two originally selected refused to take up his place if his twin brother, who was also on trial, was not also offered a contract. Leeds United told him that wasn't an option. So neither twin went to Leeds and Dad was offered that remaining place.

For both my parents, then, there was sense of a 'coming home' about this move to Leeds. It felt like they had gone full circle, travelled the world, and that from now on, it was Dad who would be orbiting us if he ever moved jobs again – which, of course, he did.

On my tenth birthday, wearing my presents proudly – a Sony Walkman and a two-tone (mustard and white) jacket from C&A – we went house-hunting again. The house I fell in love with was called Xanadu. Why my parents even went to see it in the first place, I have no idea. It was the kind of magical place I would like to think Kate Bush lives in, not a family with three kids under ten. It was futuristic

(1960s) and had a little moat around it with loads of foliage that made it look as if it was floating down the Amazon. In reality, Xanadu was on a main road in Collingham, a small village near Wetherby.

I had two cassettes for my new Walkman. Both were nicked from my dad's car; they were Adam and the Ants' *Friend or Foe* and ELO's *Xanadu*, the soundtrack to the film of the same name. Fate was playing its hand – I don't need to tell you how strongly I believed our family were destined to live in this domestic utopia. I campaigned hard for Xanadu, but was overruled.

The house my mum fell in love with, and the one we therefore bought, was a paragon of art deco architecture called Val'dor. Outside, it was white, with flat roofs and 1930s lead windows. Inside, it was bursting with incredible original features: a black lacquered bar, a mint-green sunken bath, a huge hand-laid mosaic floor, and a staircase that probably wouldn't pass a health and safety check but was pure drama. It was a theatrical-looking house with a massive personality. Mum and Dad, as per usual, seemed to be spending at the upper end of their budget, and they chose it even though the house needed a new boiler, rewiring, some new windows and probably a new kitchen. It would be a long-term 'project', which was perfect for Mum.

The prospect of a new school wasn't too daunting for us; it was presented by Mum as another adventure. In the 1980s, there wasn't a choice anyway. You didn't agonise about where your kids went to school, or what the SATs results were like. Was there a bus there that stopped outside your door? Is there a place available? Great, here's a grey skirt and a royal-blue jumper – off you go.

The main focus for me wasn't school, though, it was finding a new tennis centre. Armed with the Yellow Pages, my search led me to one in Chapel Allerton, which was a few miles from our new home. I rang up to enquire about their junior tennis programme, probably overstating my ability as a junior tennis player in the process.

'I'm sorry, we don't have any junior members at all,' a middle-aged woman, possibly wearing a pale pink twin-set, said. 'But, in theory, juniors are welcome ... it's £2,000 to join.'

In theory, most juniors don't have £2,000, I resisted replying. Instead, I asked: 'How many indoor courts do you have?'

For £2,000, I wanted her to say forty-five.

'There is one indoor court, so best to use it during the day. We do have a phone booking system, so you are not disappointed when you turn up.'

'I tend to be at school during the day,' I offer as a reason why that might not work for me.

'Well, we do have three squash courts,' she said.

What was I, a forty-seven-year-old accountant working from home? Squash was a game for middle-aged blokes with a penchant for knee injuries, as far as I could see.

'Right, I'll speak to my mum and get back to you, thank you,' I said, knowing that I would never speak to this woman again.

Funnily enough, Mum wasn't up for paying £2,000 for a tennis club membership. She assured me that the outdoor council courts in Roundhay Park would be fine, and that they would have decent lessons. As it turns out, they did – for the one month either side of Wimbledon. By now, it was October. There were no nets up and the gates were locked.

Welcome to tennis in the UK in 1980s. There was literally nowhere in Leeds I could play in October. Around this time, somewhere in Oxfordshire, the ten-year-old Tim Henman was getting quite good at tennis. Lucky for Tim that he was born in Oxford. When I read Matthew Syed's book *Bounce* a few years back, the chapter on environment and the weight it plays in sporting success felt very personal. To paraphrase him, you might have the physical propensity to become the world's greatest javelin thrower, but if you live on a Pacific island with no athletics club or coaching, you will never know nor realise your potential.

A huge part of sporting success comes down to where you live and what is around you, including coaches and facilities, and this, in a nutshell, is how I became a gymnast. If a sports scientist were to look at my physique, abilities and ambitions as a ten-year-old they'd have probably sent me off to British Cycling. But we didn't have sports ID then, as it came to be known; it was just a matter of sucking and seeing. Sometimes, accidents happened, and you end up with the right person doing the right sport. I'm pretty sure if we'd lived in a city with an indoor tennis centre, that would have been my sport. I'm not saying I'd have been any good, but I'd have given it a go.

I decided that in moving us to Leeds, my parents had ruined my life and cost me my career. 'If only we'd stayed in Coventry,' I cried, words uttered by nobody else on the planet ever. Mum thought she was being reassuring when she said, 'Don't worry, the park will be open again in eight months.'

I had to find a new sport – and fast. In our family, if you weren't being ferried around by Mum after school to a sports club, you were nobody. At our middle school, we did PE and games, but we didn't play anything competitively against other schools. We were also heading into a period of teachers' strikes, and the first lessons to be dropped from the curriculum were always PE and art. This was the average sporting experience of anybody who went through the state sector in the 1980s.

Louise had joined the City of Leeds Rhythmic Gymnastics Club and trained twice a week, so while I was assessing which sport could see me become a world champion, I decided to go along with her. In truth, I think Mum gently persuaded me to go, because it was easier to have us both in the same place for a few hours. I had been described by my parents as looking 'like a baby elephant' when attempting to do gymnastics in the back garden the previous summer, so I didn't venture into this sport with a great deal of inner confidence.

Rhythmic gymnastics often gets a bad press, with people saying things like, 'Oh, the one with the ribbon,' in a disparaging and dismissive way. Well, of course, I am going to tell you that it's a lot more than that: it's a highly technical, tough and demanding sport. There are five pieces of apparatus used, but only four in competition, with one dropped from the international circuit every few years and the other reinstated: rope, hoop, ribbon, clubs and ball. Each routine will be up to ninety seconds long and has to contain certain elements of difficulty; there is a lot of dance involved, but also the precision needed to throw the apparatus and execute the moves.

I quickly became addicted. Tracy Austin fell by the wayside, and Diliana, Anaelia, Marina, Bianca and various other Eastern European teenagers I would never meet, filled the void as my new poster girls. Bulgaria and Russia were the top two nations in the world at the time, and it pained me that I hadn't been born in Sofia.

The club was run by Anne Talintyre and Kathy McRevie, two middle-aged single women who were both prolific chain-smokers. They were as kind and giving as they were acerbic and authoritarian, former schoolteachers who devoted unfathomably long hours to all of us for very little in return. I think our subs were a couple of quid a night. Anne and Kathy were saints. Imagine, night after night, having to deal with all those teenage girls, with their moods, body issues, hormones, and friendship trials and tribulations – not to mention the parents, who often lived their own sporting lives vicariously through their kids. They were taskmasters, but they really cared – and that's what keeps you going back.

We trained at schools in dodgy parts of the city, or, in the case of the Jack Lane Institute of Sport, parts of the city that were condemned and ready to be torn down. At one stage, every other building apart from ours had already been bulldozed.

But the 'red-light district' locations and lack of decent facilities didn't matter. I loved the training. It involved strength, flexibility and conditioning, and then learning technical skills and building routines, choosing the music and practising for hours and hours until they were perfectly honed. It was all about repetition; most sports are.

It's fair to say I wasn't a natural, but I was a fast learner. I'd watch scratchy video tapes of Eastern European gymnasts for hours on end, breaking down their moves and trying them out with Louise in our bedrooms, where we occasionally smashed a window with a badly executed move with a club.

We bought cheap plain leotards and decorated them with fabric paint at the kitchen table in an effort to replicate the unattainably expensive ones worn by our heroes. We were not very proficient; these leotards usually ended up looking like they had been vomited on by a stag party.

Until the late 1990s, rhythmic gymnastics had some quirky rules regarding the music you could use in your routines. At the beginning, it was piano only, and sometimes for big competitions, we took our own pianist, which seems incredibly extravagant and glamorous. Then the rules were relaxed, and we could use any instrument, but it had to be solo. The most common choice was the guitar. I knew everything that John Williams had ever recorded. I once found an old man in Leeds to play the harmonica for me; there can't be many fourteen-year-old girls who have advertised in a newsagent's window for a harmonica player. In fact, when I think of it now, I can't believe my mum let me go to the old fella's house. I wanted him to play the theme tune to *Dixon of Dock Green*, and I paid him £20 for his efforts.

These days, any music is permitted as long as it doesn't have vocals. How much easier my life would have been if I was competing now, with access to YouTube and a whole world of online music. It definitely sounds simpler than paying old men to play the harmonica.

Louise and I listened to hours of classical music tapes in our rooms to find that one bit of solo instrument, or we'd be in the garage together, drawing stripes on our ribbons. Like most siblings, when we weren't fighting, we got on very well. We're just eleven months apart in age, known as Irish twins.

'I didn't realise you could get pregnant that quickly after your first baby!' my mum once told us.

Louise and I had very different friends and diverse interests. In spite of her angelic looks and willowy frame, she liked to settle an argument with a scrap. She was a deceptively good pugilist. She was also a beautiful gymnast, graceful and flexible, but she did have her fair share of comedic disasters. We were competing in the Northern Championships in Liverpool in a sports centre in Toxteth, the kind that never filled its vending machine and had a grille over the reception desk. Louise was on the mat with her ball routine. She needed a good score to finish in the top three. The ball is hard to control, and points are awarded for throwing it, performing movements while it's in the air, then catching it. The ball left her hand, and she went to do something complicated underneath it. When the ball came down, she misjudged it and it flew off her hand, bouncing to the other side of the mat. A lady in the front row had obviously been shopping on her way to the competition, and a large red-and-white grocery bag was sitting by her feet. Louise's ball bounced right inside. She dashed across the mat to retrieve it, plunging her hand into the bag and producing a smooth green cabbage before she realised the texture wasn't quite right. She had to reach in again, fumbling about for her ball. I'm sure most of the audience were greatly disappointed that the woman wasn't also a lover of watermelons. There was stifled laughter from the crowd. At least the shopping bag commotion woke everyone up.

I was also guilty of bringing shame to the family's sporting name. Once, in a Commonwealth Games warm-up competition, I sent my ribbon too high into the air and it hooked itself on some pipework. The music carried on playing, Prokofiev's haunting *Romeo and Juliet*, while a large crane had to be brought out, operated by two burly engineers, probably called Brian and Dave, to get the ribbon down, with the leotarded me wandering around underneath them as the audience watched on. Anyone can make a mistake, of course, but as I had already made this one three times in the warm-up, it was frankly unforgiveable; I knew exactly where the ceiling and that pipework was. The good folk of Wakefield leisure centre were not impressed. Neither were the judges – I scored a 4.2. I would have expected 9.4 if I had executed the routine properly, so I think the judges were making a point; namely that I was a twat that day.

I went home feeling a bit of an arse. It was nobody's fault but mine. My coach, Anne, was not impressed and ignored me, which was worse than being shouted at. I didn't want to let anyone down, least of all myself. Sport is a fantastic teacher; I hadn't prepared properly and the outcome was shoddy. I decided that I didn't want to be a shoddy person.

And so, finding my way to becoming a gymnast was a happy accident. Moving to Leeds had made it impossible for me to keep playing tennis, but there was obviously something inside me that was aching to belong to something and have an outlet for competition and self-improvement – and that vessel turned out to be rhythmic gymnastics.

5

High School

When we first moved to Leeds, I was quite fortunate that the city was still experimenting with a middle school system, so I had a couple of years at a 'middle school', which would be years seven and eight as we know them now, before I went to high school. This was slightly less scary than heading straight into a massive comprehensive with 1,400 pupils at the age of eleven in a new city with no mates. By the time I did go to high school, I had a gang of friends and a bit of a purpose.

The high school itself was truly physically ugly. Think, if you will, of a really tired 1960s building, all metal-sheeted panels, skinny pillars, lots of concrete, weird, muted colours of paint and a flat, usually leaking, roof. Well, Cardinal Heenan High School was even more unsightly than that. It was an amalgam of two old schools on a large site, and its one redeeming physical feature was that it had acres of playing fields. In the year I joined, we were informed that the school was due to be pulled down, which is always a lovely note on which to end a welcoming speech to the new intake – 'Look what you could have won' – as an architect's image of the new school was unveiled.

It took another twelve years for that demolition and subsequent rebuild to actually happen, thanks to 'administration issues' (no money). I can only imagine the state of the school by the time the bulldozers were actually allowed on site. There were so many classrooms condemned because of probable asbestos that lessons were often held in portable cabins in the car park – and these, we quickly learned in the winter months, were not sufficiently heated. Most of the teachers kept their coats on.

The best part about Cardinal Heenan was its exceptional teachers. This goes for any institution: flashy buildings might make things more comfortable, but it is the people who make it tick. At Cardinal Heenan, there were three who stood out as a triptych of brilliance.

John Flanagan was a ginger-moustached running machine – he's probably running the Marathon des Sables as we speak. He was head of RE and our head of year, and he looked like the teacher most likely to win *SAS: Who Dares Wins*. Nobody messed with John. When he wasn't teaching, he always had a rucksack on, as if he was ready for it to all 'go off'. His booming voice could be heard regularly, pulling reprobates into line: 'You boys, stub those fags out, run twenty laps of the field and report to my office afterwards.' And they always did. I absolutely adored RE because of him, and got an A.

Anne Woliter was my PE teacher. I am sure she taught an academic subject too, but it was on the netball court and in the gymnasium she made her impact with me, and quite a few other girls. Her delivery was in the style of a navy track-suited Victoria Wood. 'Right, girls: three laps of the courts and then into two groups of seven. Sinead's on her period, so

someone is going to have to be on both teams.' She even tried
to get a five-a-side football team together for us girls, and got
a former Leeds United player in to coach us. We couldn't get
any matches, as nobody else was playing, so eventually we
all reverted to netball. Miss Woliter believed in the power of
sport; she knew how good it was for our souls as well as our
physiques.

And finally, completing the trio was Kath McMahon.
She was head of geography, and an exceptional teacher who
brought the subject to life. She always wore a pencil skirt
and heels with a natty little fitted jacket; she loved a pussy-
bow shirt and was never seen without shocking pink lipstick
and that flowing blonde Farah Fawcett hair bouncing on her
collar. I appreciated the effort she made. When I hear people
say disparagingly about a man 'He dressed like a geography
teacher', I actually imagine someone looking more like
Claudia Schiffer.

The glamorous, perfume-wearing teachers appealed to me.
I chose Latin because the flame-haired Mrs Ausobsky drove
a white Porsche 911 (it turns out this wasn't down to some
anomaly within the government's payment structure – her
husband was a brain surgeon). There were only eight of us
in our Latin GCSE class, as most kids had sensibly opted for
the slightly more useful Spanish or French. But I had fallen
out with my French teacher over our differing standpoints
on the 1980s teachers' strikes and what I felt were his overly
militant opinions. By dropping his subject, I really showed
him, didn't I? I made him pay.

Because now *I* can't speak French.

Taking Latin at Cardinal Heenan was like being in a private school for two hours a week. Having just eight of us in
the class, and taking into account illness and bunking off,
meant that frequently there would be just four or five. I got

an A, which scientifically proves that smaller class sizes taught by Porsche-owning, glamorous teachers work.

Nunquam amittas; you never lose it.

I was so impacted by the dedication of Flanagan, Woliter and McMahon that I invited them to my wedding over a decade later. I am sure they would have preferred me to send them a crate of wine and a thank-you note for their efforts, so they didn't have to trudge up to Scotland for a couple of days. But allowing my ego to take centre stage, I thought this was the ultimate recognition of their services, the grand prize: 'Congratulations, you are the chosen ones.'

More publicly, I have written about them in the *TES*, and, as recently as 2014, when I was inaugurated as the Chancellor of Leeds Trinity University, Anne and Kath came to the ceremony. I like to think they finally realise now just how grateful I am; in fact, they probably dread getting emails from me. 'Oh, bloody hell what's she inviting us to now, Kath? I told you to change your email address.'

At a time of huge disruption, strikes, work to rule and massive cutbacks, these teachers went above and beyond. Miss Woliter, perhaps the sweetest of all, kept our netball team going, finding us fixtures and letting us practise at breaktime when she really wasn't supposed to open up the courts. She even drove us to away matches in the mothballed minibus. I can see us all now, travelling to a school forty-five minutes away: it's the middle of winter, the heating on the bus doesn't work and we are changing into our nylon short-skirts. Miss Woliter, at the wheel, throws seven Mars bars into the back of the bus for us. You don't forget great acts of kindness like that in a hurry.

She also pushed us to enter cross-country races, encouraged me to compete in the high jump at the city championships, and made sure that if any child had enthusiasm for sport, she

was going to meet it. There were those who had no enthusiasm for sport at all, but I didn't really talk to them.

(Of course I did; I'm joking.)

One of our gang was one of those people with no love for
sport. When she was thirteen, her periods started and that was
it. She was out of games for good; she was either on, coming
on or just finishing, and she had a note for all seasons.

Another of my friends seemed to miss PE for most of high
school, and only started to exercise after she went on a girls'
holiday at eighteen years old. She came home and realised
that the little pot belly she had acquired was down to sugary
alcohol, not trapped wind. She's a proper fitness enthusiast
now, so the ability and desire were always there, and her case
proves once more that it's the way we sell sport to teenage
girls that is important if we want to keep them fit and engaged
for the rest of their lives. There are so many ways to enjoy
keeping active, and many different ways to motivate and
educate teenage girls, than through organised team sport.
Just some small adjustments in the kinds of PE on offer would
reap huge rewards for the state later when those girls have
better health markers as adult women. But Anne Woliter had
enough on her plate back then; she didn't have time to reform
the curriculum as well.

Can I take a moment to tell you how important I think PE
is as a subject, and why I think it's an outrage that there is no
compulsory sport or fitness in the curriculum for any child
over eleven years old in the United Kingdom? Well, I am
going to. We have a national obesity crisis that is costing our
health service billions, but we don't value sport and movement in our children's education. The two are inextricably
linked; if you don't come from a home where healthy eating
and sport or fitness are nurtured, the only other place you
will learn about them is school. As well as the strain on the

health service, a lack of a fit and healthy workforce leads to lost tax income from those workers. And that's before you even begin to consider the mental health costs of physical incapacity. It's a no-brainer to me. If we spend more money on our children's physical wellbeing, we will be rewarded within a generation.

Right, back to Leeds in 1986.

My school mates were unbelievably supportive of my ambitions in gymnastics. By that, I mean they let me get on with it. They didn't take the mickey, they weren't jealous of any attention I got through any small successes, and they didn't mind if I couldn't make social events and nights out when I was away training. Most weekends, I was in Bedford, Lilleshall, London or Northampton, training at the national centres of excellence.

I often travelled to these national squad sessions on my own by train, or, if she was coaching at them, I'd be in the back of Miss Talintyre's car. On a trip to Bedford, she could smash through three packs of Benson & Hedges quite easily, so I travelled with the window open. This was not ideal on a sleety December day, but it was better than secondary cancer. Mum made me strip off in the laundry room when I got home, so I wouldn't bring my cigarette-smelling clothes into the house. She is so anti-smoking that for nearly forty years she has had a gold plaque at home that says 'Val'dor is a no-smoking zone' – just in case any of her friends ever thought about lighting up.

On these long journeys, as well as puffing through her annual duty-free allowance in fags, Anne used to crank up BBC Radio 3. This was a station that was never heard in our family home, as my parents were more Motown than Mozart.

'What's this?' I would ask, when I was moved by something particularly lovely.

'This is Albinoni's Adagio for Strings,' she would tell me. 'It was used to address the American people when President John F. Kennedy was assassinated.'

Then, a few tunes later: 'I like this. Who wrote this?'

'Vaughan Williams. It's called *The Lark Ascending* . . . Can you hear the lark?'

I may have smelled like an ashtray, but at least I was getting a musical education. The hours of experimental jazz on the A1 were a little more challenging, though.

'It's just noise, Miss Talintyre . . . please can we have Radio 2 on?'

If I had been doing these hours down the M1 as a teenager now, I would be wearing headphones and be in my own head listening to my own choice of music. I am grateful that I was forced into this widening of my musical knowledge at such a young age – even if I still can't listen to Dave Brubeck's 'Take Five' without subliminally smelling tobacco.

My mates carried on inviting me to social occasions, in spite of my twenty per cent attendance rate. It was probably because I didn't drink alcohol, meaning I could be relied upon to be the vaguely sensible one. Also, I was flat-chested and skinny, so I wasn't going to be a threat when it came to vying for attention from boys.

While in my sporting world, being flat-chested and skinny was an attribute, in the world of teenage boys, it was a repellent. I may as well have had halitosis. In fact, a girl with chronic halitosis but a massive round bum would have been much more successful with the opposite sex than I was. When one boy explained to me that he liked me, but I was too skinny to fancy, I warned him that the busty, curvaceous girls he did fancy were more likely to develop type 2 diabetes when they were older.

I didn't really, I just said, 'Oh.'

I wasn't that sharp-tongued or witty, and type 2 wasn't in our vernacular back then.

Girls whose bums and boobs popped up over the summer holidays went from zero attention to hottest in the year overnight. I, on the other hand, had spent the summer sleeping face-down in an attempt to prevent my breasts from ever appearing; a ritual that was as unnecessary as it was scientifically unsound, as there has never been a large-breasted woman in our family. (Years later, in the late nineties, when Eva Herzigová's famous 'Hello, boys' advert was on every billboard, I purchased a pair of chicken fillet inserts for my new Wonderbra and thought back with amusement of the lengths I had once gone to to avoid the very breasts I now wanted to boost.)

Wearing a leotard for my hobby meant I knew of every bump, lump or development on my body. I have since recognised that I had a subconscious and unhealthy wish to keep my body in a state of prepubescence. Every pubic hair was whisked away, and I resisted wearing any kind of bra for a long time. I realise this is at odds with what most teenage girls want at thirteen.

'What are these?' I asked my mum, dumping a bag of 32AAA bras on her bed. She had left it in my room.

'They were your cousin Sarah's. Aunty Pat dropped them round. She thought you might want to try them on,' Mum said, hopefully. She had commented subtly a few weeks before that I needed some 'support'.

'I'm not Dolly Parton,' I huffed as I walked out of the room, roundly rejecting my first batch of bras.

It was the most painfully embarrassing period of my life. I hated that my body was changing, but more than that I hated the idea of anyone else noticing it. A few years after the road trips had started, we went on one last family holiday where

I even found a different pool at the resort to sunbathe at so that my parents couldn't see my developing body. On the final night, my dad said, 'Would you like to go for a walk on the beach?'

So off we went.

'Gabs, we think you need to wear a bra ...'

I was raging inside.

What was my mum thinking, sending him along to have that chat with me? I don't remember what he said next because I was so livid that I just blocked out his noise. A few years ago, my daughter started her period when I was at work presenting *Match of the Day* and her dad had to get her pads and painkillers, but she was totally cool with it, because they have always had a close and honest relationship. My dad, on the other hand, had barely ever been on his own with me for more than an hour before that walk down the beach.

My poor parents probably didn't have a clue as to how much the prospect of getting older terrified me. I felt that if I succumbed to the bras, I would be admitting defeat, acknowledging that my body would go full-blown woman. Before I knew it, I'd be having a period. Which is kind of the point of puberty, I grant you, but for me, that would be the end. Not a beginning.

Can you imagine wearing a thick sanitary pad under a leotard? And then leaping around a mat, lifting your leg in the air, worrying that the aforementioned pad might make an unscheduled appearance and fly out on to row four? I knew it was coming, but I wanted to put it off for as long as I could. Of course, when it did arrive, it was two days before the British Junior Championships, so I competed in my biggest competition to date wearing a sanitary pad under my leotard. Incredibly, I came second, so I then perversely decided that being on my period brought me good luck.

This is one of the joys of being superstitious; you can turn any situation into an omen.

One of my cleverest, sassiest friends was Basia (pronounced *Bash-er*) Porecka, who introduced our little gang to the joys of Polish cuisine. The Polish Centre on Chapel Town Road was very handy for cheap lunches when the teachers were on strike. Our favourite choice was pierogis, little dumplings that could be filled with anything the chef fancied. We might have a pork or chicken pierogi to start with, followed by apple pierogi for pudding. The whole place was subsidised, so there was a lot of pierogi for our pound. We'd visit the Polish Centre at least once a week, four teenagers in school uniform with a regular table in the 'restaurant' alongside old blokes from Gdansk who were enjoying some sixty per cent proof special vodka with their borscht. Social integration at its finest.

Basia was the youngest of five kids of Polish immigrant parents. Her father was a labourer and a bit of a drinker, according to Basia, and seemed quite a bolshy chap. I don't think I ever heard him speak English; he just said things loudly in Polish. He didn't like Western music being played in the house and didn't particularly like his kids going to pop concerts either. They had to lie about 'fun' things; it was like a Slavic *Footloose* round their house.

Tragically, he died suddenly of a massive heart attack on the doorstep of the family home when Basia was just thirteen. We chipped together to get her a 'feel better' present. We decided to buy something that her father had previously banned, and as we couldn't afford to take her to see U2, we bought her a bag of make-up. My mum was a little surprised and thought it was perhaps a bit insensitive, but we thought it was genius.

I am not sure why, but when we got to high school we drifted away from each other; it's strange when I think about how close we once were, and yet now I haven't got a clue how or where she is. I wonder sometimes if the peripatetic life I had as a child made me a bit too independent, unwilling to really get close to my school friends. I have often defended our nomadic lifestyle as being a factor in me being so adaptable, but maybe it also meant I was a bit flighty when it came to friendship commitment. But I am glad I can write about Basia now, because she was a great friend to me, and I loved being let into the social life of the Polish community in the north of England for a short while.

As we got older the social scene shifted to the Leeds Irish Centre. The attraction of the Irish Centre was not its cuisine, sadly – although, to this day, I would walk over hot coals for good soda bread. Many of my friends were Irish Catholics, and their grandmas baked the most wonderful 'brown bread', as they called it. Anne-Marie Kenny, my best mate, often let us stay at her gran's on a Saturday night, as it was a cheaper cab ride than getting back to our own homes, and her gran usually had a hot loaf going on a Sunday morning. We would adorn it with lashings of Kerry butter and a bit of bacon and enjoy it with a large mug of tea for a perfect hangover cure.

I actually didn't have that many hangovers, though. Saturday night at the Irish Centre was all about boys, music and – only very occasionally, for me – booze. My parents seemed very relaxed about letting me spend evenings there, even though the Irish Centre was not in the most salubrious part of town. My friends had big families, which meant there was always an older sibling, an aunt, a cousin or even a parent keeping an eye out.

There has rarely been a night out in the history of womankind that has lived up to the excitement and anticipation of the 'getting ready' phase. When you are fifteen years old and you don't go out very much, that anticipation can begin as long as four weeks in advance of the actual evening.

The potential snog target for the evening in question was a moving one; flirting was a slow and painful process. If a boy you liked was in a different (usually Catholic) school, it could take weeks to reach any kind of fruition.

'My mum's cousin is from the same village as him in Mayo, so the next time I see my mum's cousin, I will try to find out if he has a girlfriend.'

'When are you seeing your mum's cousin?'

'Christmas.'

The idea of ringing a boy at his house was terrifying. Unless you'd sent a carrier pigeon round warning him to stand by the phone, that call could be picked up by anyone who lived there. The idea of his father or mother answering the call, then bumping into my father or mother at church and telling them I had been calling their boy made me feel sick. Not that either set of parents would care, I realise now, but it would lead to weeks – if not months – of ribbing from the whole family. Being the eldest meant I was furrowing every teenage trench, and my two younger siblings joined in with the teasing – before slipping seamlessly into the stream of my pioneering work.

'Can I go to a nightclub in Leeds on Saturday?' Me, every few weeks for a year.

'No, you're too young.' My mum, every few weeks for a year.

'Mum, can I go to a club in Leeds on Saturday night?' Me, a year later.

'Only if you take your sister.' My mum, clearly over the negotiating phase of parenting by now.

'But she's a year younger than me! And I asked a year ago.'

'Well, don't go, then.'

That's basically the contents of a book called *Being the Eldest*.

The Irish Centre was a middle ground. It was grown-up but not seedy, and it was positioned safely away from the other temptations of Leeds town centre. Fashion was optional. I spent most evenings there wearing thick, dark tights under denim shorts. Occasionally the shorts were flowery, but the tights were always black. Footwear was steel toe-capped Doc Martens or cowboy boots (I met some cool gymnasts from London and broke away from Doc Martens for a while), and the whole ensemble was completed by a woolly cardigan that might eventually come off to reveal a plain coloured T-shirt. Hair was big and unruly, and make-up was minimal but inexpertly applied; we didn't have any social influencers showing us what to do. It's really a wonder I managed to get a snog at all wearing such enticing clobber; no wonder my mum wasn't worried about letting me go out. I have barely a single photograph of this period, because we didn't take cameras out with us. We didn't have phones, we barely had a *mirror* – and let me tell you, kids, it was heaven. We were allowed to be imperfect.

The music at the Irish Centre was loud and anthemic. There were live bands in the early part of the night, often with an Irish connection; bands that could have been the Pogues but weren't. Occasionally, there was a ceilidh. Tommy Ferguson, who ran the Irish Centre, had an ear for talent. One night in the 1980s he booked a band from Manchester called Oasis; they played for £100 and a few pints.

Dancing was not of the bump-and-grind type I would later come across in the nightclubs of Leeds; it was more of the jumping-up-and-down-on-the-spot variety. White

Irish-heritage boys find this kind of dancing much easier to handle, so there was a fifty-fifty gender split on the dance floor, creating a sweaty vibe. The décor was basic, the communal areas felt more like a school, and the main room had a stage and a dance floor with velour-covered chairs and tables around the edges. It was peak northern working-man's club chic.

When I was building up for a competition or had an early training session the next day, I didn't have any of the alcohol that had been sneaked into whichever house we were getting ready at. Anyone partaking was usually pissed by the time we rolled out of the cab at the Irish Centre. The nights there might have felt like a giant house party, but the centre wanted to keep its licence, so didn't serve any of us underage kids. Any 'topping up' was strictly of the mine-sweeping variety, helping ourselves to discarded snakebite or Malibu and Coke – all the chic drinks.

These Saturday-night experiences left me longing to be a bit more Irish. My Grandma Sheila's dad, Great-Grandad John, was from County Cork – that's all the Irish I had in me. Her brother Terry and his side of the family still had the family name, Devaney, which originates from 'Son of Dubheamhna', a clan in County Down.

Being asked, 'Where are you from?' at the Irish Centre did not mean which part of Leeds; it meant which corner of Ireland.

'Cork,' I would say, putting on a subtle Cork accent. Don't get me wrong, I loved my Welsh family and roots but there wasn't a Welsh Centre in Leeds to hang out in so these were my Celtic cousins.

The thing I envied most was the way my friends could slip into the houses and lives of each other's families, simply because they were from the same county in Ireland. They had a shared heritage and a sense of belonging. In the summer holidays, they'd head back to the mother country to live with uncles and aunts in Mayo, Sligo or Roscommon. They'd sneak out, party until late and hook up with the farmer's son they'd snogged last summer. It all sounded so brilliantly feral. They were getting sexual experiences in another country with people the rest of us didn't know, so they could say what they liked about it; there was no way we could verify it.

'Yeah, we're heading back to Wales this summer,' I'd chirp up in an attempt to compete with their Celtic adventures. I didn't offer any further information, because in truth it was a trip to Cardiff for two days to see Gramps (Dai) and Gran (Mary), who still lived on the cheery council estate where my dad had grown up. We'd stay in a Holiday Inn and eat at a TGI, and we'd visit my cousins, a fun trio of sporting lads, but a lot older than us. I wasn't exactly running barefoot round Pembrokeshire, snogging lads called Dylan and Aled.

In 2018, Nana Sheila had her ninetieth birthday party at the Irish Centre in Leeds. The teenagers still tried to snaffle alcohol, and the dance floor was still full for 'Tainted Love'. Nana Sheila fell over in the toilet, but said it wasn't the gin. Old people I didn't recognise told me they hadn't seen me for years. And it was still £2.50 for a Bacardi and Coke. Reassuringly enough, nothing had changed at all.

6

Bradford

By her own admission, Mum was never a huge football fan, but she was a big fan of the day out. She just about knew which coloured strip Dad's team were playing in; her own outfits, however, were immaculate even when we were playing down the divisions. She didn't go anywhere without a full manicure and a perfectly coiffed head of hair, and lower league football was no different. Her commitment to grooming has never been anything less than world class.

I adored the ritual of it all: the getting ready to go; the atmosphere when the crowd started chanting; the half-time snack of salt and vinegar Seabrook crisps so acidic they took the skin off the roof of your mouth; reading the programme, then playing a guessing game with my sister – 'How old is the full back?' Then, afterwards, the full-time games of 'it' in the car park with the other players' kids.

When I was younger, I didn't really know what was going on for most of the match. I genuinely believed football matches were made up of two thirty-five-minute halves for many years, because we were always late arriving and then left for the players' lounge at half-time, five minutes early, to avoid the rush for the bar. But even if I didn't understand it, I felt part of something – and that is what draws you in, and makes you go back for more. I loved match day. I loved whichever team my dad was playing for.

The 1984–1985 season was thrilling. Dad's team were winning every week, and promotion was on the cards. I started to pay more attention to the actual football.

On Saturday 11 May 1985, we already knew Bradford would be crowned champions before the final game of the season against Lincoln City even began. The whole day was set up for celebration. There was to be a massive party after the match, and the players were off to Spain the following day to continue the festivities.

Footballers are always being asked for tickets to games, but for my dad, this particular day was a logistical nightmare. He had so many friends and family wanting to join in with the fun that Louise, Daniel and I were turfed out of our usual directors' box seats and told to sit on our own one block over. We were quite happy, though, as we had unlimited Sports Mix and crisps to keep us quiet. Louise and I were in matching pastel-coloured suits from Marks and Spencer, hers peach and mine lemon, with floral shirts underneath and new shoes that were a bit too tight. This was an occasion, a day to celebrate.

Mum stayed in our usual seats with dad's parents, Grandpa Dai and Grandma Mary, who had come up from Cardiff. Just before half-time, Mum made her usual early exit to the bar with our grandparents. 'Do you want to come now, or wait until half-time?' she shouted from the back of the stand.

Half-time was only four minutes away when we made one of the most important decisions of our young lives. 'We'll come now,' we said, and made our way over to her.

Daniel didn't bother coming with us to the players' lounge. We hadn't noticed, but he slipped off somewhere else, which wasn't so unusual. The lounge was already quite busy, as a few others had had the same idea as Mum, hoping to beat the rush. Our lemonades had been poured, and we were searching for somewhere to perch, when a man ran in from the direction of the stand we had just departed. 'The stand is on fire – get out!' he shouted.

But there was no rush. People carried on chatting. Should we finish the lemonade? Barely anyone moved.

'It's on bloody *fire*! The stand is on fire – get out!' Just seconds later, his second cry was accompanied by the sight and smell of smoke coming in through the top of the door.

Now there was movement.

There was a frantic rush of people to the tiny door that led to the back of the ground. It was the size of a normal internal domestic door. Finally, it was opened, and dozens of us spilled out on to the street.

The air was already filling with acrid smoke. Everything looked like a sepia photograph, tinged with orange, and the smells were intensifying. As the roof of the stand went up, it was the stench of tar that dominated; we'd had some holes in our flat roof at home fixed not long before, and this was the same smell, only amplified a hundred times. It was overwhelming.

'Where's Daniel? Where is he?' Mum was beside herself with panic. She kept trying to get back inside through the door, but people were still coming out.

Louise and I were silent, totally overwhelmed by fear. We didn't know where Daniel was. He was with us – and then he wasn't.

The plumes of black smoke were now reaching twenty, thirty, forty feet into the sky. Mum wouldn't leave the back of the ground until she'd found him, but the police and officials were trying to usher us away from the danger zone, which was growing. The flames were accompanied by that sinister crackling, snapping sound that you get when a big fire takes hold of an old building. The heat was intense; cars parked a few feet away from us were too hot to touch. Soon, they would start to melt.

Then, in the midst of the chaos, Daniel appeared through the smoke, just before we were moved on by police. One of the players had found him and shepherded him up to the lounge. Apparently, he had run off to my dad's office, which was below the bar, near the changing rooms. Dad normally had a stash of sweets in his desk, and all the staff and players knew Dan, so he could wander around on match day as he pleased. The player who found him, Don Goodman, would later learn that his ex-girlfriend, Jane Sampson, had died in the fire.

By now, of course, the players had been taken off the pitch and the match had been abandoned. For several minutes, though, there had been a surreal scene of chaos erupting in the stand while the match continued.

In the footage from that day, John Helm, the commentator for the BBC, can be heard to say: 'There is a small fire in the stand . . . ' Then he carried on commentating on the football, because nobody could possibly believe that the small fire he'd mentioned would become the disaster it did, just minutes later.

Most of the players and management started helping police to clear the ground, still wearing their playing kit. Large numbers of the fans from the stand we had left were flooding to the front, throwing themselves over a six-foot wall on to the pitch. Some of their clothes and hair were on fire as they landed pitch-side. Many others, though, went to the back of the stand, trying to escape the same way they had entered the ground.

When they got there, they discovered that the doors were locked and the turnstiles were closed. Most of the people who died in the Bradford stadium fire were among those who had gone to the back of the stand to try to escape. This was where they left from every week, after all. But they had never tried to leave *during* a match, and didn't know that it was the norm to lock the doors and turnstiles.

How do you make a decision in the midst of a disaster? What informs your brain? Your past experiences, probably. You choose left or right – and, with that, you choose life or death.

In 1985, it was rare for a match at this level to have cameras present, unlike today, where almost every professional game, and many amateur ones, are recorded for some broadcaster or another. *Grandstand* was on the TV in the pub we had been sent to, and because of the nature of our match, there were cameras present at Valley Parade, Bradford's ground. This meant the BBC were able to go to live pictures. From the window of the pub, we could see the forty-foot flames rising from the stand we had been sitting in just minutes before, while on the TV, the cameras showed us what was happening inside the ground: the panic and carnage as people ran for their lives.

'We understand that there are a few people with serious injuries,' said the broadcaster.

The adults looked at each other in a way that said they knew this was woefully understated.

And they were right: it was grossly inaccurate. Fifty-six people died, and many more were seriously injured and left with life-changing physical and mental conditions. Some families lost relatives from three generations in a single day.

We were a very lucky family. Every single one of my dad's guests got out alive, despite many of his tickets being located just rows away from where the fire was eventually found to have been started by a discarded cigarette. Dad cut his leg jumping out of the window of a bar that was below street level; he'd been helping to clear it of guests, and the door he'd entered through was no longer passable. But that cut was the only physical injury sustained by any of us. Mentally, I cannot tell you how deeply that day has impacted his health, but I think it probably played a role in his slide into heavier drinking and more pronounced mood swings.

On the day itself, he saw things he has since said he can never unsee. He looked back when a police officer warned him not to. He went to dozens of funerals in the weeks after the fire. He was forever in a black tie, with swollen red eyes. It was an incredibly dark time for the whole community, and in our family it was a disaster that hung over us all for a long time. The club put itself at the heart of the healing process, and as painful as it was, I think it was a vital part of the club coming back from that disaster. For Bradford to play again, thrive again, and to achieve Premier League status fifteen years later, was enormous for the city.

Bradford was one of a few tragic football disasters of that era that would change the way we watched and enjoyed football forever. The Heysel Stadium disaster, where thirty-nine fans died, happened just weeks later, and then four years later was the Hillsborough disaster, where ninety-six Liverpool fans died. I am not trying to group them all together – they all happened under very different circumstances, and every single life lost is a waste and a black mark for the sport. But together, they did eventually contribute towards the adoption of hugely significant changes to grounds, including the banning of standing areas, improved safety and adjustments to the way matches were policed. On top of that, there were massive developments made in the treatment of burns victims after the Bradford fire.

There are many books and reports written on these disasters, and I can't add anything to the weight and importance of those. All I can tell you is that those families who lost loved ones at Valley Parade never got over their loss. I interviewed families and witnesses for a documentary I made a few years ago on the thirtieth anniversary, and the sadness and pain were as visceral as ever. The ramifications for some of them have affected the next generation and beyond, and I'm sure the same is true for those impacted by the other disasters.

For our family, there was eventually what my mum called a minor miracle. Nine months to the day after the Bradford fire, on 8 February 1996, my brother Jordan was born. My parents had not planned on extending the family, but in the summer of 1995, when my very slim mum was finding herself more tired than usual, swollen after her evening meal and not fitting into her clothes, alarm bells rang. They waited until she was four months pregnant to tell us.

Mum had been asked to have an amniocentesis test because, at thirty-five years old, she was considered a 'geriatric mother', and was at greater risk of having a baby with Down's syndrome. She refused to have the test. Her reasoning was that after we all came away from Bradford safe and unharmed, this baby came into the world regardless of whatever challenges the baby may or may not have; it was a beautiful gift and a wonderful addition to the family.

Daniel was thrilled. He was desperate for a little brother, and he was convinced the baby was going to be a boy, even though we warned him there was a fifty per cent chance it might not be. Mum's pregnancy shifted our focus away from the disaster of Bradford; it gave us hope. And, as a young girl heading into puberty, it helped to scare me away from any idea I might have had of becoming a teenage mum – or doing the thing that would turn me into one. I didn't need 'the talk'; watching my mum's pregnancy close up, and then offering my services in the early months of Jordan's life as a night nanny, was more than enough to keep me focused on my studies and sport and away from boys and their dangerous appendages. Clever Mum.

As for the baby's name, well, that was a family decision. I was championing a name that would reflect our Welshness: Morgan or Myfanwy for a girl, or Rhodri or Aled for a boy. But in the end, Jordan, as in the River Jordan, was chosen by unanimous vote.

I like to think his middle name was a small victory for Wales, though. Jordan Lloyd Yorath was our seven-pound Bradford miracle; our phoenix from the ashes.

7

Blue Peter

I can pinpoint the exact moment when I realised what I wanted to do with my life.

I had toyed with becoming a barrister when I was eleven, but a relative told me it was a hard career to get back into after babies. Can I just stress that I was eleven? Why on earth would I be concerned about work–life balance and maternity packages? How did she even *know* it was hard to get back into? Why didn't she just say, 'That's a wonderful thing to do, good luck'? Whatever that ambition-crusher's motives were, it worked. I stopped saying that I wanted to be a barrister, although I was still deeply fascinated by *Rumpole of the Bailey*.

After that, I toyed with a few other career ideas, but nothing stuck.

'You want to be an optician, an undertaker or a hairdresser. That way, you'll never be unemployed,' Grandad Fred told us. He was right, but not one of his nine grandchildren followed this advice.

The only thing I knew for certain was that, unlike my

brother Daniel, who was getting very good at football, my sport was not going to lead to a professional career. I would never earn a penny throwing a hoop. As I have mentioned before, very few women, as far as I could see, made a living from sport. Gymnastics was always a passion for me rather than a potential profession. I wanted to be the very best I could at something – and maybe there was an element of keeping up with the boys. If I became very good at gymnastics and got international colours, then maybe my dad and brother would have respect for what I did. The ultimate prize was becoming an Olympian, of course, and in my mind, if I achieved that, then I could do anything I wanted. It would be like getting the keys to the kingdom.

Even though being a gymnast wasn't a job, I could see there were careers around sport. I did once tell a careers adviser at school that I wanted to be a sports psychologist, and she told me that 'wasn't a thing'. Which I knew to be a lie, as I had used a sports psychologist at the National Training Centre in Lilleshall, but at seventeen years old, I was not up for having a back-and-forth ding-dong with a careers adviser who seemed determined to tell most of us that being a librarian was the best option.

Representing Great Britain for the first time was an exhilarating experience. It was the 1986 Junior European Championships in Athens. I travelled with two other gymnasts, Hermione Heavy of Coventry (unfortunate name for a gymnast) and Liz Arnold of St Helens. The organisers put the teams up in hotels around Athens. I noticed when our bus dropped off other countries' competitors after training sessions that Great Britain's hotel did not have as many stars as Germany's. But on the flipside, we did drive past the Acropolis every day – and while I was doing that, my friends back at home were in double maths. I was in my sporting heaven, wearing a GB tracksuit, seeing the flag raised in the stadium, hearing the anthem ... We didn't win, but they had to practise playing it, just in case we did. In the end, we came thirty-eighth, forty-ninth and fifty-third, so we didn't even come close to troubling the anthem or flag technicians. The only anthems that ever actually needed playing were the Bulgarian and Russian ones, but I guess they had to go through the pretence of rehearsing.

Over the course of eighteen months, I travelled to Spain, France, Belgium and Germany with Great Britain, but there was one domestic international I was desperate to be selected for: the Silentnight Beds International at Wembley Conference Centre. In 1988, I got the invite. I would be walking out behind the Great Britain flag and the competition would be televised on Channel 4. As if that wasn't enough, I was also going to appear on *Blue Peter* on the BBC the week before the competition to try to boost ticket sales. My teammate Alicia Sands and I would make up a gymnastics routine with which we would open the show live in the studio to the iconic *Blue Peter* music. After this, we'd demonstrate how to perform some basic moves to Yvette Fielding, one of the presenters. *Blue Peter* was on BBC One three times a week at 5pm. It was watched and loved by millions.

We arrived at the Shepherds Bush studios a few hours before the show to rehearse. I had never even been to this part of London, let alone to the world-famous 'horseshoe', the name given to the building I had seen so many times on TV. This was the home of *Swap Shop* and *Live & Kicking* – all of the Saturday morning TV I had grown up with – plus, of course, *Match of the Day* and *Grandstand*, the shows that punctuated our weeks.

There were journalists, newsreaders, comedians and entertainers sauntering through the lobby with places to go and shows to make. It was a hive of activity and ideas; it almost felt like we were on the film set of a TV show before we even got to the actual set, because the building itself is so iconic. The BBC had some very large studios back then, and *Blue Peter* was filmed in one of the biggest. In the studio, there was an area of carpet laid out that was around the size we would normally perform on, but we had to adjust our routine to accommodate the height of the lighting rigs and the ceiling. There were cameras to avoid hitting and areas of the carpet that the director preferred us to stick to because the light was better there, so we made the appropriate modifications and worked through the routine a few more times.

After we had rehearsed for an hour, Yvette appeared, and we showed her the kind of moves we wanted her to try out on the show. She was exactly what a *Blue Peter* presenter should be: fun and hugely enthusiastic, but comically crap at the gymnastics.

Then it was into wardrobe and make-up. Back in the 1980s, the BBC employed make-up artists and even wig-makers who occupied a permanent department. Nowadays, everyone is freelance. Back then, though, you might be getting your face painted for *Blue Peter* next to Dawn French getting made up for a *French and Saunders* sketch or Angela Rippon getting powdered for the news. It was impossibly glamorous – exactly how I had hoped it would look and feel. They gave our young skins a quick once-over in the chair, and then we were ready to go live.

The floor manager counted down to the music: 'Four ... three ... two ... one.'

The camera's red light came on, and then it was us: just me and Alicia in our turquoise leotards, doing our stuff with the hoop on national television. The thirty seconds or so we had choreographed whizzed by, and then Yvette tried out her moves, giggling as her hoop rolled off set. We had a chance to tell the audience that there were tickets left to watch us at the weekend, and before we knew it, the other presenters, Caron Keating and Mark Curry, had joined us. They thanked us, and then quickly moved on to telling the viewers about an appeal to build toilets in Delhi, for which the kids needed to save their old washing-up liquid bottles.

Minutes later, we were in our tracksuits and heading to the hotel in a black cab with a *Blue Peter* badge to show for our efforts. It was a whirlwind of wonderfulness.

But I had something else to show for the day, something more personal, because a spark inside me had been ignited.

I had loved the whole thing. The live studio environment had been so exhilarating: the light on the camera going red, the immediacy of it all. I didn't want this to be the last time I experienced any of this. *This* is what I want to do. I wanted to work in an environment like this every day. And I didn't even care how hard it might be to get back into work after I had kids.

I didn't tell anyone, not least my maternity leave-obsessed relative. I mean, the idea was utter madness. How do you get a job in TV? I had no idea, so I did what all young people in the 1980s did: I wrote a letter. My previous letters to a man on TV had been addressed to Jimmy Saville, who was also at the BBC. Thankfully, he hadn't responded. However, as he was a fellow Lioner (person of Leeds), I did sometimes see him running past our house with his strange cronies, wearing his luminous-coloured string vests, gold lamé shorts and rainbow headbands. How did we not suspect?

The much nicer telly man I wrote to next was the director of *Blue Peter*, Lewis Bronze. Unbeknown to me, Bronze was a legend in *Blue Peter* terms, overseeing 850 episodes in his time there and picking up an MBE in the process. In my overly confident and familiar letter, I told him that I wanted to be a TV presenter, preferably one at *Blue Peter*, and asked him what I should do next. I resisted the urge to ask about maternity leave.

I was hoping he would send me a to-do list in return. Lewis did write back to me; he told me to work hard at school, get a degree and keep doing sport and other hobbies. I was grateful he wrote back, but this was no to-do list. It was more the kind of advice your great aunt might give you in response to almost any question you can think of.

I don't think it's a coincidence that my passion for and commitment to gymnastics grew at the same time as my academic ability. Sport has an uncanny habit of showing you a bit more about life than you think. At around the time I started high school, I decided to subtly reinvent myself academically. A lot like in the gym, I wasn't necessarily a natural, but I had a half-decent brain and I related my sporting life to my schoolwork; with a bit of extra effort, I could get somewhere. Mum encouraged my new-found academic confidence.

'When you apply to university, it isn't enough to be clever and have good grades. You need to have a packed CV to make you stand out.' My mum hadn't been to university – nobody in our family had – so I am not sure how she knew all of this. It was like when I was into acting and doing LAMDA exams with a drama coach outside school; she told me I should think about Cambridge as a university because I could join Footlights. Mum's background was solidly working class – how did she even know what Footlights was?

My mum was clever. She passed the eleven-plus and went to grammar school. She did her A levels, and wanted to go to college in Kent. But when she met my dad, he somehow persuaded her to go to Manchester Polytechnic and do beauty therapy, so that she could come home regularly by train across the Pennines to see him. Clearly, strident feminism hadn't really hit Leeds in the late sixties. I often wonder what her 'sliding doors' life would have been like; the one where she studied art, or even architecture. Would they have stayed together? As I've said, she did eventually start a property business in her early forties, proving it's never too late to follow your dreams. Maybe it was her subliminal feelings of unfulfilled academic potential that gently nudged me into believing that I could be and do anything I wanted – within reason (and before imposter syndrome kicked in). The most important lesson she taught me is that whatever else you do for your kids, leaving them with decent self-esteem is one of the greatest gifts of the lot.

A few weeks later, I was invited back on to *Blue Peter*. They were doing a feature about Sports Aid, which was the way amateur sportspeople like me were funded before the National Lottery came along. I received a few hundred pounds towards travel and equipment, which not only helped my parents but made me feel that I was special. The idea that I had been selected as someone who had potential made me want to work even harder.

At the *Blue Peter* studios, I was to appear alongside other funded athletes, including famous swimmers, hockey players and some male gymnasts. This second trip wasn't quite as adrenaline-filled, as I wasn't performing live gymnastics, but it confirmed what I had already decided on the first: that this was the world I wanted to work in.

Eventually, Lewis Bronze left *Blue Peter* and set up his own production company. When I was working for ITV2 in 1999, our paths would cross again, as I hosted a show his company made about health and fitness. As I walked on set, the first thing he said to me, with a cheeky smile, was: 'I see you followed my advice.'

Often, we never get around to doing the basic and obvious things, like writing a letter, sending an email, or just reaching out, but doing so ensures you will at least make an impression on somebody's day. And you never know – your letter might just land at the most opportune moment.

Those two visits to the BBC were among the biggest turning points in my life. We need to step back and remember that in the late eighties, there were four TV channels and no internet. We didn't have cameras on phones, and you couldn't set up a YouTube channel on a whim. Access to a career in broadcasting was not easy, and I was not well-connected. Looking back, if I hadn't gone to the BBC to appear on *Blue Peter*, I'm not sure where else I would have found my 'in'.

Over the years to come, when I was trying to find internships and asking for help, it was what I saw and experienced that first day in the BBC studios – and the letter Lewis sent me afterwards – that fuelled my fire.

8

Auckland

In November 1989, our family was awaiting big news. My sister and I had both nailed our colours to the Welsh mast for the Commonwealth Games. We were the top two ranked gymnasts in Wales by virtue of being the only two Welsh gymnasts in the Great Britain squad, and the Wales Federation was allowed to pick up to three gymnasts to take to the Games in Auckland at the end of January 1990. Louise was much better than the third-ranked gymnast, so it wasn't unreasonable to assume that we would both be able to don the Wales leotard and head off to the other side of the world together for the ultimate sibling adventure.

The Commonwealth Games was an important step towards Olympic qualification, because it was the only other multi-sport event that we could compete at. Unconventionally, the whole team would be announced in the Welsh newspapers – athletes, cyclists, shooters, gymnasts and all of the others – in one grand missive, like a list of births, deaths and marriages. Our family couldn't wait to find out. We knew

that the newspapers would have the information and be ready
to print by 8pm the night before. Dad rang one of his football
journalist contacts, who wrote for the Welsh *Daily Post*, and
asked him to confirm who the rhythmic gymnasts for Wales
were going to be.

We sat with bated breath around the telephone.

'Rhythmic gymnast, not *gymnasts*,' the journalist said.
'There is only one. It's . . . G. Yorath.'

I couldn't actually hear the journalist deliver the bombshell, but we knew that there was bad news because Dad's
face dropped.

I thought we had both missed out.

But no – I was going. It was the greatest news of my young
life, but it came with the worst news for our family. Louise
was devastated, and in the long term, it was a moment that
effectively ended her passion for competing in the sport. She
quit gymnastics shortly after. Don't feel too bad, though; it
was also partly because she won the *Daily Mirror* Face of the
Year 1990 and went to live in London to be a model with the
agency Select at sixteen years old.

But in that moment of life-shaping news, as we sat in the
living room, staring at each other with our emotions hanging in the air, my mum and dad had to dig deep into their
parenting handbook and work out how to be delighted for
me while giving my sister the right amount of consolation.

It was a tough one. Dad hugged Louise before he hugged
me, which always bothered me as a teenager, but as an adult
and a parent, I fully understand. Sport isn't everything; winning isn't everything. The mood was certainly more sombre
than celebratory, and I trudged off to bed feeling a little
bit guilty.

The next few months were all about sacrifice and dedication. I was in the first year of my A levels at Notre Dame

Sixth Form College in the centre of Leeds, right opposite Leeds University library. While I was still at high school, the Diocese of Leeds had decided to combine all of the city's Catholic sixth forms into one. At first, I was disappointed by this, having seen reaching sixth form at Cardinal Heenan as the holy grail of school life. One of the things that got us through GCSEs, acne and awkward body changes was the knowledge that one day, we too would be beautiful and sophisticated like the sixth formers we worshipped from afar. And with that sixth-form status would come access to the common room, complete with tea and coffee, and the opportunity to trade our homogenous, sexless uniform for a little black suit, like a junior NatWest banker. But instead of achieving these heady heights, we were told our sixth form would be relocated to the centre of Leeds, merged with those of the other Catholic schools – and they would scrap the uniform altogether. Along with the uniforms, we also waved goodbye to sport and anything extracurricular, and instead were offered a kind of low-budget university experience, where you went in for lectures and some form time, but otherwise could pretty much come and go as you pleased.

In the end, this new system actually worked out well for my gymnastics aspirations. I was combining A levels in economics, politics and history with the extra hours of training that were needed to ensure I was at the top of my game in New Zealand. My alarm went off at 5.15am, so that I could be on the No. 9 bus at 5.45am to get to Carnegie College (now Leeds Met) in Headingly, where the very kind caretaker let me in at 6.30am for ninety minutes of ballet and conditioning. I was on my own – no coach, no other gymnasts. After a quick splash of water on my face in the toilets, it was time to get on another bus to sixth form. After my last lesson, I would either go straight back to the gym at Carnegie, where my coach and the other gymnasts would now join me, or across Leeds to the old international swimming pool to do my cardio, an hour of swimming. I had one day off a week, but never weekends. Wales appointed Lisa Black, an ex-GB gymnast from Tring who had competed at the 1988 Seoul Olympics, as my coach. She drove up to Leeds and stayed with my family over the weekends and the Christmas holidays. We even persuaded one gym to open for us on Boxing Day.

One evening, a week or so before I was due to board the Air New Zealand flight to Auckland, I got home from training to see my friend Anne-Marie's vintage bright orange VW Beetle on the drive. I didn't immediately click what was happening. Anne-Marie was at a different sixth-form college, so we didn't see each other every day. I assumed that maybe she'd popped round to say hi. I walked into the kitchen to see Daiana, Collette, Sarah, Claire, Anne-Marie and Anna, my gang, all beaming smiles and shouting 'Surprise!' with a cake. It took me a few minutes to realise that this was my surprise send-off party, and that they'd arranged it themselves.

Mum said something later that night, after we cleared up, that stayed with me. She said that what I had with my pals was so important: to have a group of girls who weren't jealous or possessive about what I did. They wished me well to go off and live my dreams, and then come back and be a teenager with them. 'I think that's quite rare,' Mum said. I don't think I fully appreciated how lucky I was.

A few years ago, I took my kids to see *Matilda* in the West End. When the cast came forward for their bows at the end, the incredible young actress who had played the title role looked out at the audience, searching for someone. I assumed at first she was looking for her mum or dad, but then her eyes alighted on a girl of around thirteen who was sitting just in front of us. Her best friend, probably from drama school, I decided. The friend was whistling and cheering to show her mate, the Matilda on stage, that she had just delivered a knock-out performance. They locked eyes for ages, 'Matilda' beaming with joy at the approval of her best friend. I started to cry and couldn't stop; the connection between these two friends was just beautiful.

We got back to the car, and I was still sobbing. Lois, my then seven-year-old daughter, asked me why I was crying. I tried to explain. I told her the narrative I'd just invented, the one about the love and support the girl sitting in front of us had showed her friend. I understood more than ever what my mum had meant that night; I looked back and saw my friends and their unjealous, unconditional love and friendship.

My daughter looked confused, mostly because she couldn't work out how I had ascertained all of that information from one snatched look between two teenagers.

'How do you know?' she said.

'She doesn't,' said her dad. 'She just made it up.'

All roads led to Auckland, but via the 1990 British Championships, which took place over a weekend at the end of January, near Milton Keynes. I came third overall and took a few silver medals on the individual apparatus finals, which meant I beat a couple of the England team. This was an enormous psychological boost: the hard training had been worth it, I was in peak condition, lithe and light (thanks to my Christmas diet of satsumas and cauliflower), and ready to storm New Zealand.

On the Sunday evening, armed with a stash of medals, Lisa and I drove from Bletchley in north Buckinghamshire, where the Championships took place, to Sophia Gardens in Cardiff for a send-off dinner with the entire Wales team. It all got very real, and at the same time it still seemed totally surreal. Earlier that week, I had been sent a suitcase with my uniform: blazers for the opening ceremony, V-neck jumpers, T-shirts, shorts, leotards, tracksuits for training and, of course, specific branded casual wear for the twenty-four-hour flight. Even in 1990, the kit was a little dated and the fabrics highly flammable, but I overlooked the style deficiencies, and potential fire hazard that I might become. I was just so proud to be wearing the golden plumes.

The send-off dinner took place in a giant sports hall decorated with crêpe paper chains. There was obviously much agonising about which Welsh musical act to book to send us off in style; the Manic Street Preachers hadn't yet been formed, Tom Jones was probably in LA, and Max Boyce wasn't right for the target audience, so Bonnie Tyler it was. Not that we were allowed to stay for the full 'Total Eclipse' ensemble. Lisa Black was reassuringly strict. We had an early coach departure to Heathrow and a long flight ahead. There was no time to mingle; we could make friends later. It must have been odd for Lisa. I was sixteen years old and she was twenty-two. Just a couple of years before, we had been teammates, but now she was in a position of authority and power. Luckily for Lisa, I don't have a rebellious bone in my body. I keep waiting for my rebellious side to kick in, but so far, so compliant – and I am forty-eight at the time of writing.

Rhythmic gymnastics is always scheduled at the end of any multi-sport Games; it starts when the artistic gymnastics is finished. As we arrived four days before the opening ceremony, this meant we had almost sixteen days to prepare. We were there way too early, but I imagine the Wales Commonwealth Games committee had saved a lot of money by choosing these flights. Plus, once we were in the Village, they didn't have to pay for our food and drink. The Village was almost empty when we got there. England hadn't arrived yet, and there were only a few Kenyan runners, some Scottish bowlers and a few Samoan weight-lifters wandering around as we got our bearings. The dining hall was an enormous circus tent with food stations dotted all over, which offered every food you can imagine at every hour of the day. Fancy rice and beef for breakfast? No problem. A niçoise salad at 2am? Here you go.

I had some dried apricots and nuts for my first meal – crazy times. I hadn't sweated and abstained hard over Christmas shrinking myself to 54kg only to go and blow it now on a chocolate milkshake, fried chicken and rice for breakfast. I was very much aware of what I was doing. I didn't think I was fat, like I had read people with anorexia believed. I was aware I was lean, perhaps even underweight, but I was on a massive calorie deficit diet for a limited period of time. That's how I justified it.

But it wasn't healthy. Now that I understand much more about nutrition, I realise that I could have eaten better and got so much more from my body without getting any bigger. But we had quite unsophisticated support around the sport at the time. There wasn't much said about diet beyond 'don't get fat', and occasionally we would see a sports psychologist, who we would complain to about being told to 'not get fat'. Until the National Lottery came along, this was the same with most Olympic sports in the UK. It was all a bit potluck, rather than exact science.

Not long before, the British Gymnastics Association had hired a Russian coach called Irina Viner, so things were about to change. Viner arrived at Lilleshall with a suitcase of caviar, some Rive Gauche perfume and a floor-length mink coat, a 'Russian' straight out of Central Casting. She was an absolute genius, and as ruthless and direct as you would hope a Muscovite gymnastics coach to be in 1989. For a few days she sat and watched us train, saying nothing. Her mouth occasionally made a smile, but her eyes never did. You could almost hear her thinking, *What the hell am I going to do with this melee of mediocrity?*

She walked up to my sister one day and grabbed her face between both hands, saying, 'You should go to Hollyvood and vee a movie star.' It was her subtle way of saying, 'You are very beautiful, but you will not be staying in my squad for much longer.' Others were dumped from the squad without the compliment to their looks, so Louise was, in that way, fortunate.

When she eventually returned to Russia, years later, having reformed rhythmic gymnastics in the UK, Viner coached multiple Russian Olympic medal winners. One of her biggest successes was Alina Kabaeva, who took the all-round gold at the Athens Olympics in 2004.

Vladimir Putin is said to have taken a shine to Kabaeva and eventually left his wife Lyudmila for her. The former gymnast then found herself as a member of the Russian Parliament for ten years, holding a number of key positions, which is not a euphemism.

The seating arrangements in the food tent in Auckland consisted of rows of benches and large refectory tables, designed to encourage us to 'mingle' with other countries. The Commonwealths, after all, are known as the 'Friendly Games', and it turned out that lots of the athletes take that quite literally. I'm sure you've heard of the rumours about the goings-on in athletes' Villages: rampant sportspeople going wild after their competition is over? Well, it's all fairly true.

Lisa and I saw some Welsh-tracksuited blokes, so we made a beeline, dropping our trays on their table and shuffling up next to them. As I plonked myself down, I realised who I was sitting next to, and my heart almost missed a beat. We'd seated ourselves next to Colin Jackson and Nigel Walker, the two Welsh hurdlers. Jackson was a global superstar of his sport, a silver medal winner from the 1988 Olympics and probably the most famous athlete in the Wales team. And I had a massive crush on him.

'Hi, can we sit with you?' asked Lisa.

'Sure,' said Colin, with a huge smile and the air of someone entirely at ease with their own brilliance.

I don't think I spoke at all.

I just stared at his perfect skin and jawline and sculpted muscles, while he talked about the Village and what he'd been up to. For the last nine years, I have hosted athletics on the BBC, and Jackson is one of our regular pundits. Thankfully, I am more confident in his presence these days, and he is one of the nicest men you'd wish to meet. Annoyingly enough, he hasn't aged at all. He also remembers our first meeting, and has been known to tease me about it.

Village life was brilliant. It quickly came to feel very normal that we all lived like this, housed in a tiny three-bedroom Portakabin with total strangers who left their sweaty kit to dry on our window frames. Because we were such a small team, Lisa and I had to share a cabin with the male judo players. They arrived at the Games too heavy for their weight categories, and so needed to do a lot of sweating.

'Had a good Christmas, see,' one of them told me as he talked me through his food diary.

We were housed next door to the cyclists, who were always out on the grass, modifying their bikes with spanners and bolts. I was learning a lot about other sports. For example, the cyclists had very bad tan marks from their tight shorts, and also they could eat many more calories than me or the judo players put together, yet still be good at their sport. I think

I'd have put up with the dodgy tan lines to be able to have a bit of cake occasionally. Once England, Australia and then Canada arrived in the Village, the atmosphere livened up, and I never had to hear about the judo player's food diary again.

The opening ceremony took place on a baking hot day. The legendary soprano Dame Kiri Te Kanawa was singing, there were lots of grass-skirted men doing traditional hakas, and the Queen came from England to open the Games. The sun was blazing. I borrowed a pair of luminous green sunglasses from Lisa and stuck some gum in my mouth to keep away the hunger pangs as we waited until almost the end of the alphabet for it to be our turn to march around the track. As Dad was the Wales football manager, there must have been an asterisk by my name in the commentators' notes, so when the legendary BBC commentator Barry Davies saw me, he mentioned who I was related to: 'The Wales manager Terry Yorath's daughter, Gabrielle.'

Back in Leeds, my mum and dad were in bed watching the ceremony (it was 7am, UK time) and were very disappointed to see me chewing gum and wearing garish green sunglasses when Barry Davies singled me out.

'You were chewing gum, it looked a bit common,' Mum said when I rang later to see if they had spotted me.

'I was hungry.' I was a rhythmic gymnast; I was *always* hungry.

'Actually, we did say to each other when you were marching round that we really should have come to watch you. Why didn't we?' she asked, perhaps rhetorically.

'I don't know,' I said.

And I never did.

As a parent, one of my greatest joys in my life is watching my kids play sport: seeing them do what they love and learning to deal with success and failure, while creating friendships and building an understanding of teamwork. My two children happen to like sport. It doesn't matter what it is, I am just glad they have a passion – it could be music, art, science or gardening. Whatever they choose, I love to see them enjoy it. Which is why I agree with my mum: why didn't they come to watch me?

In fact, Dad didn't watch me compete once in my whole gymnastics career, largely because he was playing or managing every Saturday when I was competing, so he had a good excuse. My mum came to one competition, a Yorkshire Championships, early on in my gymnastics career, and I didn't do very well, so I told her: 'Don't bother coming to watch me anymore.'

Then I got better, didn't come last, started to do OK and win some medals, and I decided that this was because she *wasn't* there. She was the opposite of a good luck charm.

With hindsight, I wish she had dismissed what I said as superstitious nonsense and come to watch me anyway. But I think she saw my permission not to come as a convenient way out; after all, she had three other children to look after and drive around Leeds. Just getting me to training or dropping me off at a train or bus station was a logistical effort in itself, so it quickly became the norm that they didn't come. It was my thing. I had a world of friends, travel and sport they really knew nothing about.

Maybe parenting has changed, and we were in the hybrid era of children still being seen as second-rate versions of adults rather than the more child-centred society we seem to have become. I am not suggesting one is better than the other, nor am I sad for me that they didn't come to watch; I am sad for them, because there is really very little better to do at the weekend than watching your child enjoying and loving sport.

*

The Commonwealth Games opening ceremony widened our social circle. We met people from other countries, and as Lisa had been at the Olympics two years before, she was reconnecting with some of those athletes she'd met in Seoul. Now I might have been a sixteen-year-old virgin, but there was definitely a certain vibe I was picking up, which was that many of the competitors were 'on heat', for want of a better expression. Medals were the aim for most athletes, but sexual encounters were on the agenda for many, and the flirting was championship level. The great thing about a multi-sport event is that there is something for everyone: whatever you are attracted to is probably there in human form, whether you like your partners tall, short, curvy, skinny or buff. There were ectomorphs, mesomorphs and a variety of skin tones and ethnicities, with fifty-four nations competing. If you were single, then you were bound to mingle.

The Village had big, clunky cream-coloured computers dotted about, which had the biographies of every competitor in them. All you needed to know was a name or a sport, and you could find out all you needed to about that person. It was like online dating, long before such a thing existed. You just had to be discreet when you were staring at someone to try and see the name on their lanyard if you didn't want them to realise that you were about to start stalking them.

Two England athletes, Gary Staines and Ikem Billy, kept bumping into us at the computers; they always seemed to be around whenever we were sending messages or looking up the biographies of someone we had spotted that day. They were funny and interested in what we were doing, and one day they suggested we go shopping in Auckland with them. I had to negotiate with Lisa, who wasn't keen to deviate from our strict schedule, but we hadn't had a single afternoon off, so she relented.

I had one pair of jeans and one T-shirt with me that wasn't my Wales 'kit', so I donned my civvies and ventured into town. Gary and Ikem were grown-ups, in their mid-twenties with houses and cars; Gary trained in Australia over the winter months, and they both travelled the world with their sport. They were sophisticated to my very naive.

While I was busy working out whether I could afford some postcards, and if they'd even get back to Leeds before I did, Gary and Ikem were buying clothes and music and treating us to coffee. I had no money to buy anything substantial – Mum had learned her lesson from the Palm Springs trip and the Lacoste top. To be honest, I had never really been in the company of blokes I wasn't related to; I had never even been bought a coffee. I had snogged a few lads down at the Irish Centre, but they were schoolboys.

These two were men, albeit with a slightly juvenile sense of humour. Ikem and Gary finished competing a few days before we had even started, so they were out on the town, heading off to nightclubs and restaurants and getting back in as we were heading out to breakfast. The Village sees life for twenty-four hours a day, with the cyclists getting up super early to do crazy long rides and other sports finishing close to midnight. Once you have been through drug testing, you might not get back to the Village until 4am.

The swimmers get a bad rap on the party front, but it's only because they finish competing first, so early in the Championships, you are more likely to be woken up at 3am by a drunk Canadian breaststroker trying his key in the wrong door (no pun intended) than you are a gymnast, who won't be finished until the final few days. Having said that, the swimmers *do* seem to know how to let their hair down. I think it's a reaction to their very strict training regime; if you'd had a life of 5am starts and hundreds of monotonous lengths of a

chlorine-filled swimming pool since you were six years old,
wearing restrictive clothing, tight goggles that leave red rims
round your eyes and a tiny rubber hat on your head, you'd also
be up for a few wild nights out every two years. I covered the
World Aquatics Championships for the BBC in Barcelona in
2013, and it's fair to say the pundits and commentators have
carried on their partying tradition into their new careers. It
was the most fun you can have and still call it work.

Gary was always around, popping by my Portakabin to see
if I wanted to come for a coffee or go for a walk.

'Can I come and watch you compete?' he asked me one day.

*What boy would ever want to voluntarily watch rhythmic gym-
nastics?* I wondered.

I realise now there are a few reasons why a young bloke
might want to spend the day watching a sport performed
by young women in leotards. I had reservations about him
coming – for example, what if he brought bad luck? Bad luck
could come from anywhere; my life was riddled with all kinds
of ludicrous superstitions. One of them was my lucky towel, a
small hand towel used to dry my sweaty palms before I went
on to the floor to perform. It had been in my armoury for
around two years, and served me well, with my decent medal
haul from the British Championships testimony to what a
lucky towel it was. I realise I sound quite insane, but that
is what superstitions do to you. When I unpacked my case
in Auckland, I found that I had left my towel at the British
Championships in Bletchley, North Bucks, England, which is
11,360 miles away as the crow flies. There was no way I was
getting it back. I knew then I was going to have to somehow
reverse the psychology of the lucky towel. It probably took
me until my mid-twenties to untangle and abandon most of
my superstitions. Although I still salute magpies, of course.

Also, and arguably more important than the superstition

thing, I had noticed in Gary's profile that it said 'engaged' in the section regarding marital status.

'Are you really engaged?' I asked him one day.

'Yeah, I am.' He looked slightly upset I had read the biography so closely.

I found out he was due to be married a week after the Commonwealth Games finished, to an Australian long jumper called Nicole Boegman. I will confess that Nicole's impressive fifth place at the Seoul Olympics had passed me by, but had she been fit in Auckland, she would have been a favourite for gold. Sadly for all of us, Nicole had broken her leg and was in plaster in Sydney, her hometown, getting ready for her big day. I say 'sadly for all of us', because the next few years of my life were about to be dominated by a relationship that should never have happened.

'I don't mind if you come, but I think you'll be bored,' I warned him. Gary ignored my warning and came to my last day of competition. I didn't perform as well as I would have liked, and failed to make the finals. It wasn't his fault – nor was it down to the lack of my lucky towel – I simply wasn't good enough on the day. I didn't make any terrible mistakes, but I missed out a few of my higher-scoring elements as the trajectory of my throws was a bit off. In truth, I think I had probably peaked a week before; I was there too long.

My mood was low. I had built up to this Commonwealth Games for so long and now it was all over. I also had a feeling, which I didn't want to address then and there, that this meant my Olympic dream was also over, which in effect meant my gymnastics days were over. The house of cards that was my young sporting life was tumbling down.

'Come out on the town with me tonight. Let your hair down, get away from the Village. You need a break,' Gary suggested sweetly. I hadn't been out on any town, anywhere, with anyone, ever. My good mates who were competing for England had made the finals, so they still had their serious heads on. I had a choice, I could have said no – but to my regret, I didn't.

I ate all the bad banned foods – chocolate fudge cake, burgers and pizza – and drank white wine. After two glasses of New Zealand's finest, I was absolutely plastered.

At some point in the evening, while we sat on a step over-looking the harbour, and I tried hard not to throw up, Gary started a speech.

'Next week, Gabby, I am getting married,' he admitted, with a tear in his eye. 'But meeting you has made me feel so confused; I'm not sure about anything anymore.'

'Oh,' I offered by way of sympathy. *Jesus Christ, I was not expecting this.*

'I really have strong feelings for you. I wish things were different. All I want to do is take you to Sydney with me.'

'Right.' My head was spinning – not with love at this point, but with alcohol.

To give him credit, Gary never said anything horrible about Nicole, his fiancée.

While he was busy wishing things were different, I was busy wishing I hadn't had that last slice of pizza, because it was about to come right back up.

Which it did, all over the steps.

This clearly only served to make Gary like me more, because at some point soon after that, he kissed me.

I enjoyed kissing him. Kissing a man was different to the snatched snogs I had experienced before with boys at the Irish Centre. The way he held me was more tender, less urgent. I wanted to kiss him more, but he came back into the moment, probably remembering that he had a fiancée, and he pulled away from my face.

He held my hand and guided me up the steps so we could find a cab. As we drove back into the Village, the sun was rising. It was set to be a beautiful day.

Lisa soon put a stop to things. She had taken quite a moralistic and maternal tone with me after my night out; she was not impressed that I had been out on the town with a betrothed man. She was the responsible adult and had to take that line.

I sensed that a few of Gary's more sensible friends, let's call them 'wedding guests', were also dubious about his 'holiday romance'. For the few days before we flew home, we found secret corners in which to meet, sat fully clothed on each other, snogging like teenagers, telling ourselves that life was so unfair and that we hoped that in another life we'd be together. It was a holiday romance gone wrong.

D-Day arrived, and just before I was due to leave for the airport, a young man came to my accommodation with a gift. It was the official tracksuit of the Brunei team, and had been sent by Prince Jefri, brother of the Sultan of Brunei, who had been competing in the shooting. I knew nothing of Prince Jefri, and wasn't sure how he knew of me.

The young man also left a phone number on which I could contact the Prince to thank him personally. By now we were in a hurry to leave, so I grabbed my bags and stuffed the tracksuit into my hand luggage.

The twenty-four-hour journey home to Britain was miserable. I was aching with the pain of the first throes of love, the kind that consumes your every thought, when you feel physically sick to be parted. I wrote hopelessly terrible letters to Gary expressing how he made me the happiest girl I had ever been; how I wished him well and how lucky Nicole was to have him. There was a finality about these letters. I definitely did not expect to see him ever again. I know that these letters still exist, as I never posted them. I know where they are, but I can't share them, for fear that the expression 'I died of embarrassment' might come true.

At a windy, wintry Leeds Bradford Airport, the weather was much cooler than I was dressed for, so I popped on the turquoise tracksuit from Prince Jefri for warmth. After my mum had hugged me, she looked perplexed. Maybe she could sense that I had been kissing a grown man? That I had left England a girl but was returning a woman in love?

No, it wasn't that.

'What are you wearing?' she asked, and not in a complimentary way.

'It's the Sultan of Brunei's brother's tracksuit,' I replied nonchalantly.

'Why are you wearing it?'

Why was Mum so overly interested in this innocent tracksuit?

'It was a gift, and I was cold when we landed, so I popped it on.'

'Do you know who the Sultan of Brunei is?'

These days, this question might be asked because of the Sultan's unconscionable views on homosexuality; nobody should want to admit to wearing his brother's clothes. But back then, what my mum really wanted to know was if I had any idea that he was worth around £20 billion. I did not. I think my mum would have been quite happy if I had come home with a boyfriend whose family were billionaires, rather than just his tracksuit.

(I just googled Prince Jefri while writing this, and a host of stories have popped up about the many harems he has, the many wives, along with tawdry tales about his sex life and the boat he had commissioned, which he named 'Tits'. Stay classy, Jefri.)

All the chatter about the Sultan of Brunei meant I was distracted from my inner angst. I didn't mention Gary and my broken heart at all on the car journey home. Mum had made my favourite stew, and the boys came home from school wanting to know if I had learned the haka.

I knew, deep down, that it was a holiday romance, and that in a few weeks, I would be over it. But assimilating into normal life was tough. I had no focus, and my family sensed something was up with me – and not just because I had started eating doughnuts for dinner. One evening, the phone rang. It was for me. It was Gary, calling from a phone box in Sydney on the eve of his wedding.

I was about to fill a gymnastics-shaped hole in my life with a doomed relationship that was way beyond anything I could really cope with. I think, with hindsight, I should have had a plan. At some point, I was always going to reach the end of the road with gymnastics, but I came back from Auckland without another competition in the diary. My body and mind were giving up on it because they had nothing to focus on. What I have learned from top sportspeople and high-achievers in the years since is that it's so important to keep moving and adapting your goals. It means you don't get to dwell for too long on the successes, but you'll have time to do that at the end of your career. But when I came back from New Zealand, I didn't have a plan, so inevitably I fell into something that was unhealthy and messy.

Here's a tip: when a man phones you on the eve of his wedding from the other side of the world, don't accept the call.

9

When the Sporting Dream Dies

'I miss you so much. I can't stop thinking about you, my swan.' Gary had told me I was graceful and reminded him of a swan when he'd watched me compete. So now I was his swan.

'I miss you too. Er . . . um . . . how is Nicole?'

Why did I ask that? I didn't really care, but wondered how she felt about him ringing me.

'She's a bit pissed off. The weather is terrible and it's going to rain on the wedding day.'

As phone calls go, it was utterly perplexing.

Unsurprisingly, Mum wanted to know what was happening. And who this man was. Well, I didn't know what was happening; I was still sixteen years old.

The following day, I imagined the wedding, picturing the other athletes I had met in Auckland dancing on tables and having a wonderful time drinking champagne, and I really hoped that was what had happened. Seven days later, on 14 February, I came home from school to see an enormous bouquet of red roses, fifty of them, sitting on a console table in the hall.

My mum leaned over the banister and said, 'They're for you.' She raised a single eyebrow (a skill I have never mastered), and watched as I opened the card.

I had never been sent flowers before.

My first flowers: sent from a man's honeymoon on the Great Barrier Reef. I was no relationship expert, but I sensed things might not be going that well in paradise.

I think my parents were initially baffled by the whole thing. Why would anyone be so infatuated with their skinny, geeky daughter? I was as confused as they were, but of course I was also secretly flattered. My ego was loving it – I didn't appear to have a working moral compass.

Of course, when I look back now, I would suggest that Gary should have never called me from Sydney, nor should he have sent me flowers from his honeymoon. We had just shared a few kisses; I would probably have been over him in a month. I had no way of contacting him, as he lived with his wife and it was before everyone had mobile phones. I didn't have the cash nor the inclination to get trains to London to stalk him. At most, I would probably have watched his career with interest and wondered what might have been. I'd have been effectively 'dumped', and it would have been painful, but in the long term, it would have been good for me. Of course, my parents would say I was an obstinate child who knew what she wanted.

To give my parents some credit, a month or so later, after my seventeenth birthday, they summoned a meeting. Gary was due back from Australia ahead of Nicole, giving him time to drive up to Leeds to 'meet the parents'.

Gary drove up with his best mate Stu for support. Poor Stu had to sit in the kitchen with the rest of the family, drinking tea, while Dad took Gary into the living room. Dad quietly told Gary that if he ever contacted me again, he would find someone to break his legs, and he would never run again. In all the years since, Dad has never confirmed his mafia links or revealed who was going to do the leg-breaking.

That's the version of events Gary told me when he came out of the living room, anyway. You'd think he'd have been back in his car in five minutes after that threat, but he felt comfortable enough to stay for food in the company of the man who threatened to break his legs. People really do like my dad, even when he threatens violence.

Mum was slightly more reasonable. She didn't make any physical threats, but she told Gary he had to sort his life out. If he didn't want to be with his wife, he needed to leave her, get divorced, and then maybe when the dust settled they would allow me to see him. I was not really consulted; it was like an 'arranged' separation.

All of this drama made me more determined. This unassuming, perfectly nice, ordinary lad from Welwyn Garden City had become an exotic creature I couldn't have.

So, inevitably, I wanted him even more.

My back was playing up. The sciatic pain was excruciating, and lasted for days at a time rather than hours. Scans had been taken and consultant appointments booked.

'You have a physiological anomaly,' I was told. 'One of your coccyx sticks and the other slides. So that pressure means you trap a nerve on the side that doesn't want to slide, but because of what you do, it's forced to move. You'd only ever learn this about your body if you were a rhythmic gymnast or you painted the ceiling of the Sistine Chapel.'

'So, that's my next career buggered,' I said.

The consultant didn't laugh.

'What does it mean for me in the long term?' I asked.

'You need a long rest from the movement that agitates it, and eventually to do exercises that will strengthen your back. Then we can review in a few months. Take two of these a day for now.' He handed me a prescription for Voltaren 50, very high-strength painkillers.

I couldn't train. Retirement was looming; a *week* was a long time in gymnastics, never mind three months. By the end of this enforced break, I'd be overweight, out of condition and out of sight, and I knew the chances of a comeback were slim at seventeen years old. I'm also fairly sure that Gary's looming presence was a factor in me mentally giving up the ghost.

I was coasting through my A levels. I needed something to fill the thirty-five-hour hole in my week. I ran and swam, mainly in an effort to keep my weight down after discovering there was a Greggs on my route home from school, but no amount of sausage rolls could replace the adrenaline rush of competition. I even timed my lengths at the local swimming baths; was it too late to find a new sport? Yes, was the answer to that question – by about fifteen seconds when it came to the fifty-metre breaststroke.

Yearning for a man I couldn't have helped fill the hours, and the emotional vacuum led to me writing some devastatingly bad poetry. I found solace in music. Sinead O'Connor's 'Nothing Compares to You' was number one in the UK for about sixteen years. The words haunted me, but to suit my scenario I changed the days since he'd taken his love away, making it 'seven hours and thirty-five days ...', 'thirty-six days ...', and so on. Day after day. I had it bad.

I used to be an advocate of never regretting, understanding why something happened in your life and finding out what you could learn from it. I think now that might just be a younger person justifying bad decisions – and I made some very bad decisions. But maybe it's better to admit I made a mistake rather than pretending I learned anything.

I should have done what I promised to do: cut off all contact. If I had done that, then within a couple of weeks I'd have been back at the Irish Centre with my mates, snogging a boy called Declan or Frank or Seamus, or all three of them.

Instead I wrote Gary love letters, sending them to his friends' homes, and we stayed in touch on the phone. I took a pile of ten-pence pieces to college and, in my free periods, instead of writing essays and reading around my subject, I was on the payphone declaring my angst and undying love.

Within six months, Gary was on his own; Nicole had left the marital home. After some heated debates with my parents, by the spring of 1991, almost a year after we had first met, I was off too, albeit temporarily on the train to London to see my 'boyfriend' for the weekend. With his international sporting career, his flat, his convertible Golf and his natty suits, I was shamefully smitten. I know how shallow and impressionable all of that sounds, but I was eighteen years old, so cut me a bit of slack.

My mum and dad tried to stop the relationship at the start, but I have often wondered, now that I am a parent, how they might have had more success. Maybe using more subtle techniques, like showing me another way rather than just trying to block the Gary route. I was a highly motivated student, so perhaps they could have driven me to Oxford for the day and thrust another world of opportunity and excitement under my nose. Or maybe just left me there with no money to get home – OK, that's a bit harsh.

Perhaps my parents believed it was the real deal with Gary and that we'd be together forever; after all, my mum and dad had got engaged at seventeen years old. But they will probably tell you that I was just bloody minded and determined, and that they really did try to stop me seeing him.

Before Gary's divorce was even in motion, we were doorstepped by the *Sun* newspaper. It was Sunday morning and the whole family was finishing off breakfast, reading newspapers and eating fresh bagels, when the peace and quiet was broken by a knock at the door.

A journalist and a photographer were standing on our front step with some news that they wanted to clarify. 'Is your daughter having an affair with the runner Gary Staines?'

Panic gripped the family. In scenes reminiscent of a *Carry On* caper, Mum, Louise and I scampered around the house on all fours in our dressing gowns so as not to be photographed in our nightwear without make-up. At first, we just hoped that the gruesome twosome on our doorstep would go away, but they were persistent buggers, and eventually my dad decided we needed to say something.

As Mum hadn't changed out of her dressing gown and she wasn't made up, it was left to Dad to deal with the journalist. I say 'deal with'; the quote my dad gave the journalist has gone down in family folklore. After a brief conversation, Dad shut the door on the journalist and seemed quite pleased with himself. He loosely told us what he had said, and it all sounded fine. The next day, the newspaper dropped on the doorstep.

The headline read: 'OLYMPIC ATHLETE DOES RUNNER WITH SOCCER BOSS'S DAUGHTER'.

There was a picture of me in a leotard – standard for the *Sun* – and a picture of Gary running in the Olympics. Then below the pictures, was the article, including that legendary and brilliant quote.

In response to the allegations that his daughter was having an affair with a married man, the Wales boss Terry Yorath said: 'My daughter is like any other girl her age, she likes going out and having a good time.' Gabrielle Yorath was unavailable for comment.

I read the article on the bus heading to school, rereading those words again and again in disbelief: 'she likes going out and having a good time'. No attempt at a denial from my dad. If I'd read that about someone else, I'd think, *Well, if her own father says that . . . what kind of life is this girl living?* The irony is I almost never went out, and I certainly never went anywhere in public with Gary. My mum went a bit berserk with Dad for besmirching my reputation.

But life carried on, and by 10am the girl who 'likes going out and having a good time' was back in her A level history lecture. If I learned anything from that experience, it's that it really is chip paper. Nobody at school cared. Even Giacomo Ferraro, my Italian friend who actually read the *Sun*, for its racing tips, wasn't moved to mention it.

A few months later, in June 1991, my school life was over. I should have been charging straight to the pub with my mates, but that was another rite of passage missed. Instead, I walked out of a politics A level exam, took a moment to breathe in the sunshine, then got into my dad's car so my parents could drive me to Gary's flat in Earlsfield to begin my gap year.

Mum and Dad were going to a dinner in London on that June day, by the way; they weren't so desperate to get rid of me that they were making a special 400-mile round trip to London to deposit me.

I do remember Gary's friends thinking it strange that my parents were dropping me off, though, as if they were willingly handing me over. His mate Stuart asked if I came with a dowry.

There was a grand plan for this gap year. I'd travel with Gary to his international races; he'd get the race organisers to pay my airfare and I would see the world. It would all culminate with me watching him race in the 1992 Olympics in Barcelona. My Olympic dream might have been over, but his was still on course.

On the one hand, I am ashamed at the ease with which I was prepared to hijack his life without express permission. He had invited me to stay with him, but I don't think he thought I would come charging down the M1, lock, stock and barrel. On the other hand, I feel some empathy for the teenage girl who was so unsure what to do with her defunct sporting dreams that she started living vicariously through someone else. Still, at least I had an action-packed agenda of mentally nourishing international travel, with a law degree at Durham University waiting for me at the end of it. What could possibly go wrong?

10

The Rose of Tralee

The first deviation from my plan to follow Gary around the world as he pursued his international running dreams came when I found myself winning the Leeds heat of the Rose of Tralee in 1991. If you are Irish, you don't need me to explain what the Rose of Tralee is, but for those of you who have no idea, here is a brief synopsis.

The Rose of Tralee Festival takes place at the end of August every year in Tralee, County Kerry. The contestants don't just come from Ireland itself; Irish communities from around the world select a 'Rose' to represent them, including Melbourne, Berlin, Las Vegas and Dubai, as does any town in the UK with a large Irish community, including Leeds, Birmingham, London and Newcastle. Ultimately, there will be about twenty-five to thirty Roses who have won their regional heats.

Some people might describe the Rose of Tralee as a beauty pageant, but trust me, it's not. The girls all turn up in Dublin, get taken round the Guinness Factory, have lunches with

We had a lot of hair in our family (we took our fashion lead from Sadie the family poodle!). My mum chose dogs based on their lack of shedding. Aside from not losing her hair, Sadie was also a brilliant and wise dog – I won't hear a bad word about poodles!

I don't remember asking to be a bunch of grapes for this fancy dress in 1979. I didn't win this one – the static from the balloons attracted my long hair, which was annoying, and hurt. And then, as the afternoon wore on, drunk men popped my balloons with their cigars. So by the time the judging happened I had about four left and was in a brown leotard and a pair of clogs.

Believe it or not, this was an Easter bonnet parade. We had just had a new VHS video machine delivered so Mum covered the box in green crêpe and attached some ribbons. Again, I didn't win this one. Kids with intricate displays of birds' eggs and tiny ducks on their heads took the top places.

I was obsessed with going to the local convent school so, instead of paying the expensive fees, Mum bought me a boater hat instead, which was part of the uniform. I wore it as often as I could for about two years in the early '80s. Pretentious, *moi?*

The Spanish-style mansion my dad accidentally rented in Vancouver in 1981. It almost ate his whole salary but was a lot of fun to live in.

The last ever British Championships I competed in just before the Commonwealth Games in Auckland in 1990 was my best ever. I won four medals, which at the time meant everything – however, I have no idea where they are now.

Gay Byrne, the legendary Irish TV presenter, is clearly dumbfounded that the girl he is interviewing on stage at The Rose of Tralee in 1991 is in fact only 18 years old and not 48 as the appearance might suggest.

Winning the Leeds heat of The Rose of Tralee in my mum's friend Betty Goldman's fully sequinned dress. It was my good fortune that Betty had just been through both her sons Bar Mitzvahs.

Graduation day at Durham. I was the first person in my family to graduate, which
I discovered when I became the Chancellor of Leeds Trinity University in 2014.
It means I am known as a 'pioneer', for which I am very proud.

Louise and I doing a photoshoot together on the Kings Road in the late nineties
(I have no idea why!). Lois, my daughter, now has the coat Louise is wearing –
we don't waste much in our family.

The night in Barbados that Liam Gallagher decided I might be John Lennon reincarnated. Alcohol was involved, obviously.

From left to right: Lisa, Katie D, me, Tamsin (who I was with in the K Bar the night I met Kenny), Kerry and my sister Louise, the day before I got married to Kenny. I am not sure why this picture is included in the book but I do look like I might have cut carbs out before my big day.

I loved our wedding day. I wouldn't change a thing about it. Apart from the fact I made Kenny sell his ISAs to pay for it.

Kenny's farm in Scotland has a perfect view of the Wallace monument, which is where he proposed to me in July 2000. You have to walk up over three hundred steps to get to the top, so I'm pretty sure I was oxygen deprived when I said yes.

mayors and dignitaries, and then go on a tour of Ireland
doing similar things, visiting the Waterford Crystal factory
and eating so much soda bread that they reach Tralee a stone
heavier than when they set off. The girls are escorted on this
trip around Ireland by young men who are 'given to them' at
the beginning of the journey. Mostly they are young jockeys
from race yards around the west of Ireland who fancy they
might get lucky.

Once the Roses arrive in Tralee, they visit sick kids in
hospital, go to church, go to castles for medieval banquets
and are generally treated like minor royals. Then there is a
grand finale, a live TV show on RTÉ hosted by a major Irish
TV personality (back in the 1990s, it was the late great Gay
Byrne). The girls each have an interview and then entertain
the crowds with Irish dancing, Irish singing or something
totally random, like reading a poem. There's no bathing costume section, no nudity – in fact, points seem to be awarded
for wholesomeness. At the end, one of the girls is crowned the
overall Rose of Tralee, and all the other Roses sing to her. The
winner takes home a large cheque and has a year of engage-
ments as the Rose, along with a free holiday in County Kerry.

The Leeds event to find their Rose took place just before
I departed for my 'gap year'. Sean Kenny, the dad of my best
mate Anne-Marie, owned a plant hire company, KPH, which
sponsored a young woman to enter every year. It was a big
deal in the Irish community, and he'd never had a winner.
He knew about my distant relatives from Cork and my love
of soda bread, and that seemed to be enough for him.

'How do you fancy entering the Rose of Tralee this year
for KPH?' he asked me.

'What do I need to do?'

'Nothing; it'll be a doddle. You just put on a nice dress and
answer a few questions, and I'll give you £500.'

I had never earned £500 – and I didn't even need to *win* the thing. The money would come in very handy for my trip to Tokyo for the World Athletics Championships with Gary, which coincidentally was at the same time as the Rose of Tralee finals, but I didn't need to worry about the clash, as surely there was no way I was going to win. I wasn't Irish enough.

On the night of the Leeds event, I borrowed a dress from my mum's very glamorous friend Betty Goldman. Betty's son had just been Bar Mitzvahed, so she had more full-length sequin-covered gowns than the *Strictly Come Dancing* wardrobe department. She kindly loaned me a black-and-white beaded, sequinned affair with a lightning pattern down the front. It was the perfect dress for a drag queen paying homage to Usain Bolt. I wore my hair in ringlets on top of my head, and Mum adorned my ears with huge fake pearl droplets. At a push, I could have been getting ready for my fiftieth birthday party. I even wore nude tights.

On stage, we were interviewed by Tommy Ferguson, the manager of the Irish Centre.

'Now then, Gabby. Everyone knows your dad, Terry – he's a Leeds United legend and he played for Wales. So, where does the Irish come from?'

'Well, my mum.' I gestured towards my mum who was sitting in the front row with Dad, beaming. She looked gorgeous, and has bright red (dyed) hair, so that was a start. 'My mum's family are from Cork, Tommy.'

Well, that was the most uncomfortable question handled well. After that, I was cruising.

'I'd like to be a broadcaster, and if not that, because it is a tough profession, then a human rights barrister. I'm going to Durham to read law next year.' This was true, but when it came out of my mouth as I stood on the stage in a sequined dress with a corsage, it did all sound like I'd made it all up.

There was a small walk around the stage, which is when things became dangerously close to beauty pageant territory, but overall the evening was a blast and very innocent.

The judges were clearly big fans of the middle-aged *Dynasty* look. To my utter amazement, when they called out the winner's name and popped the sash on her, it was me.

My trip to Japan was off; Tralee was on.

The Rose of Tralee is a ten-day event, but the wardrobe requirements would make a royal lady-in-waiting preparing for a trip to New Zealand wince. The contestants are expected to have formal, semi-formal and day dresses, as well as white gloves, hats, costume jewellery and a range of handbags.

I am the oldest cousin of a large family, so there were no hip twenty-something relatives ready to lend me formal clothing. I simply could not afford the quantity of items required, so I started borrowing and begging my way around the more senior members of the family. My mum and her friends helped me out, and eventually even my Nana Sheila, who was then sixty-three years old, lent me a floral two-piece. Betty Goldman came up trumps again with the dress I would wear on TV, a huge, bright red meringue-style dress covered in roses. Even the brides on the TV show *My Big Fat Gypsy Wedding* would have rejected this dress as being too over the top. I was so far away from wearing the clothes I liked, felt comfortable in or would say were 'me', but that didn't really matter, as this experience was already so far out of my comfort zone, I might as well have gone naked. I was the youngest of all the contestants, but based on my wardrobe, I could easily have been the oldest.

The first night's dinner in Dublin was a rowdy affair. I hit it off with Manchester and Berlin. Berlin had a strong Dublin accent, was very quirky and wore Doc Martens; she obviously hadn't got the clothing memo, or if she had, she'd said 'Fuck it.' I wish I had been a bit more Berlin. We weren't as loud as Melbourne and Las Vegas, who didn't seem to have 'off' buttons, but we had a bit more going on than Glasgow and Birmingham, who entered the competition rather cautiously. Cork was very assured and seemed to be networking well, and Kildare also seemed to be pretty savvy. The judges travelled with us and watched our every move. By day two, we had fallen into tribes. Ours was clearly the 'we are not going to win this, but we don't really care' tribe. We knew our place: we were there to make up the numbers, the cannon fodder. The best we could hope for was not embarrassing ourselves.

On the coach to Limerick the next day, there was great excitement as sheets of A4 paper were handed out. These were the CVs and photographs of our escorts, the young men who had been selected (hopefully from hundreds of applicants, but I suspect that it may have been more like dozens) to look after us on our journey to Tralee. They were to be our plus-one at functions and tend to our every need (but not *that* need).

The escort assigned to me was called James Deane, and he was a farm hand from County Carlow. I'll be honest, I had to look in my *Guide to Ireland* to check out where Carlow even was; it's in the south-east, with a population of fewer than 60,000. James lived with his mum, who owned a village shop. His appearance was more Letitia 'daughter of Angie and Den from *EastEnders*' Dean than James 'the Hollywood icon' Dean, and my heart didn't exactly miss a beat when I clapped eyes on him as we disembarked the bus. His probably didn't for me, either.

He stood with his arms behind his back, one arm pulling the other towards it; a body language expert would say he was shy. He looked petrified. To think I had spent all those years pining for Irish summer romances, and now my very own Irish lad was standing in front of me, all five foot six of him a nervous wreck.

We were perfectly pleasant to each other, but with zero chance of romance on the cards, I did the honourable thing and let him spend his allowance (which was supposed to be for buying me drinks) on his own alcohol consumption. He was going to need it. I was having plenty of fun with Manchester, Berlin and Ulster, and none of us was in the business of husband-hunting.

What with the formal lunches and huge dinners every day, it was like lurching from one calorie fest to another. I put on almost a stone, and the elasticated waistbands of the skirts loaned to me by the senior citizens of the family were coming into their own. There was no time to exercise; we had sick children to visit, religious ceremonies to attend and monuments to be photographed alongside.

If Meghan Markle had done a week of the Roses tour before she met Prince Harry, she'd never have turned up for that first drink with the ginger-haired one. Hats off to the royals, all that dressing up and chatting to people you don't know and will never see again about things you don't understand or care about is utterly exhausting.

But we had to hold something in reserve because everything was building towards the grand finale, the live TV show on RTÉ. Mum, Louise and Jordan were coming over from Leeds with my best friend Anne-Marie to deliver moral support.

It was amazing to see tens of thousands of visitors descending on this tiny town. Locals opened their homes as bed and breakfasts, farmers gave over fields for tents and caravans. It was like Glastonbury for Irish dancers and young jockeys.

Most of the class of '91 had chosen to sing or dance on the live TV show. Cork, with her brown bobbed hair and cute freckles, was dancing in hard shoes, the kind you see in *Riverdance*. Chicago was singing a ballad in Gaelic. I thought she'd missed a trick; surely she should have gone for 'All that Jazz'. Melbourne, true to form, was planning on singing 'Makin' Whoopee' in a burgundy velvet strapless gown while draped over a grand piano, à la Michelle 'O'Pfeiffer'. Melbourne was not shy. She walked the corridors of our hotel in her bra and pants, told rude jokes, smoked and received large bouquets of flowers from 'admirers'. I wondered if she might have sent the flowers to herself to intimidate us. If that *was* her plan, it certainly worked.

Most of the contestants had chosen to perform songs, verses or dances that were authentically Irish and crowd-pleasing. I kept quiet about my talent piece, and began to wonder if reciting 'The Lion and Albert' was really the best I could do.

My thought process had been that, as I couldn't do traditional dancing or singing, I should recite something that reflected the fact I was the Leeds Rose. I wanted something that gave me the opportunity to rock a very strong Yorkshire accent – although, as you may know, 'The Lion and Albert' is set in Blackpool, and was written by Marriott Edgar, who was born in Scotland, with no mention of Yorkshire anywhere in the poem. My best hope was that the judges' geographical knowledge of the north of England would be sketchy at best. It was too late to call up Michael Flatley for a crash course in Irish dancing; I was stuck with the poem.

When I was a gymnast, I said prayers to help quash my nerves before I stepped on to the mat to perform, regularly promising God that if I could get through my routine without making any mistakes, I would go to Africa to become a missionary for a year. Until I was backstage at the Rose of Tralee, I didn't think I would ever experience nerves like those again, but as I waited for Gay Byrne to call my name, I started praying hard, adding years on to my missionary work. This being Ireland, a Catholic country, maybe the competition for God's ear was too great, because my prayers went unanswered.

All too soon, Gay Byrne's beautiful, mellifluous Dublin accent was directed at me. 'Our next Rose is just eighteen years old. She's a student from Leeds, and her name is Gabby Yorath.'

I strode out on to the stage with far too much purpose. Betty Goldman was shorter than me, and if you watch the footage, you can see my shoes as I walk, as the dress sits a few inches off the ground. My feet appear to be moving at ten to two. I walked without grace or elegance, looking as if I was about to mount a horse.

'Now,' said Gay, putting a reassuring arm around my rose-covered shoulders. 'It is Gabrielle, of course ...'

'Yeah, but people call me Gabby, because I talk a lot – as the girls will vouch,' I said, talking at a hundred miles an hour in a strong Leeds accent.

'And you're a student of what?' Gay calmed things down, talking to me slowly and with kindness.

'I just did my A levels in law, politics ... oh, sorry, no – I didn't do law. That's what I *want* to do ... I did history and economics.'

Jesus wept; I couldn't even answer a question about my own A levels. This was awful; I was dying on stage.

'Tell us about the gymnastics, now, as it's a sad story, isn't it?' He was trying to get the audience to feel for me.

But I didn't read the signs.

'Er, well, saddish ... until this time last year, I was a

gymnast competing for Great Britain, then I got sciatica and found it difficult to walk,' I said, sounding far too upbeat about not walking. I continued to mumble on about my bad back for several minutes. Even a chiropractor would have zoned out.

'Do you miss it, the gymnastics?' Gay tried once again to put the conversation back on track, trying to get the audience on my side.

'Yeah, I miss it. I miss competing, because I am quite aggressive.' *Aggressive.* Yes, I actually described myself as aggressive on a live TV show whose sole purpose was to pick a global 'Rose'. I was a thorn in my own side.

Later, Gay asked me which of my parents I was most like: my mum, who was sitting in the studio audience looking stunning, or my dad, who was away working somewhere as manager of the Welsh football team. At that moment on the coverage, there was a close-up of my beautiful mum, look-ing so glamorous. With her shiny red hair, she even looked a bit Irish.

'I'm more like my dad; he was quite aggressive as a player.' I did it again. If you didn't know me, you'd have thought that I was an MMA cage fighter thanks to my frequent references to my own unbridled aggression.

And so it went on, a toe-curlingly awful piece of TV, until it was time for Gay to ask me to perform my piece.

'Well, Gay, as I don't have a regional accent,' I said, in my strong Leeds accent, 'I thought it would be interesting to perform this Yorkshire/Lancastrian piece for you.'

See what I did there? I turned a poem set in Lancashire into a Yorkshire/Lancashire poem. It was as if the War of the Roses had never happened.

There's a reason why Yorkshire and Lancashire went to war, and it wasn't to be merged into one county on an Irish TV show by a lass from Leeds.

And so I began, holding a flat cap in my hand as if to add some weight to my claim that what I was about to do was pure Yorkshire. You've seen the Hovis advert? That's me, kids, all cobbled streets and whippets.

There's a famous seaside place called Blackpool
That's noted for fresh air and fun,
And Mr and Mrs Ramsbottom
Went there with young Albert their son.

And on I went – and on, and *on*. It's eighteen verses long. (I'm pretty sure the United Nations would class the reciting of poems more than ten verses long as a form of torture.)

I made it to verse sixteen, and then it all went horribly wrong.

Then off they went to the police station
In front of the Magistrate chap
They told 'im what happened to Albert, and . . . er . . .
And . . . er . . . and, er . . . err . . .'

I was looking out at the audience, flailing, searching for words that wouldn't come. Then came a voice from backstage: it was Gay Byrne to the rescue.

'AND PROVED IT BY SHOWING HIS CAP!' he shouted.

The audience laughed and clapped.

'Ah, yes, thanks, Gay,' I said. 'I'm glad *he* knows it.'

The audience tittered again. Tittering is laughing *at* you, not *with* you.

Somehow, after that, I managed to spit out the final two verses, and then the misery was over – for me, for the audience, and especially for Gay Byrne.

Cork won the whole thing. She wowed them in her interview with the news that later that year, she was getting married to a farmer and the honeymoon was to be 'convent-hopping' in Iceland. None of us knew there were even that many convents to hop between in Iceland.

As Gay interrogated her, we learned that the nuns would happily offer a bed to the young couple in return for a day of work in their gardens. You couldn't make it up. And she certainly never described herself as 'aggressive', did she?

She followed up that Iceland bombshell, which had probably already put her twenty-five points ahead of her nearest rival, by adding a cheeky twist to her traditional dance. Halfway through, she ripped off her long skirt, Bucks Fizz style, to reveal a slightly shorter long skirt underneath. Sexy is as sexy does.

Denise Murphy, I salute you – you smashed it out of the ballpark. I went home a loser, but the Rose of Tralee was, without a doubt, the most surreal, crazy and joyful ten days of my young life. And, for a short while at least, I had achieved my adolescent dream of becoming a bit more Irish. And even now, if I want an instant ice-breaker with any Irish person, anywhere in the world, I just say, 'I was a Rose of Tralee,' and four hours later, we're opening a joint bank account.

11

The Gap Year Gone Wrong

After the Rose of Tralee, my gap year master plan started unravelling quite quickly. After finishing in last place in Tokyo, Gary had been injured, so all racing was off. This meant no travel for me, and no race fees for him, so I started collecting jobs.

My dream of becoming a TV presenter was still smouldering, but the reality was I needed cash. *Blue Peter* didn't have any vacancies, so I became the part-time manager of a children's shoe shop in Wimbledon Village called Tootsies. It was the closest thing I could find to making Tracy Island out of washing-up bottles.

When I say I was the manager of the shop, I was actually the only person there. So, as I had to lock up and give myself permission to get lunch, I decided I was essentially the boss. It was deathly dull. I sold two pairs of shoes a day during the week, working 9am to 5pm. I wasn't on commission, so I had no incentive to sell more, but I'd have liked the company. I was asked if I would like to coach gymnastics at a school in

Balham one day a week, so on my day off I started teaching a group of 'lively' (disengaged) teenage girls how to spin a hoop. I quite liked the experience of thirty fifteen-year-olds calling me 'Miss', and I earned about the same in an hour as I did in one day at Tootsies. Meanwhile, the injured Gary had mooted the idea of going to Australia for the winter to get rehabbed and race-fit in time for the Barcelona Olympics. This was amazing news – of course I wanted to go to Australia. To be honest, right then I'd have taken Austria.

Only the plan didn't include me.

In order to stay on by myself in London, rather than go back to Leeds with my tail between my legs, I would need to earn a lot more than the coaching and the shoe shop brought in. I enrolled on a course to become a PT instructor at the YMCA in Victoria. It was very basic ('how to do a lunge'-type basic) but it got me a qualification. I hired a space at Belgrave Harriers' headquarters on Wimbledon Common and started an aerobics class a couple of nights a week.

To complete my collection of jobs, I also took on the role of nanny to an American family on Kingston Hill.

They had a seven-year-old girl, a three-year-old boy and the mum was pregnant with another baby, which was due any day. The main reason they wanted a nanny was so they could take me with them to Jamaica for a three-week holiday when the new baby was a month old. In the interview, I may have exaggerated about how I had basically brought up my six-year-old brother Jordan from birth, and I duly got the job. I cleaned, did some laundry, chopped up fruit for snacks, did the school and nursery drop-offs and pick-ups. It was great contraception for a young woman on her gap year.

The dad was a classic early nineties banker, a bit flash and prone to sweeping and slightly offensive statements. He was only ten years my senior, and seemed to think it was fine to coax me into an hour's morning run with him while we were in Jamaica, while the mum coped with the three kids alone. As a mum myself now, I can see that this might have been quite annoying.

By the time I returned from my trip to Jamaica, Gary had already legged it to Australia. I was alone in a small flat in a not-so-fashionable corner of London, juggling four jobs to make ends meet.

This was not the gap year I had envisaged.

Communicating with Gary wasn't easy. The phone calls became infrequent, and we didn't have much news to share. He was training and I was working – there wasn't much more to add.

Him: 'How's nannying?'

Me: 'Good. How's the training going?'

Him: 'Good, yeah.'

Me: ' . . . Have you eaten anything nice today?'

Any concerns that my parents might have had about me not wanting to return to my education in favour of starting a life of domestic bliss in southwest London were well and truly squashed by the mundanity of my new existence.

Not long after the Jamaica trip, I retired from my career in nannying – quit while you're ahead, I say – and took a job working for the London Marathon as an 'office girl'. Their headquarters at the time was the tiny white gate lodge inside Richmond Park at the top of Richmond Hill. Finally something to really get my teeth into: working in top-class sport, near elite athletes, for a growing global event. What a job.

In reality, I was sent on the sandwich run to Hampton Court every day, and spent the rest of the time stuffing envelopes.

One Sunday morning in the midst of all this career

'progress' and 'excitement', Gary called from Australia. We exchanged a few pleasantries, and then, just when conversation seemed to be running dry, he threw in an unexpected curveball.

'Gabby, will you marry me?'

Just like that.

'Gary ... Oh, hello? ... Gary ... sorry, the line is really bad. I'll call you back.' I wimped out.

I couldn't believe what I'd just heard. We had never talked about marriage.

I rang my wise mum. My dad had just bought one of the first-ever car phones, thank god, as they weren't at home and what I had to say to them was urgent.

'Mum, Gary just asked me to marry him.'

My mum put the phone to her chest and said, 'Oh shit,' to let my dad, who was driving, know that it wasn't good news.

She thought I was expecting congratulations for my impending nuptials. Before she could say anything more, I jumped in again. 'I just want to know how to say no to him nicely.'

She pulled the phone to her chest again and mouthed to Dad, 'Thank god.'

We then discussed how I could call Gary back and nicely say no to his marriage proposal. I knew in my heart that I was too young to commit my life to any man, and even if I was ready, I wasn't sure that man would be Gary. His trip to Australia had exposed some pretty deep cracks.

For any young men reading this, let me be clear that 'phoning in' a marriage proposal is pretty lame. Doing it from 10,000 miles away while you are quite possibly still married to someone else is really not romantic at all. I suspected that Gary might have been a bit tipsy.

Mum helped me construct a diplomatic rebuff.

'Gary, I am really flattered, but I'm going to university in September – and you're in Australia. You need to be focused on your training. You're just getting out of one marriage, so let's just enjoy being a couple for a while before we add that pressure.'

Gary took it well, and didn't seem to remember his proposal the following day. His return to the UK was imminent, but I wasn't exactly the type of girl found waiting at the arrivals gate with a home-made banner. In the months he'd been away in Australia, I'd realised that not only was Gary not going to be my future husband, I wasn't even sure I wanted him as a flatmate. Which was awkward, as it was his flat.

And so Gary came home. Time was running out on my gap year, and all I had to show for it was a very low-level personal trainer qualification, an audition for *Gladiators,* and a trip to Jamaica with a merchant banker who liked a morning jog.

Within days of Gary's return, I received that awful phone call from my mum to tell me about Daniel's death. It was like a sledgehammer came from nowhere and smashed my family – and my world – into a million tiny pieces.

12

The Rest of Your Life

26 May 1992

I packed my bag that Tuesday morning ready to head to
Leeds, not knowing when – or if – I would return to Gary's
flat. On the way to the M1, we stopped at a chemist to get
some water and a packet of paracetamol. Crying incessantly
and a lack of sleep the night before had given me a throb-
bing headache.

'What's wrong with you?' the pharmacist asked as he
handed over the tablets.

'My brother died last night,' I said bleakly.

'I am so sorry for you,' he said – and he did look genuinely sorry. Then he reached for something. 'Take this as
well.' He handed me some St John's wort and smiled kindly.
'It's free.'

I dosed up in the car, hoping to be numbed. In between
upbeat pop songs, the radio was telling me about plans for
a fifth terminal at Heathrow and the Maastricht rebels. I

couldn't believe there was any news in the world other than Daniel. The world kept on turning for everyone else.

There were tears and lots of long, loving hugs when we arrived. Sunshine was flooding the hallway. There was a different energy in the first few days after Dan's death, and a strange, unexpected sort of excitement. We were so busy, organising the funeral and meeting the coroner; guests were arriving at the house, some with cases and the intention of staying for a while; hundreds of flowers and wreaths were being delivered, and the phone rang constantly. The atmosphere reminded me in a way of one of our big family Christmases. Food was being dropped off daily by my parents' Jewish friends; normally, Shiva is the first week of mourning and prayers after the death, but they carried on bringing meals for a month. We were not ready to fully immerse ourselves in the inevitable tidal wave of grief that was coming.

The weather had stayed dry and warm, and the garden was an inescapable focal point for all of us. Dad took himself out there often, pausing at the spot where Daniel had died, taking a moment to himself away from the busy, bustling house. We planned to plant a weeping willow tree there, with a bench around it.

After two days, a tabloid photographer poked his long lens through the bushes while Dad was seeking solace. Then, moments later, a journalist came to the door. 'We understand that there has been a question of foul play in Daniel's death.'

Foul play, and all of the nasty connotations that go along with it: an implication of sordidness or illegality. Imagine being so detached from your own humanity that you could utter those words to a bereaved parent you had never met.

Dad was filled with rage. How dare they do that to us? How dare they come to our door and make accusations, founded on nothing? The Welsh FA got involved on our behalf and contacted the Press Complaints Commission. A standard apology was churned out, and a day later the journalist returned. His peace offering was the most pathetic bunch of wilting garage-bought flowers, £5 worth of weeds.

Dad shut the door in his face.

On day three of our new life, Dad, Mum and I sat with a coroner at our family dining table and listened to his explanation of the 'reason for death' that would be recorded on Daniel's death certificate. Daniel's heart had become thickened, with no obvious cause or outward symptoms, and it had become so big that it couldn't pump blood around the body, causing a sudden arrest that killed him almost immediately. The words 'hypertrophic cardiomyopathy' (HCM) became easier to say as the days and weeks and years went by. It is not a condition that always causes sudden death, and in many cases the sufferer displays symptoms, which can then be treated.

At first, Daniel's best friends were round at the house almost every day, just as they had been when he was alive. They were sixteen-year-old boys about to do their GCSEs, just trying to make sense of it all. They'd spend the day together at one of their homes, ostensibly revising, and then arrive at ours in the late evening, helping themselves to a can of Coke, nestling down in their favourite spots and chatting until the small hours.

We wanted them there; it was a comfort to my parents to feel their energy, and to learn everything we didn't know already about Dan. Sometimes they just chatted football with Dad. Leeds United had won the league, the old Division one, a month before, and as of August, a new Premier League was starting, so there was much to debate.

But when we got on to Daniel and the way he had died, not one of them could recall a single incident of breathlessness, a chesty cough, dizziness or fatigue.

'He was like a Duracell bunny,' they all agreed. He could run and run.

Eventually, we were all screened to see if we were carrying the gene for HCM. None of us were, which told us that Daniel's death was not the result of an inherited condition, but a genetic mutation. There was no sign that any of us were more likely to develop HCM than the average man, woman or child on the street, but we were advised to keep checking Jordan's heart until he was sixteen.

I couldn't accept a medical explanation for Daniel's death; couldn't accept that something so toxic was happening inside him when everything was so wonderful on the outside. The only way I could find some solace for myself was that if Daniel had been screened in the months leading up to his death, he would have had to stop playing football forever, which would have been a living hell for him.

Louise arrived home from Tokyo, and her boyfriend, Terry Bartlett, who was a gymnast training for the Olympics, came to stay for a few days. Then Gary, who had gone home after dropping me off, arrived back too. Jordan was easily distracted, and at six years old, he was loving the attention from all these visitors, who arrived with bags of sweets and gifts.

Daniel would have thrived in this atmosphere, too, seeing everyone home together again, being a great big happy family. It made me wonder why we hadn't done this in the months before. I became wracked with guilt that, during the last year of his life, while I had lived away from home pursuing my ill-fated gap year, I could count on one hand the times I had seen him.

The last time had been just a couple of months before his death. He'd got the train from Leeds to London to see me for a few days. He was due to arrive at around 3pm, so I cleaned the flat and got lots of nice food in, and then I went down to the tube station to wait for him. After an hour, with no sign of him, I went home and rang Mum to confirm which train he'd set off on.

'He should be there by now,' she said.

I was worried. I decided to wait at home; better to be near a phone than wandering around the streets looking for him. Another hour passed, and finally there was a knock at the door.

Daniel was standing there with a huge smile, looking quite chuffed with himself, holding a small overnight bag and a white sports sock. I hugged him. 'Where have you been?'

'I decided to get off the tube at Brixton because I've never been there. I wanted to see it.' A perfectly reasonable explanation in the mind of a fifteen-year-old. 'But there are just loads of markets selling records and trainers!'

'Why are you carrying an old sock?' I asked.

'It's got my money in,' he answered, as if that's how everyone carried cash.

Daniel was in an open coffin in Hughes Funeral Parlour, a few miles from our family home. One of the Hughes sons was married to my friend Anne-Marie's sister, and I had met him before on a night out at the Irish Centre. Now here he was, opening the door into the cold room where my brother's coffin lay. Daniel had been cleaned, and his body was embalmed and ready to be buried.

We had decided that he would be buried wearing his Welsh football kit. His passion for Wales grew when my dad took over as national football manager. In a pre-Sky, pre-BT, pre-internet world, the only way he could follow their away matches was by watching Ceefax on TV, waiting patiently for the screen to change for the entire ninety minutes. We'd be getting on with our evenings, doing our homework and chores around the house, and Daniel would run to the hall and shout: 'Wales one up! Rush scored.' I was so happy he was dressed in that Wales shirt and shorts; he looked ready to play.

There was a hint of a smile on his face. His skin was perfect, save for the tiny nick the scalpel had accidentally made. It looked like a shaving cut. He was blond, so I don't suppose he'd shaved much yet. I wondered how many girls he had kissed, and whether he had loved anyone other than us.

'I am so sorry Daniel. I love you so much, I am so proud of you, and I am going to do everything I can to make your life count.' Saying it to his face made it real; I had made him a promise. You don't always acknowledge your feelings towards your siblings when you are young, because they are just there, all the time.

I loved him so much.

13

Building Back

The funeral and the wake are a blur. I know Mr Flanagan, our RE teacher, gave a reading, and I know Dad did too. I know the congregation was spilling into the car park, and that there were TV cameras and press swarming all over.

In the days after the funeral, I caught a glimpse of our future. The bell didn't ring quite as often as the rate of visitors had slowed down. Those who were staying with us had now departed. And my mum simply stopped. She was broken. She didn't dress, she didn't wash her hair and she didn't eat.

In the years before Daniel's death, she had started her property business, and now there were houses in the middle of refurbishments, but she hadn't been on site for two weeks. Things needed to get moving or she would lose her investments. She'd write me a list of what I had to buy and where I had to deliver it. I drove around south Leeds in my black Fiat Panda, delivering wallpaper to decorators and instructions to builders at her request.

My life in southwest London was over; I was needed more

at home than I was in Earlsfield. Dad was due to take the Wales team to Japan on tour, and after debating with Mum and the WFA, who had given him their blessing to miss the tour if he needed to, he decided to go ahead and travel. Wales lost to Argentina and beat Japan. Immersing himself in football might have helped in the short term, but eventually, he had to come home and face the reality of a life without his beloved boy.

After a few weeks of almost nothing, mum came back to life. She washed her hair, put on make-up and started trying to work out how to live. But that tidal wave of grief was still coming at us with full force. There were tears every day, and moments of utter despair when we didn't know how we could go on, when life seemed futile, when the fear of loving and then losing anything or anyone else was too much to imagine.

'When you have a baby,' Mum told me one day, 'you worry about how you could possibly love another baby, and then when that next baby comes along, you realise it's not like cutting up a cake and dividing your love. It's a whole new cake. So when you lose a child, it's not that having your other children can make up for missing the child who has died. It's more like losing a limb and learning how to function without it. How do I walk again without that leg?' What she said made perfect sense.

Some days she hobbled a bit, while on other days she was almost jogging. The pace didn't matter; it was about moving forward, in any way she could.

Mum was on a voyage of discovery, and she wanted answers. She chatted regularly to our priest about the big questions: why we were here and what our lives meant. Things she had never really thought about. She enrolled on courses and read up around what other religions believed about the afterlife. It seemed to me that she was desperate to cling on to the hope that her boy was waiting somewhere to see her again.

I remember her saying, 'We're all trying to get up the mountain; the religion you choose to help you understand your journey doesn't make a difference. It's the same mountain,' she decided after a few months. And with that, she stopped going to our Catholic church as often. She went to see a medium and found comfort in the time she spent with her. The medium told her what Daniel was wearing when he was buried, and that seemed to be enough to convince my mum that the medium was able to reach him.

Dad didn't want to go the same way with his grief. He wasn't keen to talk to anyone he didn't know. He already had a propensity for seeing life as a series of disappointments, in spite of the success he had known. Daniel's death was confirmation to him that life was all a bit shit, to use his language. But he didn't let his anger stop there.

He decided to take deliberate steps to stop something like this from ever happening to him again. He would never feel pain like this again – because he would not let himself get as close to Jordan as he had been to Daniel. He was building himself a virtual wall, and he wasn't letting anyone behind it. The ramifications of that decision were as damaging as anything he did subsequently. If there is one thing I wish I could change from that period of our lives, it would be somehow persuading him to find a counsellor or therapist.

He later wrote a book and apologised to Jordan for removing himself from his life in that way. Jordan had to battle so hard over several years of his adult life to come back from those feelings of abandonment, but he did it, and for that I greatly admire him.

My sister Louise and I were lucky in some ways; we had experienced Dad through our formative years and we were almost adults when Daniel died, so we were able to process his behaviour better and cling on to memories of him as a more proactive and involved father.

I often think about the practical, financial side to death when I hear tragic stories on the news about young people dying. Most people don't have years' worth of savings; they might only be able to live without earning for a few months or even weeks. Into your grief and sadness, you must now factor debt or going back to work sooner than you would like to. And this was the case for our family, too – we had to find a way to start rebuilding our daily lives in the face of the tragedy we were all still grappling with.

After a few weeks, my sister resumed her modelling career in London, and Dad was starting to get back into work mode. Although I was running errands for Mum and getting free board and lodgings, I also needed to earn some cash.

I had my YMCA instructor qualification and a lifetime of sport behind me, so naturally, I became a personal fitness trainer. I wrote out a white postcard detailing my services, and popped it on the noticeboard of a newspaper shop. In doing so, I picked up my first client. The overweight and unhealthy young man who ran the newsagent's saw my card. He wanted to get fit; could I help?

I could, and for just £10 an hour, I said.

The newsagent was all about weight loss. He was about twenty-five years old, with a pot belly and no muscle tone, and he lived above the shop in a dark flat that smelt of body odour and drugs. I am pretty certain about the drug smell, because he'd often invite his stoner mates round to watch me train him. They rolled joints and sat, slumped and sleepy, on the sofa while I did star jumps in my tight Lycra shorts.

At the time, I thought it was a coincidence that they were

there every time I was due to train their mate. I now realise I was possibly being paid £10 to entertain them. There were Coke cans, bongs and sweet papers littering the floor; it was like training on the set of *Trainspotting*.

I really thought I could get him into shape, though, and imagined what a good marketing story that would be for me: *Fat to Fit in Ten Sessions*. I gave him diet tips and lifestyle advice, and he nodded away as if he were taking it all in, but he remained resolutely chubby. Thankfully, the realisation I was being played by him only dawned on me a year later, when I had long since given up the ghost of reforming him.

Despite my lack of progress with the newsagent, Mum's friends started to hire me and became my regulars. I'd run them for fifteen minutes on the streets, then do light weights and body circuits, focusing on any of their 'problem' areas – which often turned out to be tricky teenagers or husbands rather than love handles or stubborn belly fat. The gossip was excellent; the training a bit more hit and miss. I feel I might owe them refunds.

Living back at home without Daniel was tough. His presence loomed large. There was a back staircase in the house that ran upstairs from the laundry room and went through Daniel's bedroom. Often, Mum's journey to deliver laundry upstairs was arrested by the sight of his untouched bed. She would put her basket on the floor and sit on the bed, and I'd hear her gentle sobs down the corridor, then go to join her in a cathartic cry. I valued this extra time I had at home before heading off to Durham. I had missed so much of the last year of Daniel's life.

No parent ever expects to bury their child. The dream is you watch them grow up, graduate, get married and have kids; that you help them to find their path, and spread their wings. Now, for various reasons, most of us can accept that this idyllic idea of parenting isn't realistic, but you would still never expect to find yourself instead planning the order of service for your child's funeral, then meeting with the coroner, and choosing a coffin. Daniel had been wrenched from us with no warning signs. There was no illness to give us time to prepare, time to get our heads round what was happening. We debated this dilemma many times; would we rather have known, so we could have spent every waking moment with him, especially as he wasn't at all sick, or was it better for him to have died suddenly? There is no correct answer to that. The only thing we agreed on was that he had no pain and no knowledge of what was wrong with him, and for that we were grateful. He died at peace.

Apart from running round the block with my clients I'd hardly done any serious weights or power training since Dan's death, and with *Gladiators* looming I wasn't in the peak physical state I had planned to be. In fact, the opposite happened. It became apparent that I was a comfort eater; who knew? I happily hoovered up all of the Jewish Shiva food my mum couldn't face in the first few weeks: roast chicken, fish balls, lasagne – none of it was wasted. Dad took to ordering Chinese and Indian food at 9pm, and I didn't want him to eat alone, so I'd join in with him, having a second dinner. Old school friends often popped round with cake, so sure, I would eat that too. I was becoming dumpy and my face was bloated with sugar. I was happily talking – and gorging – myself out of going to Birmingham for the filming of *Gladiators*.

Even though it was obvious I was in no fit shape, Mum said, 'Daniel wouldn't want you to miss this opportunity.' She added, 'He was so proud when you were asked to do it.'

I think she was exaggerating. Daniel had a very good sense of humour, and I think he'd have found it ridiculous. I put down the cakes for a few days, went on a couple of training runs, and then found myself driving down the M1 to the National Indoor Arena.

It was apparent within minutes of arriving on the huge shiny set that this was not a show I could blag my way through. The Gladiators had been in rehearsal and were wandering around in their team tracksuits like well-oiled international athletes. I recognised a few of them from my audition day, but they didn't recognise me. I was quite literally a loser. There were cameramen, runners, riggers and lighting teams, all industriously transforming the NIA into the setting for a huge, successful TV show. ITV had big ambitions – and, by the look of things, a budget to match.

A producer took me and the other eleven contestants around the arena, explaining how the games worked – games that would soon become household names across the country.

'This is the Duel. You stand on this platform and battle it out with a Gladiator using these,' she said holding up what looked like a giant cotton bud, which we later learned was to be called a 'pugil stick'. 'You want to knock them off the platform so they fall down there; it's a twenty-five-foot drop, so today we'll teach you how to fall properly, just in case you don't succeed.'

We moved on. 'This is Hang Tough. You are on the rings and a Gladiator chases you down; your aim is to get to the other side without being brought down . . . and again, that's a twenty-five-foot drop.'

We all looked down to the padded surface below. I felt physically sick – I hate heights – but the other contestants appeared to be lapping it up. They were salivating at the prospect of beating a Gladiator. I was in way too deep; I really didn't care about anything, least of all evading someone called Flame as she chased me around on some rings. I would surrender within ten seconds.

And on it went, more games, more heights and more challenges, until finally we got to the Eliminator. This was the decider, a ridiculous assault course that ended on a steep travellator, by which point, of course, your legs would be shot to pieces, with lactic acid pouring through them, and you had to defy that lactic and run up the travellator, going against the direction of the moving belt. The kind of thing kids in shopping centres do when they've had too many sweets.

'Right! Let's get into our kit and have a go,' the producer said, gesturing with much faux gusto.

For some reason, we did the Eliminator first, gingerly trying out the apparatus on the assault course. I was, of course, hiding at the back. I could stay anonymous, creep out and go to my hotel room when this hell was over, then grab my bags and drive home. I would be eating chicken chow mein with my dad by 10pm.

'You've been quiet,' she said, looking at me – not words I was used to hearing.

'Why don't you get yourself on the travellator?'

I had no choice. I had been singled out. When the show eventually aired on TV, the travellator would catch out even the very best; falling off it was not rare, and certainly nothing to be ashamed of. But when you were attempting it 'fresh', with no lactic in your legs and in front of your peers, falling would be a humiliating disaster.

I fell.

But it wasn't just my pride I bruised; I cracked my hip on the frame of the machine. It was swollen and red within seconds. I cried hard. I was crying for Daniel, my parents, our broken-down family – and only a tiny amount for my bruised hip.

It was time to admit defeat and go home.

My gap year was turning out to be comically awful. The man I'd moved in with had disappeared to Australia for months, leaving me to find a string of dead-end jobs to make ends meet, and he'd probably had an affair while he was there. I'd missed out on the intended travel, I'd screwed up my chances of appearing on a new ITV prime-time show, and my gorgeous brother had died. There was one more bit of bad news to complete the picture; Gary's injury did not improve in time for the British trials, so his Barcelona Olympics dream was over.

After all this heartache and disappointment, there was finally some better news, but it wasn't mine. Louise's boyfriend Terry had been selected for his third Olympic Games as captain of the men's gymnastics team. Louise was desperate to go, so I became her plus-one.

We probably hold the record for the lowest budget trip to an Olympic Games ever. The Head of Spanish from the school I'd taught gymnastics at in Balham had a friend in Barcelona who would lend us a spare room. We'd get cheap flights, and all of our tickets would come out of Terry's 'friends and family' allocation. We weren't massive drinkers and bread was cheap; we could do this for a few hundred pounds, we surmised.

Every day, tickets come available in the Olympic Village, and often the participants are simply too busy to take them up. Louise and I would wait outside the Village, and Terry would pop out with whatever he could get his hands on. If they were for events we didn't fancy, we could try and trade them, swapping boxing tickets for gymnastics tickets, a couple of athletics tickets for some basketball. I'm not sure it was totally legitimate, but I'm pretty sure it wasn't illegal, either, as no money changed hands. However, that revelation

might stop me becoming President of the International
Olympic Committee one day.

Gary feigned looking 'not very impressed' that I was going
to the Olympics without him, before conveniently arranging
a boys' trip to Greece for him and six of his mates. I mean,
we were well and truly in the dregs end of relationship land,
weren't we?

Louise and I flew in on the night of the opening ceremony.
We dropped our bags at the flat, which was so far out on the
train it was almost in France, then legged it to Montjuïc, the
area where the ceremony was taking place. We couldn't get
inside the stadium − Terry's tickets weren't that good − but
we just wanted to soak up the atmosphere. It was 25 July, and
should have been Daniel's sixteenth birthday. As we came
out of the Metro station, we jumped on to the escalators and
travelled towards the glowing stadium. The night air was
twenty-nine degrees, a sticky, sweet heat that made my hair
curl. The star-filled sky had turned an inky blue, and the
chatter of dozens of languages could be heard all around. It
was magical. Olympic fans are special; they might be partisan
to a degree, with their pins and their shirts, and the American
ones will certainly let you know they are there, but they
travel thousands of miles for the occasion and the human
endeavour, not to brag about sitting top of a medal table. It
was a festival atmosphere, without the party drugs and music.

There were speakers dotted around the side of the hill,
so the speeches and concert could be heard by all who had
journeyed to Montjuïc. The orchestral music was dramatic,
but we couldn't see what was happening inside. Then, just
moments after I had whispered something to Louise about it
being Daniel's birthday, the archer sent his arrow high into
the air and lit the Olympic flame, which was a cauldron sitting high up on top of the stadium. Fireworks exploded and

the music grew even louder, and then Montserrat Caballé sang 'Barcelona', the song she and Freddie Mercury had collaborated on before his death. It was a divine and serene moment; even in that sweltering heat, I developed goose-bumps. I was certain Daniel was with us.

Louise and I spent a bit of time apart, as she was hanging out with Terry, who had managed to get her a pass into the Village. He also snuck out a few times and crept through a window into the flat to stay the night with Louise. They were young and in love and athletic. The lady who was letting us stay didn't quite see it that way; the religious artefacts around her flat should have told us to be more careful. One morning, she said she had to go away very suddenly and kicked us out, within the hour. I'm not sure she had to go away, I reckon she might have been pissed off with the gymnastic late-night caller.

Louise and I were on the streets. We had two large suitcases (with no wheels) and about £200 between us, in a city that, even before Olympic premiums, was out of our price range. It was early on a Sunday morning and the streets were deserted, so nobody could hear us screaming at each other, each blaming the other for our current predicament. We found a phone box and rang Mum, just to be sure she wasn't going to wire us a few thousand pounds to help us out. Nope, she definitely wasn't.

But she did say, 'Be sure to keep in touch, and let us know when you find somewhere to stay.' You can say what you like about my parents, but they've definitely never spoiled us – although that would have been a good time to start.

It was the closest I have ever come to sleeping rough. We headed to the beach; if we were going to be homeless, there was no point bedding down on concrete in Las Ramblas with all the other rough sleepers. The beach was close to the Olympic Village, so Louise called Terry and he kindly brought out some food for us. But, more important than the tasty cake, he'd had a rather excellent idea. His mum lived in Las Vegas, and a family she worked for, the O'Reillys, had come over to Spain to watch the Games. They were hoping Terry would be able to get them tickets, so he had a reason to call and, in passing, he mentioned that his girlfriend Louise and her sister Gabby were 'accidentally' homeless.

John O'Reilly was one of the top litigation lawyers in Las Vegas, and a cultured man, so it wasn't all about the sport for him. He was taking his family of six touring to nearby Sitges, a favourite resort of the great American writer Ernest Hemingway. This meant their apartment in the centre of town would be empty for a few days; would we like to borrow it?

We were unpacking in the apartment within the hour, raiding their selection of Pop Tarts and thanking whoever it was in the heavens that had intervened on our behalf. I think we both had a good idea who it was.

14

Not Your Average Student Life

I have a vivid memory from my first year at Durham University. I was walking down the towpath, heading back to my room after a lecture. It was raining and freezing cold, so it could have been any time from October to May. I passed two boys on a bench. They were probably fourteen years old, and smoking cigarettes. I got ten metres past them, then I abruptly turned around and decided I was going to change the direction of their lives.

'What are you doing?' I asked them.

'Smoking,' the smaller one replied, and they both laughed. They were smoking the life out of some tab ends, dragging on them hard, squeezing out every last bit of nicotine.

'I can see that, but you really should be in school. Sitting here smoking in the rain isn't going to get you anywhere in life, is it?'

Oh dear, who the hell was I turning into? I was like your nightmare walking, talking 'Good Samaritan'.

'Nah, but it's fun, like, and school is shite.' The bigger one laughed.

'I had a brother a little bit older than you,' I said. 'He died a few months ago. He was a footballer; he was going to be a professional player for Leeds United.'

'How did he die?' the younger one asked.

'He had a congenital heart disease. He just dropped down dead without warning. Nothing – not even a pain in his chest. That was it, his life and his opportunity gone. Boys, just . . . Just don't waste your lives.' I walked off, happy I had intervened in the course of history.

'Sorry about your brother,' the little one called after me.

I like to think those boys went on to become human rights barristers for Amnesty International after my inspiring pep talk, but I realise it is far more likely Amnesty International had to intervene to free *them* from a Thai jail.

I had always been a 'joiner in' at school. I loved a sports club and a social cause, and always enjoyed extracurricular activities, so it will come as no great surprise to hear that I was racing round the Student Union in freshers' week signing up to as much as possible.

But there was something more to it than my old love of 'joining in'. I definitely had more of a sense of purpose now. I had looked across the precipice of life and, as obvious as this sounds, it was the finality of it all that kept shocking me. Little things, like those boys smoking by the river, would remind me every day that Daniel's journey was stuck at fifteen years old. When I heard news of his old friends and what they were up to, it was always a gentle reminder that other people had moved on to the next stage of their lives, but he couldn't.

I didn't want to waste any opportunities – who knew when my own time would be up? It wasn't a case of being morbid. For my own sanity, I couldn't be fearful of death or wrap myself up in cotton wool, taking no risks in life. I had to get out of the blocks every day and go hunting for life and its meaning. I was a young woman on a mission.

There's seizing the day and then there's grabbing hold of it with both hands, squeezing out every last drop. The latter was my preferred technique. After just a few weeks at Durham, I had joined the Union Society (debating chambers), the Drama Society, the college boat club (I didn't last long there) and the Law Society. I was also coaching some local gymnasts, and I had taken part in a netball session with the college team. I wanted to act, too, so I joined a theatre group that was taking a play to the Edinburgh Festival. It was an adult version of *James and the Giant Peach*. I played the spider, who was a nymphomaniac (the cricket was a heroin addict). I was 'joining in', alright. On top of all that, I had made one very important phone call to Giles Squire, the boss of Metro FM, the commercial radio station that served Newcastle – but more on that in a moment.

Durham is the third-oldest university in the UK and once had a reputation for collecting Oxford and Cambridge rejects, but the collegiate system there appealed to me. I hoped that living in a smaller community meant I would be able to forge relationships that would last more than a term. It felt cosy and it was aesthetically very beautiful. The choice seemed even more pertinent after Daniel's death; being just a ninety-minute drive from our home in Leeds felt very important.

I'd got lucky with my college, St Hild and St Bede. Not knowing anything about the collegiate system in Durham, I had left the college choice open on my application, which apparently nobody ever did. Hild and Bede was a much-coveted College, so I was lucky to get in.

As we drove into the grounds, Mum, who'd never been to Durham before, took in the cloistered buildings, the thousand-year-old cathedral in the distance and the students arriving in Range Rovers with trunks rather than suitcases. After a few minutes, she said, 'Well, you did always want to go to private school.' It did all look very Malory Towers.

It's true: I'd been obsessed with going to private school when I was younger. I wanted to wear a boater hat like the girls at St Joseph's Convent in Coventry. My mum's reasoning for keeping us in the state system was not based on her idealistic politics – she was a fan of Margaret Thatcher back then – but because she reasoned that if she paid for *me* to go to a private school, she'd have to do the same for all her children, and if anything went wrong financially she would have to pull us all out of school.

We compromised and I persuaded her to buy me a boater hat, which I wore at weekends and for christenings and weddings.

I'd never met anyone who had been to a top public school. I didn't know anyone who had a country home, went fox hunting or played 'lax' (lacrosse). But Durham was teeming with them.

I was out of my depth in much of the conversation. I remember chatting to a good-looking Old Etonian in freshers' week and asking where he lived.

'We have homes in Chelsea and Gloucestershire,' he answered.

'Cool, so you can stay in London at the weekend and go clubbing, then relax in Gloucestershire during the week,' I naively surmised.

'No, the other way.' He rolled his eyes. 'We shoot in the country at the weekend and live in London during the week.'

What a waste, I thought to myself. *They've got that the wrong way round.*

Durham was a social melting pot that could be difficult to navigate. As well as the boys who wore Barbour jackets and sports kits saying things like 'Eton Football First XI' on the back, brought golf clubs with them and were already plotting their first weekend away at someone's country home before they'd even had a pint in the college bar, there were also state-educated boys like Dougie, Steve and Euan, who lived on my floor, hailing from a range of mill towns on the M62 corridor. Euan studied philosophy, almost always had his curtains shut and got migraines, but he'd still let you into his room to chat, even in the midst of a crippling attack. They called themselves 'Northern Scum'. The two groups didn't mix all that much.

I was something of an anomaly. I was northern and state-educated, but I had a car with me at college, which put me closer to the middle of the Venn diagram. The southern public-school kids took up most of the parking spaces. Most of them drove Golf GTIs, although a sassy blonde – possibly called Sienna – with a signet ring had a new convertible, and someone came back from Christmas break with a Land Rover Defender.

I drove my black Fiat Panda, which came with a picture of a large panda on each rear wing, into the car park under the cover of darkness, but it didn't go unnoticed. Unbeknown to me, for most of my first year, my peers at college assumed I was a passionate advocate for the environment and the World Wildlife Fund.

'I think you'd really like this event we're holding. It's about the exploitation of elephants in Thailand for the purposes of the tourism industry,' said someone with a double-barrelled name I had only vaguely smiled at once.

'What?' I replied, genuinely confused. I didn't hate elephants, but I wasn't sure what I'd said to make me a candidate for attending a save-the-elephants event.

'Your car? You're a member of the WWF, right? No?'

'Oh. No, it was £250 cheaper than the one without panda stickers,' I explained.

All this social stratification was quite confusing. I didn't want to only mix with my 'type' so, ultimately, I decided to ignore it. Surely university was about broadening horizons, not narrowing them, and I liked who I liked. If you were a nice person, we could be friends, wherever you were from. But I was also totally fascinated by the confidence the privately educated kids seemed to exude.

If you took it at face value, it might be easy to see it as entitlement, but that would only apply to a minority and didn't tell the full story. There was a social confidence that was learned – or maybe even bought – and the rest of us had to work hard to catch up. Stories about different students did the rounds that just seemed implausible to my northern ears: 'Oh, she danced in an INXS video in the summer', 'He's best mates with Prince William', 'She's James Bond's stepdaughter.' The stories were all true.

My room was miniscule and positioned in the eaves. It smelled dampish and had random heating, but on the plus side it was in the main building, so I always had visitors popping by for a cup of tea. I suspect that the pastoral team at the college might have done this deliberately, given the tragic summer I'd had.

Next door to me was a second-year lad called Ed Jones whose best mate was Dom Collins. Dom was in the National Youth Theatre and loved a soliloquy. His favourite late-night hobby after he'd had a few drinks in the college bar was knocking on my door and telling me to dump Gary.

'You can't possibly love him. Love is merely a construct you've hijacked to justify the fact he left his wife, but he didn't leave her for you. He used you to exit. You are now hanging on to an ideal that simply does not exist. All the while, you are losing days, weeks and months of your life here, where you should be taking in the beauty around you and having experiences in an environment you will never know again.'

I might have made some of that up for comedic effect.

Dom had loads of curly blond hair and wore a long, colourful striped scarf like Dr Who. Whatever the actual content of his speech, he was right; I shouldn't have been at university with a boyfriend who was ten years older than me.

It didn't take long for things to untangle on their own.

Gary went off to a training camp in South Africa. I knew it would be gutless to end things over the phone, but I did it anyway. I didn't really have a choice. He wasn't sure when he was coming home, and I needed to be free.

The only phone was a communal one in a booth in the corridor, and at one time or another we'd all found ourselves in the queue for the phone behind someone who'd brought a pack of digestives and a kettle into the booth with them. The idea of queuing to use a phone now seems almost biblical in its primitiveness, doesn't it?

'Sorry . . . won't be long here. Just finishing with my long-term boyfriend.'

Three years of longing, pining, waiting for him to be free, of secret rendezvous, losing my virginity and, more latterly, of domestic drudgery were over.

It wasn't all terrible with Gary, but I think he'd agree it probably should have been left as an unrequited holiday romance in Auckland.

I felt like I had been released when I put the phone down that night. I was nineteen years old, and for the first time, I felt my age. I had spent too long wearing clothes that were older than me, worrying about taking chicken kievs out of the freezer in time for dinner, and I'd spent too many Saturdays looking for pine tables for the kitchen.

Gary had known me before Daniel's death and after, and in some ways that was comforting. The next relationship I ventured into would only know this version of me. In fact, it dawned on me that for the rest of my life, any new acquaintances wouldn't have met Daniel, which made me feel sad. It felt like I would forever be explaining what had happened.

My relationship with Gary did, however, lead to something very positive that happened to me at Durham. While I don't generally put things down to 'fate', there was something serendipitous about meeting Giles Squire at a New Year's party held by one of Gary's friends, Steve Cram. Giles was the boss of Metro FM, which was a classic old-school local radio station. It permeated lives in a way that radio had the power to before the internet was invented. Giles was very good at his job and Metro FM's content was award-winning. It was a commercially thriving station, and there was a real buzz about it. The team there clearly felt a real pride in what they were doing.

At the party that night, I had told Giles I wanted to work in TV.

'Come and see me when you come up to Durham,' he said, which may, with hindsight, have been a way of getting rid of me and moving on to other, more interesting guests. It didn't matter. I had his number on a scrap of paper, and I guarded it with my life for the next nine months.

I called him within days of arriving in Durham.

'Gosh, you're keen,' he said, after I admitted it was still freshers' week.

Keen is never really a compliment, is it? It's always a bit loaded – unless you are describing someone as a 'keen gardener' or something like that. Regardless, I ground Giles down and he agreed I could come and see him for a catch-up coffee a few weeks later.

I went to our meeting without any expectation of a real paid job. I was hoping for a warm drink, a biscuit and some work experience. Giles got to the point quickly; he'd actually only allocated me ten minutes in his packed diary.

'I would like to be Jeremy Paxman, or maybe Zoe Ball,' in answer to his question about my professional aspirations, keeping my options open.

Ignoring my rather wishy-washy answer he said, 'What we'll do is start you in the newsroom. You'll learn to write copy and compile bulletins, and then read them. You'll learn to record interviews and edit them, so you can go out and deliver a story on your own. Can you do a 1pm–7pm shift?'

'Yes. Great. Amazing. Thank you.'

'I would hope that by Christmas, I'll be paying you for a news reading shift. Speak to Lynne, my PA, and she'll get you on the rota with Mary who heads up the newsroom.'

'Wow, Giles. Thank you. How much do you actually pay for a news reading shift?'

'Sixty quid.' He laughed. It became a running joke with Giles that I was always keen to get my invoices signed off and paid by the time I had left the building.

Giles flew a helicopter and lived in a mansion in the countryside. He could laugh, but £60 per shift would change my world.

And so began my double life. In my first year at Durham, I had eight hours of lectures a week and four tutorials, so for at least two afternoons each week, I pottered up the A1 in the black Fiat Panda, which frequently broke down for fifteen minutes just past Washington. Once I was up and running I was put on the weekend rota. It wasn't much fun sitting in a layby at 5am on a cold December morning waiting for the car to start again, but as anyone who knows that area will tell you, it's all uphill after Washington, and the Panda needed a breather.

The car didn't have a radio, ironically, so I had a ghetto blaster on the passenger seat that sucked the life out of £10's worth of batteries every week. Quite rightly, it is illegal to drive while holding a mobile phone. Back then, I had one hand on the steering wheel while the other changed the batteries in my ghetto blaster at eighty miles per hour.

I hope my kids have skipped this chapter.

With the exception of those studying engineering at Durham, who seemed to have a nine-to-five day of lectures, I couldn't understand why you wouldn't have a job while at university. I had essays and reading to complete, but that might take me to twenty hours of academic commitments, if I was being really diligent. This was not a popular point of view among my peers, and probably not one I would have held myself had I not spent my gap year working four dead-end jobs. I didn't share my radio ventures with my friends at the beginning.

'Where have you been all afternoon?' Dom or Ed would ask.

'In the library. I had a big essay to research.'

It was a watertight lie. Nobody who did arts subjects went anywhere near a library until at least the final term of their first year, when they were searching for people who had actually been to some of the lectures to 'borrow' notes ahead of exams.

My first paid news shift was sprung upon me one afternoon in December.

I went in to 'shadow', and was handed a news bulletin and told to read it on the top of the hour. It was a clever move; they ambushed me. If I'd been told the night before, I probably wouldn't have slept.

I had read through the bulletin a few times in the office beforehand, checking for any potentially dodgy pronunciations I'd need to look out for. When the jingle played to signal the news, I took a deep breath in and out and tried to calm the butterflies in my tummy.

The first story was a sad one. It was important to get the tone right.

'Good afternoon. It's two o'clock, and this is Metro FM. Police in Houghton le Spring have released details of the body they found last week in a water-pilled fit.

'Er . . . water-filled pit.'

I don't remember the other stories, because I was consumed with shame at getting such a sensitive story wrong.

Giles was waiting outside the studio when I emerged. 'Well done.' He winked. 'You'll get it right in an hour.' And I did. That was the beauty of radio; you could make a mistake and correct it almost immediately.

Getting through a bulletin word-perfect was my goal. Soon after I began to achieve that goal regularly, the DJs were having chats with me off the news and bringing me into their shows a bit more.

One day a few months later, Ian, a funny guy who worked on the sports team but wasn't quite an editor or journalist, ran in, urgently waving a piece of paper at me and mouthing, 'Breaking news.'

I didn't have time to read it first, but I trusted Ian that it was obviously very important. What could it be? A plane crash? A Royal wedding? I had only read one story so far, so I adopted my most serious newsreader voice and launched into Ian's story.

'News just in . . . Durham . . . have taken another wicket at Chester-le-Street against Lancashire.'

I was devastated. It was a breaking *sports* story, and I should have read it about six items later. Ian mouthed 'Sorry,' through the glass window as I moved on to the next story.

'The Waco siege, which ended in a devastating fire yesterday ... '

At least the listeners were under no illusions about how highly I valued sport.

The radio station was a tonic. Student life is great, but it's pretty much filled with students. At Metro FM, I was working alongside people of different ages, from a range of backgrounds and different levels of education.

Aside from learning an actual skill and earning a living, I was able to confide in and develop friendships with some great folk who taught me a lot about being an adult. What's more, they didn't care what mark I got for my last essay, nor whether I had snogged Huw in Ritzy's the night before.

I thoroughly recommend having a double life at university, acquiring a job or getting into some volunteering. I'm pretty sure it helped create a bit of balance. I already knew real life could be pretty mundane after my year of choosing pine furniture and heating up leftovers with Gary. I wanted to carve out something a bit more exciting for myself, and my weekend job was the first step on that road.

Metro FM was where I earned my first pound as a broadcaster, just four and a half years on from that fateful day at the BBC when I appeared on *Blue Peter*.

15

Slow and Steady Wins the Race

I met Zebedee in the toilets of the Student Union in fresh-ers' week. Her real name was Helen, but she bounced everywhere, like the character from the children's TV show *The Magic Roundabout*. I am fairly sure we came up with the nickname in the toilet that first night.

When two students emerge from a toilet and one has chris-tened the other Zebedee, you could be forgiven for assuming drugs were involved, but I promise you they weren't. Zeb had a mountain of blonde curls and wore round gold spectacles. She was petite and very upright from her days as a junior school gymnast, and to top it all off, she had a very slight Gloucestershire burr.

'I'm from Cheltenham ... but I didn't go to Cheltenham Ladies' College,' she warned me as she washed her hands.

'OK, that's cool. I don't know what that is.'

She laughed. I think she found my naivety refreshing. We clicked straight away.

Both of her parents were teachers. Zeb wasn't at university

to waste three years before she got a job in PR; she was a real academic. Her degree was in French and Russian, and she'd already read *Anna Karenina* in Tolstoy's native tongue. If you were friends with Zeb, by definition you must be OK. She exuded positivity and didn't seem annoyed by my 'seize the day', 'living my life for two' demeanour. I understand now that it was a demeanour that might have aggravated less enthusiastic types – even I get a bit annoyed by me when I think of how driven I was at Durham.

In between my studies, my job at Metro FM and all those extracurricular activities, I did find time to start snogging a boy called Steve from another college, St Chads. He played rugby and studied archaeology, and was also quite handsome.

Things were fun with Steve; he was a sweet young man and it was all very carefree. It felt like the kind of relationship someone my age *should* have, in contrast to the years I'd spent with Gary.

Steve bought me a necklace that said 'Gabrielle' for my birthday. It was specially made, he said. I knew the relationship was doomed at that moment. It was a lovely thing to do, and yet it made me a bit cross. He never called me Gabrielle – what was wrong with Gabby?

And why did Steve always have brown sauce on his lips after he ate a bacon sandwich?

I was revealing myself to be something of an angry person.

Steve was actually very lovely. But I wasn't ready for lovely. If he'd presented me with a unicorn wrapped in a rainbow for that birthday, I'd have said it was the wrong shade of white.

I wasn't sleeping well, and we had exams coming up. We knew the score: fail your first-year exams and get kicked out or redo the whole year again, paying for the tuition yourself. I put my insomnia down to the new weekend shifts I had undertaken at Metro FM; getting up at 4.45am meant I regularly had four hours' sleep on both weekend nights. It then took me a couple of days to get back into any normal sleep pattern, until eventually there *was* no normal sleep pattern.

The first anniversary of Daniel's death was coming up. I would be going home for a memorial service, but it was in the middle of the exams, so the build-up was especially wretched. I cried a lot in my room on my own, and I didn't answer the door when I heard Steve knocking.

Eventually, we had a full blown row over a game of tennis one day, so he stopped knocking.

My dad loved a sleeping tablet, which should have been enough of a warning for me to never take them, although he downed his sleeping tablets with whisky for added knock-out effect. *If I just had a few,* I thought, *they might see me through this rough patch.*

I hadn't been to a doctor for a year, not since Daniel died. Looking back now, it's strange to think that I didn't visit a medical professional at this time in my life. If I experienced tragedies like the Bradford fire and Daniel's death these days, I would have gone to a counsellor and spoken about what I had experienced. But back in the early nineties, we didn't place the same value on mental wellbeing. Trauma simply got buried.

'I'm not sleeping, but I'm exhausted. I feel upset over silly matters and yet I find other people get too hung up on things that don't matter, not in the big scheme of things,' I told the old man in the white coat who was sitting in front of me in the austere clinic. He was my doctor, apparently. He didn't know me any better than the chair I sat on.

'I'm going to give you thirty sleeping tablets. See how you go and then come back next month, once your exams are over.' He handed me the prescription and sent me on my way.

No questions at all, questions that might have helped him find out I was grieving for my brother and not coping very well with my new life at university.

That night, I fell asleep within minutes and woke up ten hours later. The next day, I was groggy and grumpy, but I had slept, so it was a fair trade. I didn't ring home and tell them I wasn't feeling great, because their pain was always much worse. Everyone was struggling. I felt my calls home needed to be upbeat and positive to counter what they were going through, which I later learned was the start of the long march to the end of my parents' marriage.

But I did tell my mum about the tablets.

'Why don't you try not to take them? Maybe just knowing they are there if you really needed them would help you fall asleep?' she asked wisely.

'I'll see.' I didn't promise.

Then, an hour later, Northern Steve shouted down the corridor. 'Terry Yorath, the Wales manager, is on the phone, Gabby!'

Dad never called me at college.

'Dad, are you OK?'

'Hi Gab. Your mum told me you got sleeping tablets from the doctor.'

'Yeah, I've been a bit stressed and I can't sleep. And I have exams coming up.'

'Please don't take them. I've struggled my whole life with sleep. I started taking them when I was nineteen and they don't help; you just end up needing more of them, and then they don't work. Try not to use them.'

'OK, Dad, I'll try,' I said. 'Love you.'

The thoughts I'd shared with the doctor – about other people getting hung up on things that didn't matter – were weighing me down. I was no better than anyone else, of course. But maybe I had subconsciously been flippant about the issues and tribulations my peers were dealing with, because I felt none of them could be as bad or as sad as what I had experienced. *If only they knew what I know. That would put things into perspective for them*, I'd think to myself. I'm not sure what you'd call that mental state – insight dysmorphia? A lack of empathy?

Zeb's concerns about where she was going to live next year were legitimate, not trivial. Steve's anxiety about getting in the top rowing boat was understandable. Dom wanting the main part in a play was not insignificant.

Internally, I had dismissed these things as being low down on the scale of sad, consequential things, where *my* understanding of sorrow was at the very top, of course. I didn't elucidate on these matters; I didn't need to. It was easily inferred by my lack of genuine interest or concern. 'Hey guys, what will be will be', 'If it doesn't kill you, it makes you stronger.' I wasn't exactly oozing with understanding and supportiveness, was I?

If I did have an insight into the 'bigger picture', I needed to keep it to myself and be more human for my friends, try to get back some empathy. Nobody at my college was looking to hang out with Yoda.

I went to my room and grabbed my trainers and the packet of pills. When I was a few miles into my evening run, I opened the packet and put the pills in a bin. I ran back to college, full of endorphins, feeling that a little light had gone back on inside me. I knew what I needed; to run more – and laugh more. Everything was too serious.

There was a boy who kept smiling at me in the college bar, then I'd catch him staring at me across the dining hall. We'd lock eyes for a few seconds too long, and then he'd blush and then I'd blush. He was a second year, six feet two inches tall and athletic-looking. He only ever wore baggy navy track-suit bottoms and T-shirts by tennis brands. He drove a blue Escort van that had blocked up windows in the back, something you'd expect a plumber to drive rather than a student. I'd seen him carrying Wilson tennis bags, and I'd heard his friends call him Geordie.

'Geordie fancies you,' one of them told me as we queued for dinner.

'Geordie?' I pretended not to know who he was. But my heart started beating a little bit faster.

'Ian Baggett. You know, the tennis player with the van,' his friend Crabby continued. 'Are you going out with anyone?'

'Not really,' I said.

Ian was a very good tennis player, but he'd probably found the sport too late; he was well into his teens before he had picked up a racket. Like most boys brought up around Newcastle, his main sport had been football. He still harboured dreams of becoming a tennis player, but had a geography degree to finish first. He'd heard I had fallen out with my previous boyfriend over a game of tennis, which was partially true, and he told me he'd give me a lesson one day if I wanted. I took him up on his offer, and that's how it all started. Hooking up with someone in 1993 was really very simple.

We had the perfect university relationship. His friends were some of the most popular people in college, and his friend Jenny became one of my closest female allies. My friends thought he was great. He played his tennis, and I went to work at Metro FM. We were both northern and proud of it, he was especially proud of his working-class roots, although he was happy to mix with others from different backgrounds. He was a state-school kid whose A level result in maths had been the highest in the region, but he was not a super geek. He was balanced, and I needed some of that. He came from a steady home; nothing had ever really gone wrong in his life.

When I needed to be asleep early for my 5am starts for work, he'd stroke my hair until I dozed off, then he'd head out raving or nightclubbing. He loved illegal raves, which were held in farm buildings in the County Durham countryside, and would stay up dancing until 7am on nothing but Evian water; we were both a bit suspicious of people who needed to take drugs to have fun. I loved that Ian could dance. He loved that I worked for Metro FM, the local radio station he'd grown up listening to.

He was always up for a political debate, but listened thoughtfully if your opinion was different to his, and he proved his patience by working with me on my tennis. He was an entrepreneur; at the end of each term, he'd go to the most popular newsagents in Durham, where all the students bought their sweets and snacks, and buy up stock that was due to go out of date over the holidays. He'd fill his blue Escort van, then pull up outside the various college summer balls and sell the sweets for a profit. He was Del Boy rolled into Andy Murray, Brian Cox and Billy Elliot.

Ian's family lived thirty minutes away, in a house in the middle of a forest on the edge of a mining village called Rowlands Gill. His mum was a housewife who sewed and cooked, and occasionally had bed-and-breakfast guests. His dad was a woodwork teacher who loved cycling and was obsessed with the Tour de France. They were a beautiful, uncomplicated family, and Ian was very much the product of that. He was the reason I finished my first year at university much happier than I had begun it.

I was never going to lose my drive and the ambition to make something of my life, but in Ian and his family, I saw a different way to be, and they showed me that I could put my faith in other people once more. It was the first big emotional commitment I had entered into since Daniel's death. Looking back now, it's interesting I chose to be attracted to someone with such solid roots from such a loving, protective environment. Life had delivered enough drama; I didn't need to seek out any more.

16

How to Get an Exclusive

The university summer holidays felt far too long. Not a popular sentiment, I grant you.

I was offered so much work at Metro FM that summer that I didn't need to go home for long; I just needed somewhere to live within fifteen miles of the radio station. At first, I stayed in an empty student house in Durham, with no TV or radio and only one pan to boil my penne pasta. It was set to be a fairly monastic, low-rent summer.

I had turned down the offer of a room at Ian's parents' house due to my obsession with independence. Eventually, though, I relented; there is only so much plain pasta one can eat, and then one night someone tried to break in while I was sleeping, so I rolled up my sleeping bag and legged it to the woods near Newcastle, where the Baggett family lived.

It didn't start very well. I found Ian's family home claustrophobic. It wasn't the size; I just wasn't comfortable with parents being so attentive and kind. I'd wake up to find his dad had washed and serviced my car. His mum ironed my clothes, even when I said I would do it, and they fed and watered me well. They couldn't do enough for us. I wish I'd accepted their hospitality with more grace; I truly cringe now at my resistance.

But I was twenty and a bit angry with them all for being so happy. Their blissful home was such a sharp contrast to our shattered family life.

One day, instead of saying thank you to Ian's dad when he mentioned he'd driven my car round the block to check something he suspected was wrong in the engine, I replied, 'Are you insured to drive any car then, Peter?' in a bitchy, sarcastic tone.

Peter looked hurt, which immediately made me feel like shit.

Later, Ian suggested wisely that gratitude might have been a more appropriate response.

'Your parents do too much for you; they're scared of you being independent,' I snapped.

'You could just be gracious and say thanks to them, and keep your thoughts to yourself,' he suggested reasonably.

Instead of relenting, I changed tack. 'I don't get why they don't want you to be a tennis player. They're just scared of you being disappointed; they're stopping you achieving your ambitions.'

They loved him and they didn't want to see him hurt. I get that now, but back then, I was confused by the stability he had. It was all a bit unfamiliar to me. I think the more my own family unravelled, the more I tried to defend it as being normal and character-building.

As capable as I was of being a resentful provocateur, I think, in my better moments, I gave Ian some confidence to try things that were outside his comfort zone. When his gran died, she left all her grandchildren £5,000. This was not money Ian had been expecting.

After some debate about what to do with the money, I helped persuade him that he should buy a cottage in a village near Durham to rent to students. The cottage we eventually found in Bowden needed work, but he could do that cheaply with his dad over the summer holidays. Working on this project together would also help his dad feel more invested, as his parents were worried about him buying a property. My mum's property company was going well, so she helped Ian get his mortgage and advised him on the refurbishment. And he was off; that summer was the start of what would eventually become a very large property empire, which he presides over to this day. I am very proud to have played a tiny part in helping to persuade him to take a risk.

Another great love began that summer. It all started on 25 August 1993, a beautiful summer evening, just before the start of my second year.

Earlier that summer, in their preparations for Premier League football, the newly promoted Newcastle United bought a twenty-three-year-old Cypriot midfield player called Nikki Papavasiliou. As well as her property company, my mum had started a small sports management business and she was Nikki's agent. Nikki had a wife, who was also called Nikki, and they had a baby, whose name I can't remember, but it may well have been Nikki too.

Mum helped them rent a house in Chester-le-Street, which cricket fans will know is between Durham and Newcastle. As we have established, my mum is a good businesswoman, but she's never been a lover of a full ninety minutes of football. So, once the deal for the 'Nikkis' had been signed and he was handsomely wearing the black-and-white stripes, Mum had a genius idea.

Rather than her having to drive up from Leeds every week to go to his matches, as an agent might be expected to, I would pick up female Nikki from Chester-le-Street in my Fiat Panda and take her to the matches. I'd watch the match, help her look after the baby, and then she'd go home with her husband afterwards. I was happy to earn £10, which is all Mum offered, and I got to watch a top-flight football match. Mrs P was only two years older than me, so we could be mates, whether she liked it or not.

Newcastle beat Everton one-nil that first night, and I loved it. My new 'escort' job was going to be perfect. I had an exciting team I could get behind, and was watching them with someone who had a vested interest. You know the saying about things being too good to be true.

Nikki only made seven appearances for Newcastle United. I'm not sure exactly why it didn't work out for him, but I got the feeling that Mrs P wasn't that impressed with the Fiat Panda, and I heard rumours that Mr P thought the value of his contract was *after* tax, so it was a bit of a shocker when HMRC sent them a letter asking for a few thousand pounds. Ultimately, the small baby, a strange language and no family (even with a helpful Durham University law student befriending them) wasn't a winning combination for the Papavasilious, so they headed back to sunny Cyprus with a large tax bill.

But I couldn't leave St James' Park.

This was a team with an alluring combination of swagger, long hair and plenty of local grit: Andy Cole, Peter Beardsley, Rob Lee, Barry Venison, Steve Clark, to name but a few of the players who would come so close to glory a few seasons later. Add to that mix the charismatic King

Kev as the manager, a national hero and a local icon, and it was clear a revolution was afoot; a revolution I wanted to be a part of. On every match day, there was a buzz in the air, the hope and expectation tangible; people talked of little else. The football stadium in Newcastle, St James' Park, is unusually placed, as it sits right in the middle of the city a short walk from the train station. It dominates the skyline like a citadel. Sir John Hall, the son of a miner, owned the club in the days when having a few hundred million pounds was enough to run a Premier League football club. He was a well-respected businessman (he'd also taken over the local rugby, ice hockey and basketball teams), and he was lining up exciting global names to wear the black-and-white stripes. It felt like we lived in the United Kingdom of Newcastle.

Is it any wonder I got sucked in? Since Dad had taken over as Wales boss, I had stopped going to matches regularly, as international football is sporadic and involves expensive travel. But football wasn't just something my dad did to earn a living; it was at the heart of our family, and offered me a connection to Daniel – soon, his peers would be playing in the first teams I was watching. I checked out birthdates in programmes, looking for players born in 1976, then I imagined them as teammates or rivals of Dan's.

People often say they are surprised I don't support Leeds United. I do have a soft spot for all the teams my dad played for, because each one evokes memories of my childhood, but the misery and occasional ecstasy that comes from being the child of a footballer and then football manager is always subject to the transitional nature of the job. Never get too close to the team, because soon we'll be ringing Pickfords, on the move to god knows where for god knows how long. Only a cold-hearted football-hating fool would have spent their Saturdays in a Durham bedsit writing essays on employment law when they could have been in the cathedral of football being seduced by the black-and-white army. It also helped that I worked at the radio station, which had the contract to cover all the live matches.

Ian was a Geordie, and had been a regular in the Gallowgate End at St James' Park since he was a small boy. He filled in a few of the gaps with his historical references, little vignettes like: 'At half-time, they couldn't be bothered going to the toilet because it was too packed, so they'd do it in the stand, and because I was so small, they'd lift me up, so I didn't get piss on my shoes.'

If you've never supported a football club or even been interested, you might not understand the significance of listening to the radio at 4.50pm on a Saturday. When all the scores are in, the full classified results are read out. For many years of my youth, and even into my professional life, that voice was James Alexander Gordon; he had a mesmeric effect on football fans.

When Dad played for Leeds United, we were often left at my Nana Sheila's house for the afternoon so Mum could go to the match. As I've said, it wasn't the football so much as the occasion she loved; in fact, ten days after I was born, she went to Wembley to watch Dad in the FA Cup Final against Sunderland. I'm not sure what they did to women in childbirth in the 1970s, but the flared trousers she wore that day were so tiny around the waist that my sister and I couldn't fit into them as teenagers. And we were international gymnasts. The shirt was see-through, save for some strategically placed pockets on the breasts, so clearly no leaking boobs for my mum. She'd had the outfit made and tailored with a fitting a few days after my birth. I was nine pounds ten ounces, by the way, so I didn't exactly slip out. By way of contrast, ten days after I gave birth to *my* children, I considered it a victory when I managed to make my own toast.

I always remember the music coming on the radio with the results on those Saturdays at Nana Sheila's. Once I had heard that, it meant an hour later, Mum and Dad would arrive to pick us up. A Pavlov's dog response. They'd rush in, smelling of expensive perfume and cologne, Dad in a suit and Mum in a fabulous outfit with a fur coat propped on her shoulders, and they'd whisk us off home in time for a babysitter to take over so they could go clubbing. That's what happens when you have three children by the time you are twenty-seven.

While I was falling in love with Newcastle United, Dad was with the Wales national team, who were doing well in their World Cup qualifying campaign. Belief was growing that they might make it to the finals in the USA. They had even overtaken the Welsh rugby team in popularity (it helped that the rugby team were having a disastrous time, haemorrhaging players to Rugby League). As was always the case with Welsh football, there were a few top-class players, some average top-flight players and a few from lower down the leagues, but in this team, there was one player who had captured global interest: a once-in-a-generation player. His name was Ryan Giggs.

In 1991, at just seventeen years old, Giggs had been capped by Dad for Wales and Sir Alex Ferguson at Manchester United. With his mop of fantastic dark hair and his swarthy looks, his face was a regular feature on the front cover of teen-age girls' magazines, never mind the football magazines. In short, he was a heart throb. Men wanted to be him, women wanted to be with him, and brands wanted him to be their face. I won't deny that he made the trips to watch Wales' qualifying matches in Cardiff much more enjoyable.

I took Kerry, one of my best friends from my gymnastics days, down to the Arms Park to watch the penultimate World Cup qualifying match against Cyprus. Kerry was an Arsenal fan, no johnny-come-lately to the Giggs juggernaut.

Wales won two-nil, and the World Cup dream was alive and well, with one match remaining against Romania. Cardiff was buzzing. Kerry and I decided to hit the town. We headed to a nightclub called Browns. Dad dropped us off and had a word with the bouncer, who knew him. I assumed that he was trying to get us in for free, or asking the bouncer to keep an eye out for us.

In the club, we spotted Ryan Giggs having a drink with a friend. Bingo.

'Go on, Gabs, get over there,' Kerry insisted. Kerry is a singer and an actress, and has never been backwards in coming forwards.

'No, what am I going to say?' I was less sure about approaching the hottest name in world football.

'Er, why don't you try, "Hi, Ryan, I'm Terry's daughter. Well done tonight." That would be a start,' she suggested reasonably, nudging me in the back.

I wandered over, with Kerry hot on my heels.

'Hi, Ryan,' I said, with the emphasis on a super-confident and friendly 'Hi'.

'Oh, hi,' he said, less confident, but still friendly, as if he knew me. Maybe he'd seen me with my dad? I now know that famous people do that all the time. They say 'HI,' as if they know you, just in case they *have* met you before, or because you might be important to their career. Once they work out you are not important, the not-nice ones ignore you.

'Well done tonight. You must be pretty pleased.' Pathetic opening gambit.

'Yeah, it was a good performance.' He was being pleasant and responding as if I was a journalist.

'So, guys, where else should we go out in Cardiff, when we leave here?' Kerry was better at this stuff.

It was noisy, so Ryan's friend leaned in to answer. As he did so, another head popped into our quartet.

It was the bouncer my dad had spoken to outside the club. Where had he come from?

'Now, Gabby, I'm really sorry. Your dad gave me express orders that I had to intervene. He said he didn't want you talking to any footballers.' His deep Cardiff-accented voice boomed so loudly that anyone within a twenty-metre radius knew we were not to be talked to. He was six feet six inches tall and about four feet wide.

'But this is Ryan Giggs ... he's younger than us,' Kerry reasoned.

'No footballers.' The bouncer was adamant that my night was over. He looked me in the eye and gestured for me to move. 'NO FOOTBALLERS.'

'Sorry, Ryan. My dad is Terry Yorath,' I said, by way of explanation.

'Right.' He looked relieved.

'Hey, do you think I could interview you for my university newspaper?' I asked, as a parting shot.

'Yeah, I don't see why not. After we've qualified for the World Cup.' He laughed.

If I couldn't hit the dance floor with Ryan Giggs, at least I could get a world-first; he'd never done a print interview before. Neither had I, of course. I'd been bluffing about the university paper; I'd never written for them, but I was pretty sure they wouldn't turn down a Ryan Giggs exclusive.

A few weeks later, Wales failed to qualify for the 1994 World Cup in the USA. They were beaten by a late goal from

Romania. None of the home nations qualified. England had been humiliated by lowly San Marino on the same night, conceding a goal that ended their campaign. After the final whistle in Cardiff, someone let off a firework in the stadium that killed a sixty-seven-year-old Wales fan called John Hill; it was a truly depressing evening. The next day, my dad was told by the WFA that his contract would not be renewed; he'd need to reapply for his own job. Football can be a very cruel game.

Ryan was true to his word, though, and came good on the promise of an interview. My mum had been in contact with his mum, Lynne, the previous year, when she was hoping Ryan might join her sports management business. Lynne was helpful in getting my interview with her son off the ground. We agreed it would take place at her house. I persuaded Metro FM that I could get some clips for the radio as well as my copy for the student newspaper. Because of this, they agreed to lend me a radio car, a cream-coloured Austin Metro that was quicker and more luxurious, and also marginally less embarrassing than my Fiat Panda.

After my three-hour drive across the Pennines, I arrived to find Ryan had six friends hanging out with him in his living room. It is not unusual for footballers to have lots of pals hanging round; over the years I have spent hours with the mates of Premier League stars while we wait for the 'main man' to arrive for their interview. Usually, it's the unmarried ones or the foreign ones who have no family in the UK. Nowadays, it doesn't intimidate me, but back then – well, I was already nervous. There was no way I could conduct my first-ever interview in front of an audience. Sensing my unease, Lynne ushered the mates out of the room, and made Ryan and I some tea.

I pressed 'record' on the cumbersome machine borrowed

from Metro FM and reached for a Dictaphone they had also lent me. For good measure, I got out a notebook too.

And we began. I asked him about Manchester United, and his aspirations for his career. I also tried to get him to confirm whether he was dating a soap star – that was more to satisfy my own nosiness than for the eventual article.

Nothing earth-shattering was asked, as you might expect from a total rookie, but there was one random question that makes me wince even now. Ryan did well not to burst out laughing.

'When you are driving, do you look at the car in front, or do you look four or five cars ahead?' It was the question of someone who had recently passed her own driving test.

'I look at least four cars ahead,' he answered correctly.

'And is that how you play football?'

'What, looking a few players ahead?' He tried to make sense of a nonsensical question.

'I mean, are you always aware of where ... every-one else is, on the pitch?' My mind had gone blank; I couldn't think of any other Manchester United footballers. None. Not one.

'Yeah, I see what you mean. Yeah, I think I have good peripheral awareness.' He was very kind to me.

It was time to go. I got my equipment together and didn't bother checking that it had all worked. As I made my way out to the cream Metro for the journey home, I tried to find my keys, fumbling around in the street while juggling radio recorders, Dictaphones and notebooks.

I realised I must have left them in the house.

'Sorry Lynne, it's me again,' I said, as she opened the door. 'I can't find my car keys.'

I went into the living room. Ryan's six mates had returned, but the keys weren't there.

'They might have dropped out of my pocket when I went to the toilet . . . ' I was having a shocker.

I came back from the toilet empty-handed to see Ryan's friends tipping his mum's sofa upside down, trying to find the keys in a frantic attempt to get rid of me. Thankfully, one of them found them.

A few hours later, after I had cringed all the way from Manchester to Newcastle, I arrived back at college and went to play the interview back. The radio recorder had managed to catch about five minutes of my hour-long 'fireside chat'.

The quality of the Dictaphone recording wasn't broadcastable, but I could just about make it out well enough to transcribe. It wasn't a total disaster; I managed to write a 1,000-word article, and made the front page of *The Palatinate*, the student paper, the following week. A few nights later, I saw a TV advert for the *Sunday Times*.

'This week, we have a world exclusive with Ryan Giggs. The Manchester United superstar gives his first EVER interview. Only in this week's *Sunday Times*,' the voice-over said, while beautiful, well–lit shots of Ryan Giggs, clearly not in his mum's living room, filled the screen.

My interview might only have been read by a bunch of students in Durham, and it might have been average at best, but the *Sunday Times* was wrong; mine was definitely the first.

That Christmas, Ian bought me a framed picture of Ryan Giggs from a market stall for my room at college. I'm sure he was being ironic, but Giggs remains the only footballer I have ever had on my bedroom wall. My room was burgled a few weeks later; they took my dirty washing, a word processor, a kettle and some shoes, but they left Ryan behind. Maybe the burglars were being ironic, too.

I got a buzz from being published and seeing my name as a byline, but I enjoyed the sitting-down part of the interview

the most. I was good at chatting to people, genuinely interested in what made them tick. I knew I wasn't going to turn
into Michael Parkinson overnight, but now I had an idea of
why I might be doing all those unsociable shifts at the radio
station. I had a focus.

17

Love in the Evenings

By the Christmas of my second year, I was back in college halls. I had briefly attempted to share a house with a group of PhD students. They had huge brains, but were very messy. The thing I really couldn't hack about the house, though, was the cold. We failed to notice when signing the lease in the warmth of summer that there was no central heating; no heating at all.

My avariciousness in grabbing the biggest bedroom in July had backfired. By November, I could write my name in the frost on my mirror in the morning. Fearing a winter of pneumonia and depression, I abandoned my independence, (there's a theme here, isn't there?) and begged the college principal to have me back.

I took courses in labour law, human rights, public international and philosophy of law, the kind of courses that don't trouble the students looking to make millions in the City on takeovers and mergers. If I was going to be a lawyer, then I wanted to work for Amnesty International or an NGO that was a force for good. I was full of altruistic intent, if not actual action.

I grew up fretting unnecessarily about money. We were never poor, not like my dad had been growing up. But Dad did have a habit of hiding tax bills in his sock drawer in the hope they'd go away, so there were often arguments and emergency meetings with accountants. It always felt to me like we were on a financial tightrope. Even though on the outside we had a big house and a gold toilet in the downstairs loo, there were periods where money seemed to be a bigger concern than it should have been.

Sometimes, Mum and Dad took us out for dinner to their favourite Italian restaurant, the Flying Pizza. We had a budget of £5 each, and that included a drink. I could get a calzone and a lemonade for £4.50. So while I wasn't driven by money per se I think the metaphor for my motivation in life when it came to cash and material wealth was to be able to choose whatever I wanted from the menu.

That year, Giles Squire gave me my first big break: my own radio show. Metro FM had a sister station called TFM, which was based in Stockton-on-Tees. Giles wanted me to take over the Friday and Saturday night *Love Show*, which went out from 11pm to 2am. I would drive the desk, play the tunes and read out the love dedications.

My show fee was £80, an improvement on my news reading shifts, but it meant I still didn't have a weekend social life at university. However, I was savvy enough to realise that I was gaining experience in a career that might otherwise have taken me another couple of years to get after graduating, and that these graveyard shifts meant I wasn't massively exposed. I could make mistakes and learn on the job.

I say it was my own show, but there wasn't much I could do with it. I didn't even have a producer and there was no budget. The inmates of Holme House and Durham Prison provided me with most of my programme content. Their hastily written love letters arrived on blue prison notepaper, stuffed inside small brown envelopes with the prison stamp on the outside. I had piles to wade through before the show. None of them were contenders for the Pulitzer.

To Doris,
I'll be oot in seven months, wait for us pet and I'll mak it up to ya. This song's for you babe.
Ur
Mick
PS Can you play 'Freedom' by George Michael.

Dear Brenda
I miss you loads, more than last time, see you next year.
Luv Bruce
Can you play 'Don't Leave me This Way' by the Communards?

And on and on they went. Initially, I wondered what Mick and his like had done; had they hurt anyone? After a few weeks, though, I was getting bored of these simplistic, badly written letters. We weren't actually allowed to say that the men were in prison, so I decided to use my creative writing skills and embellish their lives a little bit.

'This one is for Brenda, who lives in Barnard Castle. Brenda, I have a lovely letter from Bruce. He's a beautiful writer, isn't he? He says, "I've had a contract working away for a while now, and Brenda knows that I took this job so I could provide a better life for her and the kids. And I will do." He goes on to say that he misses you so much and the thought of holding you in his arms next year is what keeps him going. When he gets home, he can't wait to take you on the holiday of a lifetime. But he says he'll need to go shopping first, as this job has made him lose weight! He says he is indebted to you for the commitment and love you have shown him. And this song is for you. It's U2's 'I Still Haven't Found What I'm Looking For' ... But I don't think he means you, Brenda.'

I was slightly concerned that Bruce might get out the following year and hunt me down, but not concerned enough that I didn't carry on 'editing' the letters.

It was a long, lonely shift. If I needed a trip to the ladies', I'd search out an especially long song to cover me; one night, I found an extended version of 'Latest Trick' by Dire Straits. The side of the CD said it was eight minutes and thirty-five seconds long. My persona for this show was a slower, less frenetic version of the real me. I spoke as if I was advertising a Magnum ice lolly, in a low and slightly suggestive voice. Think Fiona Bruce with a hint of Yorkshire.

'It's that time of the night where I give you a real treat: its Newcastle's very own Dire Straits with "Latest Trick".' I faded the intro up, then sprinted to the toilet.

There were speakers all over the building playing the station output. I spent a minute enjoying 'Latest Trick' while looking at my face in the mirror, picking at a few spots, and I went into a cubicle for a leisurely wee. No urgency, this was a long track. I might even buy a coffee and a Twix on the way back.

As I sat down, the song disappeared. *The speakers in the ladies' must be playing up again,* I thought. I didn't panic.

A few seconds later, there was a crash on my cubicle door.

'Gabby, Gabby! The phone's goin' mad! Get yorsel' oot heor! The music's stopped.' The security man, the only other human in the building, was apoplectic. His idea of the phone 'going mad' turned out to be a single call from the station controller, who happened to be listening at home and wondered why the music had stopped.

I pulled up my jeans and ran to the studio. Not so Fiona Bruce sultry now.

'Well, that was wonderful, wasn't it,' I lied, sounding more like I had just got a new personal best in a Park Run. 'Let me tell you about a lovely letter I had from Christine; she's missing her man Brian,' I panted, while fumbling for a new CD to whack on.

Once the next track was playing, I grabbed the Dire Straits CD box. Sure enough, it was three minutes, not eight.

'Not long enough for a wee,' I scribbled on the sleeve.

Ian was still harbouring hopes of becoming a tennis player, but decided to do a PhD and maybe have a shot at the SBS, the Navy's answer to the SAS. He was so clever, he could have done almost anything he wanted, but the only thing he really wanted to do was become a tennis player.

That summer, I was less stressed about proving my independence and I happily moved into the house in the woods with the Baggett family so that I could carry on working at the radio station. Ian was prepping for his PhD and playing tennis; it was an idyllic time. I was even starting to enjoy letting the lovely Peter and Eleanor do things for me.

The tennis centre where Ian played was hosting a big Challenger event with international players (the Challengers are one level below the ATP Tour so the standard was very high). We spent a lot of time at the tournament, and on the final night we went to a party held by one of the host families. I wore a tight white cotton T-shirt dress that finished at mid-thigh but had long sleeves and a high neck. 'Legs or chest, but never both,' was my mum's rule about dresses. I felt as beautiful as I had ever done in my life.

I think there may only be a handful of times in my whole life when I can honestly say I felt that way. Women can be really terrible at recognising when they are beautiful. I am often asked, what would you tell your younger self? I think I would say: 'Trust me, you look great now – don't waste any more time thinking about it.' I used to spend hours poring over magazine pictures of some supermodel's thighs, wondering how many weeks of starvation it would take to achieve such a look, only to be told years later by editors that the picture was probably airbrushed, and the model probably fainted after the shoot due to malnourishment. Accepting your physical self, whenever that happens, is one of the best things you can ever do. So if you can, do it sooner rather than later.

I'd just spent two weeks visiting my sister Louise in Las Vegas, where she was working as a gymnast, acrobat and all-round performer with Cirque du Soleil. I'd had the time of my life, dipping my toe into her very cool Las Vegas world. I'd returned tanned and fit, with a spring in my step, an inner confidence and a new wardrobe, which Ian mistook for fla-grant infidelity. I guess he thought I'd had a very glamorous and decadent time in Vegas. When I got back, Ian went from being a man who had always displayed very little in the way of jealousy, to suddenly being consumed by it. He wasn't cruel or aggressive with it, he was just awfully suspicious, which got a bit draining.

That night at the tennis party, as I sashayed about in my white dress, he circled me as if guarding his territory, but it didn't matter. It was as if I was a magnet for attention. A small Argentinian tennis player with long blond hair, and a tall, good-looking German player with dark hair both smelled

Ian's insecurity and preyed on it, flirting with me and topping up my glass with white wine. I lapped up the attention, and our conversations became more suggestive.

The German, Patrick, pushed a crumpled piece of paper with his phone number into my hand as we were leaving. I threw it away the next day but thought about him a lot more than I had expected to.

Ian was angry and accused me of flirting. I apologised, because I had been, but deep down I felt that the flirting was the outcome of a self-fulfilling prophecy.

A few months later, I was working at TFM, the radio station in Stockton-on-Tees, when Mum called my new mobile phone.

'Your dad has a phone number for you. Some German guy phoned the Welsh Football Association today and wanted to leave his number for you to get in touch.'

'What was his name?' My heart missed a beat.

'Er, I have it here . . . Patrick. Have you got a pen to write this number down? I don't know what it's about.'

I knew what it was about. I was hugely flattered that the German had tracked me down. I wasn't going to bump into Patrick anytime soon, so he'd never know that I had received his number. I could have pretended to write the number down and just never called him.

But there was a little part of me that wanted to believe in fate; that thought perhaps it was the universe taking me on a different journey. Instead of coldly acknowledging that I was in control of my own future, it was easier to imagine that something else bigger than me was guiding my fingers around the phone, dialling his number that October night.

Patrick sounded thrilled to hear from me, and we struck up a flirty, easy phone relationship.

It escalated quickly. For a couple of months, I flew around

Europe to meet Patrick, going to Vienna and Bochum near Düsseldorf, his main bases. I told Ian I was away with cousins that he hadn't met. On one occasion, I even said I was away at a murder mystery weekend in Wiltshire (I had never even been to Wiltshire) with my old gymnastics friends and no phones were allowed. He wasn't stupid and could smell my guilt. I was a terrible liar, and I hated the feeling of deception.

But man, it was exciting for a short period of time.

However, it wasn't all beer and bratwurst with the German, and I wasn't about to decamp to the Black Forest permanently. The 'affair' took a strange turn. I had visited the Christmas markets in Bochum and was eating fondue in Patrick's new kitchen when I made a very odd faux pas.

The house was new – it was a bit like a prefabricated Huf Haus – and I noticed the builders had left little round orange stickers all over it, in very odd places. When I sat on the loo, I saw one of the stickers on the wall straight ahead of me. I decided to peel it off. As the day went on, anytime I noticed a sticker, I removed it. Later, over dinner, I told Patrick how helpful I had been.

'I peeled off all those orange stickers,' I said, happily dipping my fatty meat into the gooey cheese.

'YOU DID *WHAT*?' he said, in his very angriest voice.

'The stickers that the builders left behind. I got rid of them for you,' I explained.

'What colour?' he asked, more calmly but still a little bit too unappreciatively for my liking.

'The orange ones.'

'THEY ARE MY MOTIVATIONAL TRIGGER POINTS. I SEE THEM AND PRACTISE POSITIVE THINKING.'

'Oh ... erm ... sorry.'

I was beginning to understand that sometimes it's the journey rather than the destination that's the most exciting part of a story. One trip to see Patrick would have been enough, but I was a repeat offender. I kept going back for more. I had already stopped getting butterflies on the plane before seeing him. I wanted out of this messy affair. A further trip to London to see him on his way home from Doha convinced me that whatever this was it had run its course.

Perhaps I should have just lived with my guilt; eventually it would have dissipated, and I wouldn't have broken Ian's heart. Instead, I decided to make myself feel better by offloading the toxic bile building up inside me. I told Ian exactly what had been going on.

Unsurprisingly, he didn't react very well.

I played Paul Weller's 'Wild Wood' on a loop and cried for days in my room at college, surviving on sachets of Cadbury's hot chocolate.

Ian wanted nothing to do with me.

I rang Patrick, thinking that if I officially called it all off, Ian would be happier.

'I'm really sorry, but I don't think we should see each other again.' I kept it simple – after all, there had been no 'I love you's between us. I was expecting a very pragmatic German response, maybe something like, 'I agree, it's not really working, is it? And after all, you ruined my personal motivation programme by removing my orange stickers and I haven't won a match since.'

But the German went all Latin on me. 'Agh, I see you are a fucked-up bitch too,' he replied.

'Sorry?' I was on the communal phone in the corridor at college, putting my hand around the receiver so the waiting queue couldn't hear me being psychologically analysed by an angry tennis player.

'I thought you were normal, but you are fucked up too.'
Apparently, I was confirming some theory he had about
all women.

'Right then, Patrick . . . *Auf wiedersehen*, pet.'

Ian and I did manage to patch things up, but the wound
was gaping. I did truly love him and his steadying influence,
so I was just going to have to earn his trust back. Of course,
if you hurt someone and then expect them to forget all about
it and go back to how things were before, you are incredibly naive.

I was incredibly naive.

In 1995, a few weeks before the start of my finals, I was called
in to see Giles Squire at Metro FM. The conversation went
something like this.

'Gabby, you've done a great job over the last few months
on your show and filling in on the other shows,' he said.

'Thanks Giles. Thank you for the opportunity, I've really
enjoyed it,' I lied. In fact, I was starting to fall out of love with
the *Love Show*. It was, ironically enough, soul-destroying. I
wasn't sure if this was an appraisal or a sacking yet, though,
so I stayed neutral.

'I have an offer for you. I'd like you to become the new
co-host on *Breakfast* with Mark Thorburn.' He smiled.

I had not seen this coming. 'What, full-time?' I asked.

A month before, juggling revision and lectures, I had done
a couple of days with Mark on the breakfast show to cover
his co-host's holiday. I hadn't realised it was an audition, or
that she was about to be given the elbow.

'What's happening to Michelle?' I asked. 'I mean, how is
she going to pay her mortgage?'

'Don't worry about Michelle. Yes, full-time! A two-year
contract, £22,500 a year. Monday to Friday, on air 6am

to 9am.' Giles was straight to the point, as always. I liked his style.

'Twenty-five thousand?' I asked, more in hope than expectation. I'm still not sure why I thought I had a shot at bargaining, but I knew Mark was on around £50,000 and I felt half of what he earned was fairer. I wasn't the lead presenter and was still very inexperienced, so I didn't expect to match his salary. I didn't realise then that, twenty years later, there would still be a debate about the large pay gap between me and male colleagues doing the same job. Even the ones with the same experience.

Giles smiled and nodded in agreement to my not-so-exorbitant demands.

'When do you want me to start?' I asked.

'Monday 3 July,' he said. 'Until then, just focus on your finals and don't worry about doing any late-night shifts or news. I'll take you off the *Love Show*.' The best words I had ever heard.

Goodbye Meat Loaf, Chicago, Foreigner, Barbra Streisand and Bryan Adams; adios to the fake love letters. Hello Mariah Carey, Everything But the Girl, Take That and 4.30am alarm calls. I was, in reality, swapping one kind of exhausting end of the day for another, but it was a higher-profile exhaustion. With a bigger pay cheque.

Dad had taken a job in Lebanon at the beginning of 1995 as the national team coach. Lebanon was barely out of its decades of bloody civil war and the country was still riddled with the scars of that time – quite literally. He'd eat dinner in cafés scarred with bullet holes and sunbathe in the St George, once the chicest hotel in the Middle East, now half-bombed but still trading. You could sip a cocktail at the bar, but three floors up, wires and concrete were hanging out of the abandoned bedrooms. Like his surroundings, Dad was still heavily scarred and bruised from the death of my brother Daniel. They made a fine pair, him and Beirut.

Mum and ten-year-old Jordan were not going to relocate there, so Dad was alone. Alone with his thoughts, no hand-brake on his drinking and in a country that still experienced nightly shelling.

The job was fascinating; he had players who were Suni Muslims and players who were Shiite Muslims, and his first job was persuading them to pass to each other. And then there were the Christians, who he also had to encourage to join the same training sessions. Lebanon were not expecting to qual-ify for a World Cup; the aim was the Asian Cup. Football, as it so often is, was a symbol for their rehabilitation back on to the world stage. It would have been an enormous boost to the morale of the nation.

I visited Dad for a week after my finals. I found Beirut intoxicating. There was an energy around the city; it was a true twenty-four-hour town. The telecoms system wasn't fully functioning, so people would hook themselves into the grid from their nearest telegraph post with some wires and a bit of guesswork. Streets in the less well-off areas were often covered in a large canopy of wire, so dense that daylight could scarcely penetrate. The country was chaotic, with traffic symbolic of the lawlessness, cars regularly finding a route that was quicker if they went the wrong way up a one-way street or highway. Most windscreens were shattered or cracked or simply missing, and the bodywork of the average car looked a day away from the scrapyard. The sound of gunfire was common. I don't think innocent people were the targets; it seemed to be a way of attracting attention. The Lebanese people I met that week were so proud of their country. They didn't care it was a bit rough around the edges; they saw hope and possibility where there had been none. Which is all I could wish for Dad.

I left admiring the spirit of this beautiful nation, with a new-found love of mint tabouleh and a severe bout of dysentery after overindulging. Summer ball season was in full swing on my return to Durham, so all of my outfits were hanging off me as my weight dropped and my inability to keep anything inside me dragged on and on.

'What have you done?' the skinny posh girls gasped in admirable delight at the sight of the gap between my thighs.

'I have been eating in Beirut,' I explained.

Finally, I had supermodel thighs – for a few days, anyway.

I was due to graduate on Thursday 29 June, so I would have three days off before starting my career and effectively the rest of my life. Hosting a breakfast show means getting up before the milkman every day, but it's the flagship show on any station, as it gets the biggest audience and sets the tone. This was an enormous opportunity, and it had just fallen into my lap. Well, that's how it felt at the time. When I write that now, I see how ridiculous it is. It didn't *fall into my lap*; I wasn't a lottery winner. I had worked my butt off for three years on all of the rubbish shifts. I had earned this chance. But in England in 1995, and as a woman in particular, it would be vulgar to think I was anything other than lucky and grateful. I had assumed that after Durham, I might stay on in the northeast working for Metro, but I'd seen myself picking up scraps, covering for the other DJs while they were on holiday.

I made a deal with myself that if, after the two-year contract, I wasn't on national radio or television I would go to law school to become a barrister. As much as I loved local radio, I knew I needed to set my goals a bit higher. I didn't want to feel too comfy and just fall into a life in Newcastle. Ultimately, I had my sights set on London.

If my background in sport had taught me anything, it was that a bit of pain usually means progress. And let's be honest, there's nothing more uncomfortable than living in the capital city on a low wage, going to work on packed trains and living in expensive but subpar accommodation with no garden. I wasn't alone; London was a lure for many of us graduate northerners, it was almost as if you didn't have any fire in your belly unless your ultimate goal was to share a house in Clapham with some trainee accountants.

For me, and the industry I had set my sights on, there was simply nowhere else in the UK that offered as much opportunity. Back then every single national broadcaster was based in London. So in 1995, the M1 was the road to opportunity.

Ironically, during my A level years, the northern music scene was all anyone cared about; the Hacienda in Manchester and bands like the Stone Roses and Inspiral Carpets were globally revered. But even Oasis had moved to London by 1995, so that was where I intended to follow, assuming that the streets were paved with gold. (Not that I was following Oasis per se. I did see them live at Whitley Bay once, when Noel had a strop and left Liam on stage on his own for a while. Then someone threw a penny at Liam, so he left for a while. It was like a revolving door of Gallaghers, until eventually they managed to stay on stage at the same time for one song. At least I can say *I* was there, even if they weren't.)

Years later, I was on holiday in Barbados with my husband, and we met Liam and his then-wife Nicole Appleton at the hotel beach bar. We drank with them from around 3pm until 3am. Liam was convinced I was a reincarnated version of John Lennon because of an argument I had with Richard

Desmond, the billionaire owner of, among other things, *OK!* magazine.

Catherine Zeta-Jones was suing *Hello!* for printing paparazzi wedding photos, but had sold the rights to her wedding to *OK!*. As we were discussing this, I told Richard that if you sold your wedding to a magazine, as Jones had, you were giving up your right to say you were a private person. I will admit I was being a bit belligerent, and I had drunk six mojitos. Also, I sat on the moral high ground, letting Richard know I had turned down a six-figure sum to sell my own wedding. He thought I was mad, and assumed that if the cheque was big enough, everyone would sell out in the end. Clearly Richard and I did not see eye to eye.

Richard had met the Beatles in the 1960s, and Liam asked him what John Lennon was like. Liam is obsessed with John Lennon, as you probably know. Richard slowly went through the members of the Beatles, one by one, teasing Liam, saying nice things about all of them, and when he got to John, he paused, looked at me and said: 'He's like that Gabby girl ... aloof.' Only Liam didn't hear the 'aloof' part. He also didn't know the back story about why Richard was a bit narky with me. All the fairly inebriated Liam Gallagher heard was that John Lennon was 'like that Gabby girl'. For the next five hours, Liam Gallagher barely left me alone. He shadowed my every move, believing I might be John Lennon reincarnated.

Maybe I am.

(I just checked, and he died seven years after I was born, so I am not.)

Anyway, back to 1995. Revising for my finals with the knowledge I had a job secured was a relief. Many of my peers were fixed up with post-Durham plans – banking, law, PhDs and teacher training – but plenty more were a bit rudderless.

Here's where the social divide reared its head once more. The kids from more privileged backgrounds didn't seem to be as worried about having start dates for jobs. They might do some travel or work for their godfather in the City; maybe they'd spend the summer in the south of France or do one more ski season. I didn't know what a 'trust fund' was until I went to Durham, and I can honestly say I am glad I never had one. My desire and hunger to get out, work and create a life for myself would almost certainly have been stymied if I had known I had £40,000 a year tax-free for life, as one of my peers did. I certainly don't think I would have got up at 4.45am at the weekend to read news bulletins for £60.

I was hovering just below a first-class degree going into my finals, and I eventually missed out by a couple of per cent. On balance, I think the fact that I had done three years of work in local radio allowed me to cut myself a bit of slack. I am not very good at that, cutting myself slack.

I must do better.

Our results were posted on the noticeboard of the law library. As is tradition, I went up to see them for myself and then rang home, standing on College Green in the shadow of Durham Cathedral on a gorgeous summer evening. I was incredibly proud; I was the first person on both sides of my family to graduate. I'd never experienced this rite of passage, the picking up of results. I had missed my GCSE results coming out because I was training in Coventry with the national squad, so Mum picked them up for me and rang me. Then I missed my A level results because I was working in a children's shoe shop in Wimbledon Village, so those were posted to me.

'Hi Mum, just calling to say I got a 2:1,' I said, excitedly.

'OK, good, you must be happy. Now, on Sunday, how many of your friends are coming for a barbecue?'

'I'll get back to you, but I think ten.'

'I need to get enough food in, so let me know by tomorrow.'

And just like that it was all over.

As we cleared out our rooms and packed up our lives on the last day, I stopped on the stairs to say goodbye to a friend.

'I've just worked out that I've only had two days without a hangover since I started here,' he told me as he popped a half-drunk bottle of Jack Daniels on top of three years' worth of history books.

'I think I've had two days when I *have* had a hangover.' I laughed, but inside I was anxious. Although I had loved every minute of my time at Durham, and I was now starting my dream job, I was fairly sure I should have got pissed a bit more.

18

Breakfast

S tarting your first day of work used to be a landmark
moment. In 1980s sitcoms, the young person puts on a
suit or a uniform and is given a pat on the back by a parent,
and maybe even handed a lunchbox of sandwiches by the
stay-at-home-mum character (we didn't have Pret a Manger
back then). And then we see the 'child' head out into the
big bad world, stepping on to a treadmill of nine-to-five,
five days a week, for the next forty years. Well, the days of
having a job or even a career for life are long gone, and our
kids will probably do jobs that we don't even know exist yet.
I guess my generation were one of the first to experience
this 'employment fluidity'. I certainly never expected Metro
FM to be my working home for life; my aim was not to
become the CEO. The Thatcher years in Britain had taught
young people that they could be their own bosses, and being
an entrepreneur was lauded. It worked out better for some
than others.

Having worked for Metro FM for three years while I was

a student, I knew what I was doing and where I was heading on that first Monday morning; nobody had to show me where the toilets were. But it was still a landmark day for me. I had a good contract and the biggest show on the station. It was, in many ways, the perfect start to my broadcasting life. I was learning so much in a safe environment, with people who had known me for a few years. I was living with my 'in-laws' and at that time, I would say I was living my dream life.

There is one big problem with a breakfast show, however: sleep, or the lack of it. It was about to become one of my great obsessions, as it is with any breakfast show host or any regular early shift worker. On Sunday 2 July 1995, the night before my first breakfast show on Metro FM, I finally fell asleep at around 2am with my alarm set for 4.30am. I didn't worry about that first night of insomnia. I was nervous and excited, so the first night would be the hardest? Right?

Wrong.

Adrenaline got me through every show that year, but the slump afterwards, well, that was tough. The agonising decision about whether or not to sleep during the day was often taken out of my hands as I succumbed in an armchair or on my bed. Simply sitting down to take off my socks could see me knocked out for an hour.

I read that I should drink coffee just before a daytime nap for maximum impact from the caffeine; that I should sleep with a lavender eye mask; that I shouldn't eat after 6pm; and that I should always exercise before 1pm. I was a sleep bore.

'How are you?' was always met with 'I'm well, aside from sleep ...' Then the eyes of whoever had asked the question would glaze over as I listed my nightly routine. Argh, the irony that I could make anyone else fall asleep within a few minutes of opening my mouth.

Once I recognised that I was a sleep obsessive, it was easier to go with, and two to three hours' sleep a night became my new normal. I was a proper worker. I didn't have a summer job or a weekend shift; there was no turning back. The flip side to the alarm crashing into your dreams in the middle of the night is the secret club you become a member of: the early workers' club. I was in charge of picking up the newspapers on my way to the studio, so the newsagent was the first 'club member' I spoke to every morning. He didn't see me at my best.

I rarely had a shower, for the sake of speed; instead, I had a facecloth body wash and a squirt of deodorant, and then I'd quietly climb into whatever ensemble I had left out the night before. The beauty of radio in the pre-digital broadcast age was that nobody ever saw you. Your voice was the only medium by which the audience could judge you. I wasn't hideous; I just didn't bother with make-up until about three-quarters of the way through the show, when the rest of the building was starting to arrive and come to life. Out of respect for them, I brushed my hair.

I'm so glad I had the chance to enjoy those years of freedom, to be totally unbothered about who might want a selfie or the content I might have to produce for the radio station's website. Radio now is almost as visual as TV. Most breakfast shows are live-streamed, which in effect turns them into TV shows. I was able to focus on my job, oblivious to the frizz on my head and the spots on my chin.

The next person I saw after the newsagent was the overnight security guard at Metro FM. When I turned up, he was about to clock off, with the more glamorous receptionists due to arrive at 8am.

'What you doing for the rest of the day, Brian?' I asked him one morning. I will be honest, it might also have been Dave, Mick or Bob.

'I'll have a few pints on the way home, then catch some kip. The Toon are playing tonight, so I'll bathe the bairns and watch that on ma telly.'

'A few pints?'

He went on to describe the underground breakfast drinking clubs dedicated to shift workers that were to be found all over Newcastle. It blew my mind. I wasn't really a drinker back then, so the idea of pints at 8am was beyond my comprehension. Not that I am a morning drinker now.

The newspapers were vital in helping us produce our early content. I say helping, what I mean is they *were* the early content. We used little razors to cut out our stories of interest, gossip mainly, then delivered them with our own 'interesting' slant.

We ran competitions almost every day, giving away cash, cars and holidays, and we also produced 'comedy' items after the show. Mark and I created characters who performed prank calls. Our favourite was an old northern couple, who would accidentally phone American car showrooms or hotels and try to buy things that they didn't sell. This style of 'comedy' was fashionable at the time: playing a character allowed you to say rude or dismissive things to real people, which sounds suspiciously like bullying when written down. At its best, it was Caroline Aherne as Mrs Merton, and at its cringiest, it was Paul Kaye as Dennis Pennis on *The Sunday Show*. Kaye can rest assured that even his cringiest outing was nowhere near as unfunny as Mr and Mrs Braithwaite working out how to get a pick-up truck back from Ohio to Washington. 'No dear . . . not DC . . . Washington, Tyne and Wear . . . hello? hello? Are you there, Brad?'

But gossip and sketch writing played second fiddle to the traffic and travel news. If the skies were clear, the traffic news came from 'the Flying Eye', a helicopter whizzing over the

Team Valley, telling the people in their Ford Mondeos and white vans below that the traffic they were sitting in was static. The fact that they were sitting in it going nowhere would probably have been enough for them to work that out for themselves, but the Flying Eye was incredibly glamorous and it was Giles's baby, so it stayed.

The other perk of being in the early workers' club was witnessing a part of the day that very few others did. The drive from Ian's parents' house to work was breathtaking. I loved seeing the sun rise and watching the animals plod around in the woods, looking for breakfast, and hearing the birds waking up. Then came the joy of the first coffee and slice of Marmite on toast, usually at around 6.30am during the first news bulletin. Driving home from work at 10.30am also had its bonus points; I never ever sat in rush-hour traffic.

My first month's pay cheque was due when I received an unexpected letter from my mum.

Dear Gabby,

Hope all is well.

This is a list of all of the things you have put on a 'tab' when you have been home over the last year or so.

Car repairs £189
Newspapers £18
Tampax £8.50
Travel and transport £179
Coat £89
Cash £200
Fruit £38
Haircut £30

Can you send me a cheque, please?

Love Mum x

I was devastated. I've had to make up bits of the list, as I can't remember exactly what was on it now, but the real killer was how uncannily close the total was to the amount I was about to receive in my first pay cheque. It was almost as if Mum knew what I'd earned and when my payday was. It was an absolute sucker punch. I called her, hoping it was a joke.

'Mum, it's me.'

'Hi,' she answered.

'I just got your bill,' I explained, hoping she'd say something along the lines of 'Only joking!'.

She didn't. 'Yes?' she asked.

'Are you serious?' I was a bit livid now.

'What about?'

She was winding me up, surely?

'You're going to make me give you almost all my first-ever full pay packet for the kind of things that "normal" Mums just buy their kids?'

'You borrowed money or asked me to buy those things, saying to me, "I'll pay you back,"' she countered.

'But . . . but . . . TAMPAX?!' I squealed.

I was sitting on the bottom of step of Ian's parents' house. I looked around, seeking inspiration for my argument.

'Ian's mum wouldn't do this.'

She didn't reply.

'Bye, then.' I put the phone down and cried.

I'd been getting up at 4.30am every day for a month, and at the end of it I would have enough money for a McDonald's Happy Meal if I settled my account with Mum. I wallowed in self-pity. Even Ian, who thought my mum was great, lent some empathy. 'I'll grant you, that's very keen of her,' he agreed.

I wrote the cheque and paid the debt.

My mum has meted out some hardcore parenting lessons over the years, but that was a particular toughie. Some of the other lessons were more strategic. Once, I was standing in the bathroom, watching her and my beautiful sister tweezing their eyebrows. I was seventeen and Louise was sixteen.

We were talking about sex, something I hadn't had yet – but I was dating a man ten years older than me, Gary.

'I will definitely lose my virginity before I get married,' I said, confidently.

'How do you know you'll be any good at it?' Mum retorted, plucking away at her eyebrows without so much as a flinch.

It was the perfect response to a highly competitive seventeen-year-old who might be thinking of losing their virginity. I waited at least another six months. I wasn't going to 'do it' until I was a bit more confident about being *good* at it. She'd scared the life out of me. I mean, I didn't even know you could be *bad* at it. Did people mark you out of ten? This was awful news.

Anyway, years later, as a much-practised non-virgin, I was getting into the rhythm of my life as a breakfast show host when, after a couple of months, I was called in for a chat with the bosses.

'We noticed that you hang out with the sports team after the breakfast show every day and seem to enjoy the football,' said Big Jim Brown, the man in charge of news and sport. He was right. I dawdled at the sports desk every day, gossiping about transfers and trying to get snippets of news that I could take home to impress the Magpie-loving Baggett family.

'Yeah, I love it. I'm a Newcastle fan!' I said, wondering where he was going with this.

'So, we wondered if you would like to do touchline interviews at St James' Park for us at the Newcastle United home games. You'd interview the manager and players before and after the match,' he explained.

'A Saturday job?' I laughed.

'Well, actually, there are a few mid-week matches as well.'

'I'd love it,' I said, accepting the job offer. 'Will somebody train me or tell me what to do?' I asked as an afterthought.

The previous touchline interviewer, let's call him Geoff, was getting on a bit; he wore a pork-pie hat and a trench coat, and Big Jim felt that someone a bit younger might bring more vitality and help to persuade the players to stop for interviews. They had got into the habit of walking straight past Geoff. I was certainly a bit different. I was a twenty-two-year-old woman, for a start, and I had a penchant for short skirts and ankle boots. I guess the bosses were hoping that I might be able to persuade a young, red-blooded professional footballer to stop for a chat. I look back now and fully understand that my first break into sports broadcasting was reverse sexism. I wasn't being promoted because I was good; I was being given a chance because I was a young and fairly attractive woman who happened to enjoy football. I can't phone Jim Brown now and get a definitive quote on that, because he sadly died just short of his fiftieth birthday, but I am fairly certain they were his motives. Today, you might find that a bit creepy, but in 1995, he gave me the break that would change my life and I am forever grateful.

One of my first interviews was with a player called Darren Huckerby, who had signed from Lincoln City for £400,000, which was a lot of money back then. I was sent to the training ground at Maiden Castle to do the interview. It was a crisp autumnal morning and we sat on a wall outside.

'You must be thrilled to get a life-changing opportunity in the Premier League?' I said, to kick off.

Darren nodded his head.

'Could you speak, please, Darren? It's radio,' I said.

We had both failed. I'd asked a closed question that only required a yes or no answer, and Darren had nodded in a radio interview. It was the perfect storm: a meeting of two novices without a clue.

Match days were exhilarating. I'd arrive a couple of hours before kick-off, and after I had chatted nicely to the gate man for a few weeks, he allowed me to park right by the entrance. I was on first-name terms with the receptionists, and felt like one of the family very quickly, which is testament to the type of club Newcastle United is. In the press room, we'd have a cup of tea and a biscuit and discuss the team news, and then I'd do the pre-match interviews. I'd watch the match with the commentary team and then head down pitch-side for the post-match interviews. Thumbing through the programme, I'd scan the names of the players and their biographies, always noticing those who had been born the same year as Daniel. *Would he be starting in the first team at Leeds United by now?* I wondered. He would have been nineteen, so it was entirely plausible. I imagined how his life would be panning out, the headlines he'd have made and the success he'd be enjoying on and off the pitch. The job made me feel close to him.

The breakfast show was going well, too. My mornings and Saturdays were now full, and then to fill any remaining minutes in the week, Tyne Tees television asked me to go in for a screen test for a show called *Tonight*. *Tonight* was a new format show that would go out at 7pm after the regional news. It was pretty much like a local *One Show*, about ten years before the national *One Show* had been invented. It involved random stories about the local badger population, lollipop ladies and archaeological digs; then there was cooking and live music, with some sofa guests thrown in. It was all packed into a frenzied thirty minutes, and done on about a hundredth of the *One Show* budget. I didn't get the main hosting job, unsurprisingly, as I had zero TV-presenting hours under my belt, but the editor said they'd call me to do some reporting. Then, as I was leaving, the producer asked if anybody in the office had any riding experience and was free on Friday.

My arm shot up in the air quicker than I knew was physically possible. On top of that, nobody else volunteered. It looked like I had landed my first TV role. The only problem was, I didn't ride. I had ridden a few times as a child, but that's not *riding*, that's visiting a stable and stroking a pony.

I left the *Tonight* office at lunchtime on Monday, and by Tuesday afternoon I was making my way to some stables near Durham for a riding lesson. It didn't go very well, so I booked another one for Wednesday. Friday was looming, and it appeared I had not got one ounce of natural horsemanship. I could barely make the things move. I say *things* because at first, I insisted the issue was with the horse, not me, and tried out a few before conceding that it was indeed me.

I booked another lesson for Thursday. The cost of the lessons, the riding boots and travel to Durham every day outweighed my fee for Friday's filming by about £200. This was an investment, an 'opportunity cost', I decided. Some time on the Thursday, the producer called to explain what I would be doing; naively enough, I hadn't even asked.

'You need to be in Yarm by 10am,' he said.

It was going to be tight; I didn't get off air from the breakfast show until 9am.

'Here's the address,' he continued. 'You'll get measured up for your armoury as you arrive.'

'Sorry?' I said.

'Armoury,' he repeated. 'You're taking on the world jousting champion. I mean, we know you won't beat him, but you'll have a few duels and charge at each other with your jousts ... in all the chainmail ... then you'll go for a hack, interviewing him on horseback. He's got the world championships in Antwerp in a few weeks, so we want to big him up.'

'Right.' I didn't know what else to say. The sensible thing would have been to pull out.

'It'll look great. They've got you all the gear: the breast plates and the suede thingy-ma-bobs you wear on your legs. I've got to get to a meeting. Joe's your cameraman, he's great. Good luck. Bye.'

There's being keen and then there's being an arse and putting your life at risk. My enthusiasm to make it in TV was starting to fall dangerously close to the second option. I couldn't pull out, though. I'd just have to be on my game – and hope I had a kind horse.

Have you ever seen a jousting horse? If you imagine the horses that run the Grand National might be about sixteen hands, a jousting horse is usually around eighteen hands. They are gargantuan. The armour was uncomfortable, heavy and restrictive. On the plus side, it could save your life in a battle, so I understood why I needed it. It was a stunning day, with the low winter sun lighting up the orange and red leaves still left on the trees. The scene could not have been more perfect.

The jousting world champion was a very nice man, but he could smell a fake a mile off, and no doubt got a whiff of the strong stench of my fear mixed in with that.

'Why don't you perhaps think about not holding the actual joust? It takes years and years to perfect holding it, and it's quite hard to handle a horse like this anyway, no matter how experienced you are.'

'That's a great idea,' I agreed. 'I mean, I don't want to spoil the film, but I think it's safer, don't you, Joe?'

The producer and cameraman already looked disappointed with me.

Somehow, despite wearing twenty-five kilograms of armour, I got up on the horse. The world champion was practising, joust in one hand, galloping across the fields as if facing an imaginary opponent. It really was quite an impressive sight. The opponent in a few moments would be me.

My horse wasn't responding to the nuanced signals I was giving him. The skills I had honed at a riding school in Durham just days earlier seemed to be failing me. It was almost as if I didn't *have* any skills. The magnificent beast stood still and refused to move.

More than twenty years later, my daughter is a show-jumper, and I now know that very well-trained horses know when they have a novice or idiot on their back, and they simply shut up shop. That's if they are kind; if they want to have fun, they take off and dump you in a bush. At least I wasn't being dumped in a bush.

The crew's frustration was growing. Horses don't like frustration. Crews don't like delays.

'How much riding have you actually done?' the world champion wondered.

I didn't answer.

After another hour or so of me trying to get the horse to gallop, then canter, then trot, all bets were off.

'Right, how about you just walk beside the horse with a rein in your hand, and we do the chat that way?'

'It seems such a shame, but I think that's for the best.' I sighed in blessed relief, then jumped down and took hold of the reins.

As the cameraman repositioned himself, I started to walk, thinking the horse would follow. He didn't, so I gave him a gentle yank. I wasn't expecting him to respond, but he did – before I had the chance to move my foot out of the way.

'Shit!' I screamed as a ton of horse landed on my big toe.

I ended up interviewing the jousting world champion while sitting on a bench.

With hindsight, the whole thing was an awful idea. I wouldn't go and interview Lucy Bronze in a football kit and ask her for a kickabout; nor would I suggest to Tom Daley that we get up on the ten-metre platform and do some piked somersaults (although I did present *Splash* with Vernon Kay).

But then, I shouldn't have shot my hand up and said I could ride. Lesson learned, but opportunity not wasted. Happily, the bosses liked the piece enough to offer me a strand on the show.

The new strand was to be weekly and called 'Gabbing with Gabby'. The plan was that I would meet a very well-known local celebrity in a restaurant of their choice, and we'd have dinner while I interviewed them.

I was still doing the breakfast show and my Saturday job at St James' Park, but this was a brilliant break; a paid TV job, with a free dinner thrown in. The first person booked was a boxer called Billy Hardy from Sunderland. He was the recently crowned European featherweight champion.

Billy was tipped for big things, and would eventually get a crack at the world title against Naseem Hamed. Disappointingly, Billy chose a Mexican eatery in the food court at the Metro Centre for his interview – not exactly fine dining. We chatted over fajitas and a large full-fat Coke. It's hard eating and talking, as I have continuously reminded my kids for the last decade or so.

At the end of the interview, the USP for the feature was when I pulled a specially made medal out of my bag and hung it around the neck of the guest. The medal had 'You have gabbed with Gabby' embossed on it.

What? Why? Who thought that was a good idea – and why did I go along with it?

Ego, that's why. I mean, who even was I? I wasn't Michael Parkinson or Terry Wogan. I had no legacy as a top-class interviewer. I was a twenty-two-year-old recent graduate, who probably would not have been missed from the world of broadcasting if I had decided to jack it all in that week. But somebody on the production team thought going through the experience of being interviewed by me merited receiving a medal.

Maybe it was ironic.

Oh.

I genuinely just had the realisation twenty-five years on, that it was probably an ironic medal: a reward for enduring such a tortuous experience.

My next guests were Ant and Dec, who were slowly dropping their *Byker Grove* personas of PJ and Duncan and were on the verge of becoming huge stars. We went to a lovely café called Heartbreak Soup on the then-trendy Quayside in Newcastle, pretty much under the Tyne Bridge.

Ant and Dec were lovely – as you'd expect. You don't win 75,000 National Television Awards for nothing, after all. And, as there were two of them, one of them could actually eat their soup while the other was talking. Years later, when we were all working for ITV, Dec told me that he still had his medal. I cringed so hard that I almost threw up.

I'm not going to go through every interview I did in the

'Gabbing with Gabby' strand, but suffice to say that it wasn't long before the northeastern celebrities on offer had been well and truly covered. So, unwilling to let a good idea (and a bag full of medals) go to waste, the producer extended it to cover 'people passing through the region'. That's how I ended up sitting down and chatting to popstar Mick Hucknall of Oldham, and the playwright Alan Ayckbourn of Scarborough. We also dropped the dinner part of the gig after I got quite pissed while interviewing Les Ferdinand (of west London), the Newcastle United striker, in one of the most expensive restaurants in the city. Wearing a PVC snakeskin jacket, I appeared to be bright red and blotchy, and a little slurry, which didn't make great telly. I thought I was keeping it real.

While Ian was finishing off a PhD in geopolitics and heading down to Lymington for naval officer training, I was building my broadcasting career on a diet of football, breakfast-show shenanigans and chats with children's TV hosts over leek and potato soup. To kill off any spare time, I was then asked if I would take part in a panto to help save the Tyne Theatre in which it was being performed.

The idea was that the DJs of Metro FM would appear in *Cinderella* as the DJ at the ball; we'd all be on a rota and do a few shows each a week. The publicity would help generate more ticket sales, and the theatre wouldn't need to close. Sadly, in spite of our late-night shifts at the panto, the run-down old theatre did eventually close. Years later, when Ian had become a very successful property developer, he bought the theatre and was hoping to turn it into apartments. Which I think even Alanis Morissette would agree is ironic.

Saying yes to so many opportunities during my year in Newcastle gave me more experiences than I could never had dreamed such a short period of time would deliver. There was part of me still running on that energy of *carpe diem* that had taken me to Durham after Daniel died; I was still taking on a bit more than I could chew. It was a golden period in my life, though, and I am forever grateful to the people who gave me those breaks and opened doors for me, from Giles and Jim at Metro FM to Lyn Spencer, a Tyne Tees reporter who gave me some tips on clothes and make-up and made me feel I belonged in her world. Showing kindness and support doesn't cost a lot, but it's invaluable when someone really needs a hand or a kind word.

Having said that, I was as desperate as ever to get to London to work with a national broadcaster. I just had no idea how.

19

The Road to London

On 5 May 1996, Newcastle United played their final match of the season at home against Tottenham Hotspur. This should have been the day they won the Premier League, but having been twelve points ahead at Christmas, they were now hanging on by their fingertips, hoping Manchester United would lose at Middlesbrough. In spite of this disappointing fall from the heady heights of being nailed-on Premier League champions to second-place finishers, Newcastle's season had been electric, with a high-octane style of football predicated on the philosophy 'we'll score one more than you'. The team, who absolutely loved to attack, were spearheaded by David Ginola, a man who looked more like a French movie star than a French movie star; Les Ferdinand, whose hang time in the air waiting to head the ball into the net could rival that of Michael Jordan; Peter Beardsley, the local goal-scoring hero; and Tino Asprilla, who backflipped after he scored.

I was in my usual pitch-side position, waiting to do interviews, when a cameraman approached me.

'Hi Gabby,' he said. 'I'm from Sky Sports. I've been asked to give you this card.' Then he sauntered off, casual as you like, having potentially just delivered the great sliding doors moment of my life.

On the card was the name Richard Keys and a phone number.

'Er, excuse me,' I shouted after the cameraman. 'What is this?'

'Richard Keys.' He gestured to the Sky TV studio in the corner of the ground. 'He's making a show about women in sport, and he wants you to contribute,' the fast-thinking cameraman told me.

Richard Keys was the Sky TV football host. He had been a breakfast TV host when I was growing up. Together with Andy Gray, an ex-professional player from Scotland, they had reinvented the way football was presented, and Sky had thrown a lot of money at the technology to help them do that. They *were* 'Sky Sports'.

But there was no TV show about women in sport. When I rang Keys the next day, he apologised for the fib. He told me he wanted to introduce me to his bosses at Sky, as he felt there could be a big opportunity there for me. Sky were looking to recruit more women, and he'd noticed me on the touchline at matches. Then he'd heard that my dad was Terry Yorath. Keys was a big Coventry City fan, so I guess the name Yorath was a bit of a draw – although he also claims to have discovered Kelly Cates (née Dalglish), so I guess his talent-spotting wasn't confined to the daughters of his favourite players.

I don't really want to write a lot about Richard Keys; he was dismissed, along with Gray, when they were caught talking lewdly about the lineswoman Sian Massey, and after he was caught asking pundits in the studio if they would 'smash it', referring to another woman. In one painful-to-listen-to monologue aimed at saving his UK career, he tried to argue he couldn't be sexist, because he'd helped get *me* a job and kickstarted my career. This really highlighted that he truly didn't 'get it'. It's the 'I'm not racist because I sat next to a black woman on the bus' school of logic.

The boss at Sky was a man called Mark Sharman, who was recruiting for *Sky Sports Centre*, a twice-nightly sports news show. It was live at 6pm and 10pm, Monday to Friday, and was the forerunner of *Sky Sports News*, which was launched in 1998.

By the following Tuesday, I was in conversation with Mark Sharman.

'We'd like to fly you down for a screen test,' he told me. 'You come to the studio and read autocue, and we can see what you're like on camera.'

'Do I need to interview anyone or research anything?' I asked.

'No. We'll just do the show as if it's live, as if it's that day's show.'

Mark Sharman's assistant booked me cabs and flights, and a few days later, I was driving through the impressive gates of Sky TV. It was a pinch-yourself moment. A few days before, I had been pitch-side for local radio, and now here I was, about to be screen tested by one of the biggest players in sports TV.

The screen test seemed to go well. The crew were all lovely and I felt like I had given it my best shot. The following evening, Mark Sharman called and offered me the job. I would be paid £50,000 a year, plus expenses and I would be required to be in London from late July to train and settle in, to make sure I was ready by mid-August and the start of the 1996–97 Premier League season. I managed to up him to £55,000.

Now all I had to do was get out of my contract with Metro FM, which still had over a year to run.

I arranged a meeting with Giles.

He was furious, at first. 'No, no way. I'm afraid you still

have fourteen months to go on this contract,' was his angry reply when I asked to leave.

'You can't make me do this,' I argued. I tried to remember some of the employment law I had studied a year before. I mentioned 'constructive dismissal' (which was totally irrelevant), then spouted a bit of 'restraint of trade' at him. But it was all bouncing off his hard-boss exterior.

There was silence.

An impasse.

I went for a different tack completely: 'Giles, you have a teenage daughter, and you have high hopes for her. What would you say to her if this opportunity came up for her? What advice would you give her?' I asked.

He turned to face me, trying to fight the small smile that was threatening to break out on his face. 'I would want her to take it. Gabby, I knew we would lose you eventually, but I was hoping you would stay here for a bit longer.'

'I appreciate that, I really do, Giles, and I'm grateful for everything you have done for me. I would have really liked to finish my contract, but this opportunity is right now. Sky is a huge channel, with all sorts of possibilities for me. I have to take it,' I said.

'I know.'

And that was it. My notice was handed in and I got to enjoy a few glorious weeks of Euro '96 as I planned for my new life in London. I suppose I was quite brave, really. I had nobody to live with in London, I didn't know anyone at Sky TV, and I really didn't know how to be a TV presenter, either. It was all something of a leap of faith.

My search for a new home involved Mum and I driving around my preferred areas to live, Wimbledon and Richmond, looking at gorgeous places I couldn't afford and horrible places I could. As the flat-hunting day progressed, I was forced to start slowly scaling back my expectations of a penthouse with a balcony, even though I had a decent budget for 1996 of £850 a month.

Most of my early enquiries went something like this.

'Hello, we are calling up about the one bedroom flat in Park View, is it still available?'

'Yes, it is,' a haughty, impatient woman on the phone replies.

'Can you tell me how much it is, please?' a naive girl from the north (me) asks excitedly.

'It's £650.'

'Great, we would like to see it, please. Just checking, is that £650 a month? And including ground rent?'

'It's £650 *a week*. And no, it doesn't include ground rent!' the exasperated and bored woman sighs.

'Thanks, we will get right back to you!' replies the girl from the north, who fears she will end up living in a squat.

Back on the Tyne a few weeks later, it was my last show. Mark played us out with 'Video Killed the Radio Star' by The Buggles. He looked genuinely sad that I was leaving.

A group of us DJs went down to the Quayside on a gloriously sunny day and sat by the majestic River Tyne, drinking lots of white wine and too many tall turquoise cocktails. It was a proper old-fashioned leaving drinks. Everyone was lovely to me, and one of my closest friends, the drive-time host Greg Burns, who was a year younger than me, told me he'd be right behind me, coming to London as soon as he could get himself a show. (He arrived a year later, became a stand-up comedian and got a show on Capital FM.) I went home a bit drunk, but elated that I was already on my way, with lots of good will behind me.

I know the exact date of my departure, because it was also the day of the opening ceremony of the 1996 Olympics in Atlanta: Friday 19 July. I was due to start at Sky TV the following Monday, so my plan was to head south on the Saturday morning. I had packed most of my life into a few bags. The room I stayed in at Ian's was his old bedroom from when he was a boy, complete with posters of Chris Waddle, the Newcastle player, and a box of his tennis medals and swimming certificates. Ian was still away training to be a naval officer at Lymington, so it was an odd moment, me in a single bed in an empty room in a house in Chopwell Woods, about to start a new adventure, with a small TV in the corner showing a grainy image of Muhammad Ali lighting the Olympic flame in Atlanta.

It was four years since I had been outside the Montjuïc Stadium in Barcelona with my sister, feeling Daniel's presence looming large. I hadn't wasted a moment of that time, but how far was I along the road to making any kind of peace with his death? There had been some progress in our healing as individuals, but not collectively. As a family, it felt as if we were fractured and splintered, each working things out in our own ways, some of them healthier than others.

The journey of grief is a marathon, not a sprint, and you might never finish it. Muhammad Ali had been diagnosed with Parkinson's disease in the 1980s, and by 1996, he was shaking quite badly as he held the flame aloft: a flame that had travelled around the world from Olympia, the ancient home of the Olympics, and must never be allowed to go out. There was something incredibly poignant and distressing about seeing one of the greatest fighters the world had ever known struggling so visibly, but keeping the flame alight.

As I watched this hero battling on, I felt overwhelmed with sadness, excitement, grief, hope, endings and beginnings. It all welled up inside me, and I cried myself to sleep.

*

With a thumping hangover-headache, puffy eyes and the entire contents of my life packed into my recently acquired sponsor car from a local garage, a royal-blue metallic Renault Clio with gold alloys and my name plastered down the side, I took off to chase my dream.

Eleanor and Peter had made me a packed lunch and waved me off down the drive. They looked emotional; maybe they knew that it was the last they'd see of me. They'd been wonderful, loving surrogate parents to me over the last few years, and I had learned a lot from them.

As I drove through the Team Valley on the A1, I saw the Tyne Bridge in my rear-view mirror. A wave of emotion rushed over me. I have never felt as strongly about a place as I felt about Newcastle right then. It was like I was leaving a lover. It's a city synonymous with shipbuilding, steel, coal and hard graft, and while its modern guise might be more football, students, call centres and nightlife, I think there is an indomitable spirit that runs through the very DNA of the place. I'm always a little envious of people who have a strong connection to where they come from. Because of the nomadic childhood I'd experienced, I didn't really 'come from' anywhere – but in that moment, I felt I had at least belonged somewhere.

20

Sky

Moving to London and working in TV was the dream I had pursued ever since that first visit to the *Blue Peter* studios, and now here I was, seven years later, relocating to the capital.

I had eventually found a flat to rent in the classified adverts of the *Sunday Times*, which, even in 1996, was an unusual way to find accommodation. The owner of this flat was based in East Asia for work, and he wanted £800 a month for a two-bedroom, second-floor apartment on one of the nicest roads in Richmond with off-street parking. I had a feeling he hadn't been to Richmond for a while. It was a steal.

For that price, there was bound to be a catch. Well, it was hideously decorated and had no mod-cons at all; the bathroom was painted royal blue with an avocado suite, the lounge was a deep red, like a dodgy bordello, and the main bedroom was a depressing shade of burgundy. There was no washing machine, so I had to use a laundrette, and I had to wash my hair with a plastic shower attachment in the bath.

Every room was lit by a single central wire with a bulb; no fitting or shade, and no dimmers. Mum persuaded me it was a winner. 'We could always buy lamps,' she said. For her, it was more important that the location was safe – and beggars can't be choosers.

My friends (when I eventually made some) would name Charmouth Court 'the Old Folks' Home'. There were three blocks of three-storey flats around a 'quadrant', which was a communal grass area that had, for a while, been home to an abandoned Zimmer frame. The internal staircases had an 'institutional' feel, in that everything could be wiped down. The real clincher, though, was that most of the residents were over sixty-five. You might have called it suburbia, but I felt I was in the heart of the metropolis. I had arrived.

Things were slow to progress when it came to my social life. I knew hardly anybody else in London, apart from my new colleagues, who were generally male. Unusually for a job in sports TV, I was working a regular week – Monday to Friday, with a working day of 2–10.30pm, which meant I usually got home around 11pm. I often went home to Leeds for the weekend, so there wasn't much time for any kind of social life.

On the weekends when I did stay in London, I would go for Saturday-night jogs around the streets of Richmond to pass the time. I would run very slowly so I could peer into people's homes as they were entertaining and having glamorous drinks parties, wondering when I would ever get a social life of my own. The 2020 equivalent of this behaviour would be sitting on Instagram, scrolling through pictures of other people having a 'fun' time. At least in 1996 I could keep fit at the same time.

There were quite a few of us who had been taken on by Sky at the same time, and it was a relief to find I wasn't the only one who didn't know what she was doing. For the first few weeks, we trained and attended workshops, and in one of these, I met a man who would end up becoming one of the most important mentors in my life: Ed Percival. Ed was a very special man, and I've seen him help so many people from business leaders to athletes. Whatever else I learned at Sky, meeting him was one of the most important things that happened to me in my time there.

The best way I can describe Ed is as a performance specialist. He worked with me by getting me to visualise being brilliant at my job, throwing away any negative thoughts or concerns, and helping me to create the physical sensations of brilliance so I could access those feelings really quickly, whether through a clench of the fist or by saying a trigger word. Then he'd watch a show back, and would pick up on tiny subtle movements made on camera that could be distracting for the viewer; he had an eye for detail and a brilliant way of communicating.

From my days as a gymnast, I was used to being coached, and I've always really enjoyed it. Critique and feedback are vital for development, no matter what you do. Telly can be a bit 'luvvie' at times, with everyone saying everything is 'marvellous' and 'fantastic', even when it's really not.

When I hear broadcasters say, 'I never watch myself,' I think, *Well you should, at least occasionally, because you're expecting the rest of us to.* I appreciate that watching yourself back isn't the most pleasant experience, but it's the only way to keep on learning and improving what you do.

Ed was masterful at communicating the little things he felt I could work on that would make a big difference. He had a zen-like calmness to him, and was a wise old owl. When I left Sky, we carried on working together. In all, I would work with him for almost twenty years, until his death five years ago. I haven't managed to replace Ed. I do ask trusted producers for feedback, but Ed was a one-off. I am very lucky to have had a mentor like him.

Sky were thorough. As well as training up presenters, they had a style and a 'look' they wanted you to adhere to. It was quite corporate and, like a lot of what they did back then, it was based on a US version of being an anchor. Before this, I had largely been on radio, and I would describe my dress style as 'eclectic' and 'mainly secondhand'.

I was sent shopping in Knightsbridge with a stylist called Patti. She was very cool, slightly scatty and unbelievably kind to me. Patti would grab herself glasses of champagne whenever we were offered a drink, and I waltzed along behind her in awe, feeling like Julia Roberts in *Pretty Woman*. Just four weeks before, an hour in the Metro Centre in Gateshead had been my idea of 'shopping'. Patti took me for a haircut and advised me on how the make-up artists should make my face look, and then we spent hours in Harvey Nichols as I tried on suits and she sipped some more champagne. When Patti had chosen seven of the best, we went to the till to tally up. It was then that Patti realised that I was expecting her to pay for the suits.

'Sky will reimburse you,' she said, to reassure me.

'That's fine,' I whispered, while going red, 'but I don't have that kind of money in my account today.'

'Have you got a credit card?' she suggested.

'No.'

The bill for the suits was close to £5,000. Patti could sense my embarrassment, and without another word, she whacked them on her card. I had only met her that morning, but she'd saved me a ton of humiliation. When Sky said they'd buy my clothes, it hadn't occurred to me that I would have to pay for them first and claim the money back. I was hopelessly naive. Patti didn't even roll her eyes. She just got on with it. It was an incredibly kind thing to do for a complete novice.

That night, I proudly hung up the suits on the curtain pole in the dingy burgundy bedroom: Armani, Kenzo and Prada, designers I had never dreamed I would own at the age of forty-three, let alone twenty-three. (If you work for HMRC, then technically I didn't own them – they belonged to Sky.)

Those few weeks felt like a dream, as if I had walked into someone else's life. But once the preparation was over, it was time to get on with the job. The first bulletin they let me loose on was two minutes long – I was dipping my toe into the water before the longer thirty-minute shows that I would regularly co-host with the calming and avuncular golf fanatic Dominik Holyer started.

The studio was a five-minute walk from the offices, where all the various sports show editorial teams were based in an open-plan environment; Premier League football was in one area, *Soccer Saturday* in another corner, with *Goals on Sunday* on another desk. Our spot was right in the middle.

I opted for a pale taupe Prada two-piece for my first day. Alongside the suit carrier, I had a bag containing my shoes and toiletries. As I was leaving the flat that morning, I decided at the last minute that I should bring a spare pair of pants, as I was wearing black underwear, and if the pale suit was in any way see-through, my knickers would show. You wouldn't actually see them on set, as I'd be seated, but I didn't want to be walking round an open-plan office filled with alpha-blokes flashing a black G-string. The pants I grabbed were nice, sensible M&S nude ones.

I had a few butterflies in my tummy, but generally felt I was ready. It was time to get changed and head to the make-up department, so I grabbed the suit carrier and the shoe bag and marched off.

When I got to the wardrobe department I was in a bit of a flap and couldn't find the spare nude pants, but it turned out the suit wasn't at all see-through, so I didn't think any more about it. The two-minute bulletin went well, and I made my way back up to the office to get some feedback from the editor, Nick, and the deputy editor, a brutally honest Northern Irish ex-hack who took no prisoners. He only smiled when he was about to give someone a massive bollocking.

It was his booming voice I heard as I headed into the office.

'Does anyone know where these pants have come from?' he was asking in his agitated Northern Irish accent. He had the aforementioned nude M&S pants held aloft on the end of a pen and was parading them around the room, with a half-smile on his moustached face. He was a small bloke, but was holding the pants about two metres in the air on the end of his pen, just in case anyone in the rugby or tennis departments, which were tucked away in the corner, might miss the show.

I panicked. 'They're mine – but they are clean,' I shouted. There was no point denying it; they could only be mine or Anne McCaffrey's. Anne was the only other woman regularly working on our show. She was in charge of booking reporters and film crews for shoots, and as far as I knew, she didn't bring spare underwear to work. She would later become a really great friend, but at that moment she must have thought, *Sister, what the hell are you doing bringing spare knickers to the office?*

There was much laughter as I grabbed the pants from the Bic pen and stuffed them into my bag. I mumbled my explanation for the pants to the room. Nobody looked like they cared about VPL.

The day I got home from Queen Charlotte's hospital, Reuben and Lois were seven days old. It was a heavenly time of life, although I appear to be struggling with holding two babies at the same time.

Her Majesty Queen Elizabeth asking me how I managed to feed twins. Genuinely.

The proud grandmas. Elizabeth (Kenny's mum), my Nana Sheila (great grandma to Reuben and Lois) and my mum, on Reuben and Lois's first birthday.

The night before we got married, Margaret and Hendie, friends of ours in Dunblane, hosted a big barbecue for all of our guests. Louise and I caught up with our old PE teacher, Miss Woliter.

When I started out as a football presenter, it's fair to say the landscape was fairly male and the hair was rather bouffant, even for the blokes.

My old pal Ally McCoist and I fighting over silverware. I appear to be wearing cream leather boots, for which I can only apologise.

I was the first woman to host a live football match on terrestrial TV. This wasn't it but it's fair to say I have done hundreds more since. Alan Shearer and Lee Dixon were two regular pundits I worked with when I joined the BBC.

Publicity shot for the 2014 World Cup in Brazil. There appears to be a lack of women. Things changed by the next World Cup.

The samba turned out to be my last dance on *Strictly* in 2007 but it was one of the best things I ever did. Not the samba clearly, or I wouldn't have been voted off, but the show itself was an absolute joy.

Watching Kenny play for Scotland was the most nerve-wracking and pride-filled thing I ever did, until I had children and started to watch them play sport. However, Kenny kicking for Scotland was a nightmare for me, and often was for him.

Working with the athletics crew at BBC Sport is probably the place I pinch myself most. I set the alarm clock to watch Denise win gold at the Sydney 2000 Olympics and I stayed up late watching Michael Johnson in Atlanta 1996. As for Jess – like the rest of us, she brought me to tears in 2012. Now I get to call them colleagues and mates – lucky me!

Hosting Sports Personality of the Year for the last decade has been a joy. But what big shoes we all step into when we take on that gig, and what a legacy the show has. As Gary Lineker said backstage one year, as we were about to walk out to the audience, 'it's the closest to a laxative any show can be'. Nice.

Being awarded an MBE for charity and services to women's sport, and then sharing the moment with Kenny in November 2021, is something I am incredibly proud of.

Family reunions like this one are rare. Louise came home for the first time in almost four years in the summer of 2022. After the picture was taken we played a giant game of rounders with all the kids and I disgraced myself.

Freeze the Fear was the perfect show to do as I stepped into the mid-point of life. What's more, as a result of my ability to bear the cold, I have saved money on thermal underwear and heating bills.

My gang. Reuben, Lois and Kenny are my world.

I hadn't been expecting applause when I walked back into the office that day, but neither had I anticipated having my underwear revealed to all my colleagues on my first proper day at work. I never figured out how the pants fell out of the bag, but ultimately I decided my initiation into this macho world could have been a lot worse.

And, as I had said, at least they were clean.

Sky Sports was a tough school, but I find it hard to say I was subjected to discrimination. I was there because they wanted more women on screen, for a start, so there was an air of positivity to that, and I worked alongside strident broadcasters like Kay Burley on the wider network. I first came across her on a photoshoot for the Sky TV Christmas card; I saw the way she dealt with Gray and Keys, and took note. I'd heard some fairly scathing remarks about Kay – from men, of course – but I realised at that shoot that it was because she didn't tolerate any nonsense. To be forthright is great, but it takes confidence and that only comes from experience, which can be hard to attain if you can't take the heat. Or, more importantly, if nobody is prepared to come along and make an honest assessment that the temperature needed turning down, which it probably did at Sky, and many other alpha workplaces at that time.

It took until 2011 for Keys and Gray to be sacked. I was occasionally the butt of comments and scenarios that my male peers might not have had to endure. As I wandered through the office one afternoon, one well-known male presenter shouted, 'Oi, Yorath! How many Premier League footballers have you notched up on your bedpost?'

At twenty-three years old, I lacked the verbal elasticity to knock him out with a witty retort. His gang of cronies giggled; I smiled and carried on walking. Inside, I was dying.

An older rugby league presenter stopped me in the corridor one day and said, 'Your arse is amazing right now, but sadly for you, it's one of those arses that will be by your knees when you hit thirty.'

'Well you might find out – if you're even still around when I'm thirty.' That was the best I could do – and I meant if he was still alive, not still working at Sky.

Even though I left the station in 1998, it appeared I was still fair game for Gray and Keys, long after my departure. I sat a row behind them on the flight to Istanbul for the Champions League Final between AC Milan and Liverpool in 2005. I was seven months pregnant with twins, and I was huge, much bigger than I would have been at full-term with a single-baby pregnancy. I looked like I had swallowed a space hopper. I was hosting the final for ITV, while Keys and Gray were hosting for Sky.

In full earshot of me – and anyone who might be listening in our business-class cabin – Richard said: 'So, Andy, what do you think of pregnant women?'

'I'm afraid I don't find them very attractive, Richard. In fact, I never slept with my wife when she was pregnant with our kids.'

'So you didn't have sex, Andy?' Keys asked.

'No, I didn't say that Richard.'

Then they laughed their heads off at their little 'comedy' routine.

It's rare when you put on three stone around your middle that you feel at your best or your most sexually desirable. The weight of the babies, and the fact one of them had kicked a rib out, gave me chronic back pain. I was tired, and I just wanted to slow down. This trip to Istanbul was my final hurdle to navigate before I could prepare properly for motherhood. I was embarrassed, of course, and thought their comments were especially cruel, bearing in mind they both had children and wives of their own. I imagined what their daughters would have thought if they'd heard them speak like that about me.

Luckily, by that time I had been working with lovely men like Ally McCoist and Andy Townsend at ITV, who were kind and caring, always asked after my wellbeing, and seemed genuinely excited for me about the babies. Keys and Gray were dinosaurs, waiting to become extinct. If TV is mainly judged by how many viewers you have, then I guess we won. Fifteen million people tuned into ITV that night for one of the most iconic and memorable finals ever; less than a million watched them.

To be clear, sports TV wasn't an island of filth while the rest of the world and society circled around being politically correct and virtuous. In the mid to late nineties, I reckon I would have seen and heard the same kind of idiotically sexist stuff if I was working in a top law firm or as a trader at an investment bank. It was just a very male ego-driven environment. I am sure there were probably quite a few men there who also found the alpha atmosphere a bit too much. It wasn't just a male-dominated space in front of the cameras, but behind them too. The camera operators, sound technicians, statisticians, directors and producers were ninety-five per cent male. On the show I hosted, we had one female director, Karen Wilmington, and that was it.

One of my best female allies at work turned out to be a great friend. Mel Chappell was a junior producer on the show *Soccer Saturday* and she knew her footballing onions. Thankfully, she brought me under her wing and made sure I mixed with the right people. Mel is now an agent and also honorary godparent to my kids. Her opening gambit as she

walked past my desk one day was: 'Grapes retain water.' I
was halfway through shovelling another handful of grapes
into my mouth. She swears it's not her fault I put a stone on
in a month when I swapped grapes for freshly baked chocolate cookies. Turns out the cookies made me retain more
than water.

Back then, women generally tended to be found in the
admin and HR jobs. In the corner offices where the bosses
resided, there was not one single female sitting in the expensive seats.

It's like turning a tanker, isn't it? The first movement is very
slow, and it feels like nothing is changing, but you have to
keep going, and then eventually the whole boat comes along,
gaining momentum. You can tell I didn't do physics GCSE,
but you get the gist.

My attitude was, being there and doing the job, being visible and trying to be good at it, was as powerful as anything
else I could do to speed up the change.

Presenting *Sports Centre* was fine, but only used a basic skill
set. I really wanted to do live sport; specifically, I wanted to
do live football. After all, that's what I had been doing in
Newcastle when Sky Sports recruited me.

Vic Wakeling was one of the founding fathers of Sky
Sports, the man who helped pull off the initial Premier
League deal for Rupert Murdoch. He was a phenomenal
chain-smoker and resided in the main corner office. When
I say resided, I really do mean he essentially lived there, for
an average of thirteen hours a day. He was unsmiling, but
one-to-one was friendly enough. He was a County Durham
native, so we had the northeast in common, but he didn't take
my requests to host live football seriously.

'You won't be presenting football while I'm here. You

won't be on screen after you're twenty-eight,' he said between puffs of his Benson & Hedges one day when I had secured an audience with him.

I believed him. With the news that I had about four years left of my career ringing in my ears, I started pestering Mark Sharman instead.

'Look, Gabby, even a tightrope walker has boring days at work,' he said.

'No, Mark. It's not that I am bored. I want to grow and progress as a presenter,' I protested.

'I'll see what we can do,' he'd say, and then I'd come back a few days later, knocking on his door with the same request. It was Groundhog Day for both of us.

Then one day, he requested to see me and told me he had good news. 'Right, from next season, you can host the ice hockey!'

I'd lived in Vancouver, home of the Canucks. I knew who Wayne Gretzky was. I had once held a puck in my hand. Aside from that, I was fairly clueless.

Sky were clever. They knew the audience for ice hockey was minimal (at the time it would have been cheaper to send a VHS tape to anyone interested), but it was a good place to learn the mechanics of hosting live sport.

My first live match was at the Ayr Barr Arena, and everything was going fine until a fire alarm went off. The players were guided off the ice and we waited for an announcement. I had to come back on air and 'fill' (filling is one of key skills you will need in your locker if you are thinking of becoming a sports presenter). The studio guests and I chatted for a while, and then the arena started to evacuate. After a few more minutes, the director, a loud Scottish guy called Gerry Logan, said: 'Right, cameras lock off, and everyone leave the studio . . . apart from Gabby.'

There was no fire as far as we could see, and I guess if I was going to be left in a burning building on my own, then an ice rink was probably the best place. But I certainly hadn't planned for this scenario in my pre-match preparation.

The match eventually restarted, and we ended up being on air for over four hours.

'Welcome to live sport,' Gerry joked afterwards in the bar.

I loved presenting the ice hockey. The players were like streetfighters with blades on their feet; a fight broke out in almost every match. I never worked out why they were all so angry. They certainly weren't angry afterwards when they came into the local nightclubs, chewing tobacco with a swarm of groupies around them. The league was a United Nations of hockey players, with Italians, Canadians, Russians and Americans dominating the teams. In spite of their protective clothing and elaborate face masks, there was always a stick to the face or blood on the ice from some brutal-sounding injury or other. We had fantastic access, and a reporter called Nick Rothwell, a former Canadian pro whom the players trusted. Nick would follow a stampeding angry giant off the ice and into the dressing room if they'd been red carded, or trail after them into the medical room if they were injured. It was the kind of access a Premier League football producer would die for.

One night, a wayward hockey stick had cut open the eyelid of a six-foot-four muscle-bound man. Nick followed him into the doctor's room, where the giant was fuming and desperate to get back on the ice to take revenge on the opponent who had almost rendered him blind. As the angry man simmered on the massage couch, the doctor peered into his eye with a torch.

'What's happened there, Doc?' Nick asked, although we could all see for ourselves that the eyeball was visible through the actual eyelid.

'His eyelid needs plastic surgery. I'm afraid we can't sort this here; he's got to go to hospital.'

The player pushed the doctor's hand and torch away in fury. 'I need to get back on the ice, Doc,' he implored.

The doctor looked helpless and suddenly tiny.

'Stitch it to the bone,' the player demanded. Five words I will never forget hearing.

The cameraman widened his shot, giving us a view of a smiling Nick looking queasily at the camera.

'Back to you, Gabby,' was Nick's brilliant pay-off, leaving the viewer (and sadly I do mean the 'viewer') wondering whether the doctor would oblige the player's extreme request.

I still think it was one of the most brilliant – and Partridge-like – moments of live sports telly I have ever witnessed.

21

Dad

Work was progressing nicely, but my private life was in a spot of bother.

Ian was in Hong Kong with the Royal Navy, preparing to hand over the island to China (not on his own; the rest of the Navy and Chris Patten would help too). I didn't feel like I was actually in a relationship, and I am not sure he did. I don't have the answer on long-term, long-distance relationships, but when you're young, unmarried and you don't have kids, I'm not sure they are worth the angst. I'll be advising my kids against them.

Eventually, it was all too much. There was very little trust left after my dalliance with the German tennis player, and we made the painful decision to split. I was heartbroken because I truly loved Ian, but there was no way we could carry on following our separate dreams half a world apart. Breaking up with someone you really care about absolutely sucks, but it's a different kind of heartbreak to losing your brother, and eventually I was able to put it all into perspective. Ian knew my family; he knew the raw, pained and manic me who had just lost Daniel, and he was a good, clever and kind man. I wished him nothing but the best.

When it came to the other man in my life, it was becoming clear that the old version of my dad was not coming back. He had never been a particularly attentive 'hands-on' father; he didn't read bedtime stories to us, watch school plays or attend parents' evening, which I suppose made him a regular seventies Dad. He was a 'play sport with you in the garden after dinner' dad, a 'play cards at the table' dad. He often meted out discipline, and was a traditional breadwinner. He worked hard and led silently, by example. He was also a famous dad.

Other people wanted his time and his energy just because of what he did on a Saturday afternoon, and that didn't always sit well with him. He gave them what they wanted, stories and bonhomie, but they sometimes left him a bit drained for us. He seemed to hold quite low or negative opinions of people and the world in general, and my brother's death confirmed for him that life really is 'shit'.

When Daniel died, that energy must have been tough for my normally super-positive Mum and the six-year-old Jordan, who were the only two left at home full-time. But Dad was increasingly showing a different face to the world. He was humorous and charming to others, and I was always being told by complete strangers what a lovely man he was. The guy who lived in our family home wasn't always that way. He had started to drink a lot more than usual and then fall asleep on the sofa, or get shouty with everyone before stomping off to bed. We've always darkly joked that he never seemed to get that 'funny, happy' kind of drunk with us; just the angry one.

Mum's property business was going well. She didn't partake in these evening drinking sessions. Instead, after Jordan went to bed, she took herself off to her offices, which had been built on the side of the house, and worked there until the wee hours – it's normal to receive emails from my mum at 3am, even now. Back then, fuelled with whisky, Dad started to resent her work ethic and the subsequent success that came with it. I am sure she wasn't without blame, and I know there are two sides to every story, but Dad's side to that particular story would have been a lot more compelling if it wasn't soaked in alcohol.

I hardly spoke to Dad when I wasn't physically at the family home. I thought at the time that maybe he was a bit embarrassed that I was presenting sport and encroaching on his domain. When I got offered the job at Sky, he told my mum that he hoped I didn't 'cock up', which is a very typical 'Terry Yorath' response. I once had to interview him on Sky ahead of a live match. At the end of the very straight interview, I said, 'Thanks Dad,' and he said: 'That's OK, love. Mum wants you to call her about the weekend; are you coming home?' It was a cheeky pay-off and typical of him. To the outside world it must have all seemed very happy families. And there were moments when it still was.

I know that many people reading this will have someone in their life who abuses alcohol or drugs, and many of the experiences I have had will resonate. The reason I wanted to share them with you is because I am guessing that, like me, you probably felt for a very long time that it was something you could change. Or maybe you felt that if you were only loveable enough, the person would stop abusing whatever substance or behaviour they'd found solace in.

Nearly everywhere I went in the football world, someone would ask,

'How's your dad?'

'He's great,' I would lie.

I wanted him to be great. I wanted him to be happy, but he wasn't having any of it.

Eventually, in 2003, after years of arguments and bust-ups with Mum, my dad moved out of the family home around my thirtieth birthday. I think she thought it was going to be a wake-up call; that he'd sort out his drinking and they'd work things through. But it wasn't. If anything, the handbrake was off, and things got worse for him. Now he could partake in daytime drinking without anyone nagging him to stop.

Dad drifted from our lives. He rarely rang or returned our calls, and he often lost and changed his phone without sharing the new number.

I have owned houses he's never visited and had boyfriends he never met; that's how long he'd disappear out of our lives for. All the while, I was asked regularly: 'How's your dad? He was a hero of mine,' or 'How's your dad? He's a great guy.'

I could only be honest and say, 'He's not good,' to a select few of his old friends from Leeds United, like Jimmy Lumsden or Eddie Gray, who still popped by to see him. To everyone else I'd repeat, 'He's OK, thanks.'

Then, many years later, in 2009, I was driving home from an event that I'd been hosting in central London, and the 11pm news came on the radio.

'The former Wales manager Terry Yorath has been admitted to hospital after he was found unconscious on a street in Leeds. It's believed the fifty-nine-year-old was mugged.'

I felt sick and rang Mum, who was hearing the same thing through Facebook messages, but she didn't have any more information than the little I had heard on the radio.

We rang the two big hospitals in Leeds and eventually found him; he was in Leeds General Infirmary, and unable to speak to me.

We're still not sure whether he was actually mugged; he

may have just been very drunk. He said his watch had been taken, but we can't be sure he had it on when he left his flat.

He was a fairly unreliable witness. In the few years before that night, he'd set fire to his flat and almost killed a young woman when drink-driving, only avoiding prison by the skin of his teeth. The judge let him do community service instead, because he thought Dad was a suicide risk. Dad has written about this and has expressed enormous regret at what happened to the young woman.

Maybe waking up in hospital after being found on the street was the wake-up call, the one we had all been hoping for. An acupuncturist and therapist I had been seeing talked to me of removing the silk cushion from an addict and seeing how far they would go if you didn't rescue them. Maybe this was the removal of his silk cushion.

When he eventually became more lucid, I spoke to Dad on the phone and discussed what he was going to do about his life, how he'd move on after he left hospital.

My mum was not an ex who had simply abandoned her husband; she was at the hospital every day and able to fill me in on medical updates. Dad was sketchy with detail at the best of times, and he was also hallucinating, so it was invaluable to have Mum's testimony. He was medically detoxed in hospital, which took ten days in total, and during that time all of his vital organs were checked. He wasn't in great shape, as you'd imagine, but aside from some irreversible liver damage, his other issues could be improved if he cleaned up his act. He was told in no uncertain terms by the doctor that he could die if he started drinking again, and that if he did succumb to drink again, he should not try to stop on his own, as his organs wouldn't be able to handle it; he would be risking 'catastrophic organ failure'. If a doctor ever said this to me, I am fairly sure I would never drink again, but I am not an alcoholic, and it is so hard (impossible) to put yourself into the mindset of an addict when you are not one.

It was clear Dad could not go back to his flat and hope to go on a journey of sobriety alone; he needed some tools. So we suggested, and the rest of the family agreed, that he should come to stay with me and my family in London. We would try to persuade him to enter rehab and nourish him with good food and love.

At this point, he hadn't seen our four-year-old twins for over a year. (Neither have you come to think of it; don't worry, you will meet them properly later.) He arrived late at night, and the following morning Reuben, our son, came into breakfast to see him sitting at the table eating toast and drinking tea.

'Grandad has come back from the dead!' he exclaimed as he processed the old man sitting next to him. Then he carried on eating his yoghurt.

Dad was adamant he would not go into an overnight facility, so I set about calling specialist centres and hospitals like the Capio Nightingale in Paddington, which offered day services. I also found other therapists for daily appointments and tried to put together a recovery schedule for him. My husband Kenny and I were strict with him, and told him he couldn't just sit around reading the newspaper and going to the bookmakers. He had to do jobs and help around the house. There was no purpose to his day, so we tried to create one.

'I don't have the right shoes,' he'd say, when I asked him to do almost anything.

I'd never known a man pay this level of attention to the 'right shoes'. So, we took him shopping, and bought walking shoes, trainers and lots of new clothes. I felt we were in it for the long haul. I didn't mind how long it took; I just wanted him to be healthy and happy. A bonus would be having him as part of the kids' lives.

One day, Kenny set him off on a weeding task in the garden. He showed him what to do and how to use the garden fork and a trowel. Dad was wearing leather brogues and a pair of tailored trousers, but we couldn't physically make him change his clothes, so we left him to it. When we came home, he had taken out every bulb and plant, so the flowerbed was entirely bare. And the shoes were wrecked. It was clear he had no practical skills to speak of. This wasn't a huge surprise to me: at one point, he had lived for months in his two-bedroom flat with only one light working, because he thought 'someone' would come to change the bulbs. His life as a cosseted footballer had left him totally unprepared for the real world, and my mum had always filled in the blanks for him. She even filled in the cheques; he didn't write one of those until he was well into his thirties.

At the time he was staying with us, we had a boxer dog called Sydney, so Dad became the designated dog-walker. But the walks got longer and longer. One day he was out for three hours, which for a man who had been at death's door a few weeks before was remarkable.

'I got lost,' he said.

The dog's demeanour said different. Sydney still had plenty of energy.

I didn't smell alcohol on him, but I did get a whiff of cigarettes, and suspected he might have spent a couple of hours in the bookies.

He didn't sleep well, as I suspect his blood-sugar levels were all over the place, and he often got up in the night to watch the news until the house came to life, so by mid-afternoon he was shattered. It was like having someone in the house with permanent jet lag. He ate small portions, like a little bird, and wanted sweets at night-time, when he had the biggest alcohol cravings.

We'd drive him to his appointments across London, and in the car on the way home, we'd try to talk to him about what the future might hold. It was feasible he could go back into coaching if he had an appetite for it and wanted to look after himself properly. Reuben and Lois, our children, enjoyed getting to know him a bit better, and he occasionally walked to pick them up from school with one of us.

There were little shoots of hope that he could build a life again, but blame and anger were never far away, and it was clear he needed long-term help.

'I think I can go home now,' he said one day, after just three weeks with us.

'I don't think you can, Dad. You don't have a plan,' I replied.

'I'll just do what I did before, but without alcohol,' he said.

'No, you can't go sit in the pub all day with the same people you drank with before and drink water,' I told him. 'You need a new pattern, new friends who do things other than drink.'

'I can. I'll just have a Coke,' he said, with absolute sincerity.

'You are nowhere near ready to do that, Dad. You need to go to AA meetings and carry on your progress in Leeds, and you haven't even looked into that. You need a hobby; you need to join a gym or get a non-alcohol related social life.'

After another week of him badgering me to let him go home, I gave in. We booked him a train and wished him well.

The thing about my dad is that he is very sweet and vulnerable when he is sober, and he was grateful for what we had done, but he wasn't ready to go home. We researched AA meetings in Leeds and gave him the details of where he needed to get to.

He attended his first meeting the day after he got back, then left it early and went straight to the pub, where he drank for several hours. He later told me that all the talk of alcohol in the AA meeting had made him desperate for a drink. As I say, he wasn't ready to go home.

The thing about people with addictive behaviour is that you can often see what they need, but they can't – or they won't accept it – and that is the basis for the most frustrating relationship you'll ever have. And here is a truth I know now: you will never ever sort it out unless the addict themself wants to sort it out. All you can do is offer love and not expect anything back. And here's another truth: you have to love yourself quite a lot to do that.

This all happened in 2009. It took another eleven years – and plenty more heartache – for me to get to a position where I can write that down and actually believe it.

It struck me a few years ago that my dad was probably depressed long before we lost my brother. With conversations around mental health now more prevalent and open than ever, I've started hearing other stories and accounts from people that matched his experiences. Alcohol was the numbing agent that became the problem, but the darkness in his brain was probably there long before. The self-doubt that came from never feeling good enough at Leeds United – 'I was a whipping boy,' he'd say – probably had far more serious ramifications than he realised, and then there was the trauma from the Bradford fire disaster. He had a strange superiority complex in some areas of life, and yet he'd exhibit paranoia and inferiority in other areas, such as unfamiliar social gatherings. He was the 'tough guy' as a footballer, famous for his aggressive style of play, and yet at home he'd often cry at the most innocuous things. How could someone like him ever ask for help? He couldn't, so he didn't. He found his answer in the bottom of a mind-numbing bottle of alcohol.

There were so many more years of drinking, sadness, aggression and anger to come. And every little episode, whether it's a hurtful phone call or the months of no communication, push the happier memories further away, until you really can't remember the person you used to know.

Dad has ridden through a few different enforced detoxes and relapses and then finally had a diagnosis of diabetes, which seems to have been a trigger to slow down the drinking.

Just before Christmas 2021, Dad agreed to come and see us for the first time in five years. When I say 'agreed', I mean I really had to persuade him.

'But what would I do?' he asked.

'Er, hang out and have a nice dinner with your grandchildren,' I suggested.

The day before he was due to come, he contracted a 'touch of Covid'. My brother, who had been bringing him down, rang to tell me, and we both treated the diagnosis with suspicion.

He never actually had a positive test, but the doctor said it probably was Covid. He then said it would take a week to get his results, so I was fairly sure this wasn't an entirely truthful story. The alleged appointment was on a Saturday, which seems remarkable, as almost nobody in England can get a doctor's appointment on a Saturday, and if they could, no self-respecting receptionist would book one for 'suspected Covid'. Dad was obviously not comfortable about coming to see us, and all the therapy in the world doesn't allow me to be happy with that.

I may have got to a place where I know I am loveable, where I know it's not my fault that his life has been dominated by drink for so long, but I also miss having a dad.

When I see friends' dads coming to watch kids play sport, or hang out with their families 'just because', or helping them out with daily life, it's hard not to feel a pang of envy. I know that is not a universal experience, but no amount of acceptance can ever change that. I feel sorry for Dad that he has missed out on so much of the joy that his grandchildren would have brought him, and also that he has missed about twenty years of his career. The one light that has never gone out in him is his passion for football.

I have nothing but love for my dad and enormous respect for the trials and tribulations he has been through. For a few years, I sought the company of not very appropriate older men. You don't need to be Freud to work that one out, and thank god I am happily married to a good normal bloke who isn't an addict – so hurrah to me, I didn't marry my dad.

But that doesn't mean I wouldn't like a hands-on father in my life every now and then.

However, I do know that in spite of everything, he does love us.

22

Finding a Husband

You already know that I didn't marry Ian, Gary or Steve. To be honest, I have tried to write this book without making a big deal about getting married, because quite frankly I don't want to share the limelight.

Only joking.

But I can't pretend, twenty-odd years into our marriage, that he is someone who doesn't deserve a few paragraphs in the midst of an essay about what I have learned in life and how sport has shaped all of that. All being well, soon I will have been with him longer than I have been without him. For most of that time, it's been an absolute delight and I feel truly blessed to have met him, but we all have the other days too. It's called being married.

Three weeks before we met, I had experienced a fairly unenjoyable New Year's Eve at a cabaret club in London. I snogged a cigar-smoking wide boy who had tried to persuade me to do cocaine in the toilets. While I avoided that, I didn't manage to avoid him sticking his tobacco-coated tongue down my throat. I didn't like myself very much the morning after that experience; I felt as sick as if I'd puffed his large cigar.

That's not a euphemism.

On New Year's Day 1999, I decided to stop drinking, stop going out and stop looking for a boyfriend. Instead, I would focus on being a better, healthier person. It was a fairly unoriginal New Year's resolution for a human in their mid-twenties.

A few sober, non-partying weeks into my new 'healthy' life, on 22 January to be exact, one of my best friends, Kirsty Gallacher, was having a birthday dinner in London at a glamorous restaurant called Quaglino's. Kirsty was like a little sister to me; she'd taken on my old role at Sky when I left to go to ITV, but our friendship had endured my transfer. On my way home from presenting *On the Ball*, I stopped at Harvey Nichols to buy her a gift and me a new outfit for the dinner. (Remember those days when your income was your own and you just bought stuff because it made you happy?) I went out that night feeling fairly hot for the first time in ages: new clothes, a new scent, a new me.

After the dinner, we headed to the Met Bar for drinks. In the late nineties, the Met Bar nearly always had a Spice Girl, a Premier League footballer or a member of Oasis propping up the bar. Everyone was getting quite drunk, and I didn't want to fall off the 'not snogging wide boys' wagon, so I asked my mate Tamsin if she fancied sharing a cab and an early night. (Back when 1am was an 'early night'.)

As we drove along the Fulham Road, just fifteen minutes from our respective homes and warm beds, Tamsin said, 'Why don't we stop at the K Bar for last orders?'

I asked the cab to pull over and we went to the door of the club, only to be met by a bolshy bouncer who wasn't sure why we wanted to go in for the final fifteen minutes of the evening. He had a point. It was like being back in Browns in Cardiff in the early nineties.

'Why don't you just go home? It's ten to two!' he suggested, in a rather judgemental way.

'Mate, I don't want lifestyle advice – I just want a drink,' Tamsin argued.

'Oh, come on, old chap ... let them in.' A friend called David Ross was walking behind the bouncer at that exact moment and spotted us. He obviously had a bit of pull with the doorman.

I was already turning towards the road to find a new cab.

'Gabs ... come on,' Tamsin implored.

'OK. Just one!'

'I know those guys,' she said excitedly as we walked in, pointing to a group of very tall men in the corner. 'They're Wasps rugby players; we did a VT with them last week, they're lovely.' Tamsin was a producer at Sky Sports and worked on the Rugby Union coverage.

And with that she was off, chatting to the very tall men with big muscles and cauliflower ears. A Scottish guy called David whom I had been out with a few times a year or so before, not the David who'd persuaded the doorman to let us in the bar, saw me and offered to buy me a drink. As he walked back from the bar with two glasses of Chardonnay, another Scottish guy, who was with the rugby players, glided in and took the wine glasses from him in a very swift move, handing me one while knocking back the other himself.

David had been muscled out – and lost his wine.

That man with the glide and the free Chardonnay was Kenny. He was very jolly. We chatted about his rugby career, his farm in Scotland, my work and what we had been doing that weekend. Then David came back in for a second go.

Kenny wandered off, and that might have been the last I ever saw of him.

He returned to his mates, where he said to one of them, 'I've just been chatting up Gaby Roslin round the corner.' (Gaby Roslin is a broadcaster who hosted *The Big Breakfast* in the nineties with Chris Evans.)

'No, you haven't, you idiot. That's Gabby Yorath,' his friend Simon corrected him.

Kenny decided to come back over and tell me about the mix-up, which he thought was hilarious.

Then, before we knew it, we were married with kids and a large mortgage.

Well, not quite.

It was kicking-out time at the K Bar, so we wandered over the road to a restaurant called Vingt-Quatre, which, as the name suggests, was a twenty-four-hour eatery. It was jam-packed, and we ordered full English breakfasts and tea and coffee, together with my mate Tamsin (I'm not a total arse, I wasn't going to leave her behind) and Kenny's mate Peter Scrivener, who also played for Wasps. We sat there until around 4.30am, eating, chatting and laughing.

It turned out we all lived in Chiswick, so at the end of the night, we agreed to share a cab.

I was shivering as we waited for the taxi, so Kenny put his arm around me. I felt protected and warm, and like I didn't want him to remove it, ever.

'What are you doing next weekend?' he said, with his arm still in place.

'I'm taking my hairdresser to a health farm,' I replied. It was, bizarrely, the truth.

'Oh, shame. I thought you might like to come up to Edinburgh and watch me play for Scotland; we're playing Wales.'

Damn. What I wanted to say was, 'I can cancel' and then kiss him. Instead, I said, 'Another time.' It was one of the greatest chat-up lines I had ever heard, and I had to knock it back for a night at Champneys and a pedicure.

I'd just bought a four-storey townhouse that backed on to a marina and had a small swimming pool and a waterbed. It makes me sound like a lottery winner, but I was just very lucky, as the people who had owned it had tax issues and fled the country. I'd just sold the flat I owned in Richmond for double what I had paid the year before, so I was in an absolutely fortuitous manoeuvring position.

'Do you want a nightcap?' I heard myself say as the cab pulled up outside my house.

At this, both Peter and Kenny got out of the cab. Kenny hastily bundled Peter back in and waved him off.

I had promised to show Kenny the waterbed, which was in a bedroom I didn't use.

I lay on the bed (fully clothed), demonstrating how sick-making it was to try and sleep on. He ran across the room and jumped on to the bed, with which I flew in the air and landed hard on the floor on the other side. That's physics for you.

'Oh god, I am so sorry,' he said. We were both laughing uncontrollably; I suspect an evening of Chardonnay helped to numb any pain. Kenny sat down next to me, rubbing my back while still laughing. I sat up, feeling a bit dazed, and then we finally kissed.

My kids might read this, and my mum definitely will, so let's move along; nothing to see here.

The next day, he was heading up to Edinburgh for the Five Nations, as it was called then, so we didn't see each other that week. The following Saturday, I sat on a bed at a health farm in Hertfordshire and watched Kenny kick the goals for Scotland as they beat Wales in their opening match of the campaign.

'He seems quite good at rugby,' my friend (and still my forever hairdresser) Zoe said, as we watched the match.

Kenny appeared to be the hero of the hour, as the normal goal kicker broke his leg during the match, which was a shame for him but an opportunity for Kenny. I wasn't an avid rugby-watcher back then, but even I could see he was having a stormer.

The relationship got off to a wonderfully (uncharacteristically) relaxed start. Kenny would be home for a week, where he'd be training and playing with Wasps, then away for a week with Scotland during the Five Nations. We did old-fashioned courting; we went out for dinner or for drinks, and I watched him play for Wasps and met his teammates. We got to know each other and liked what we found.

Kenny had lost his dad at nineteen to pancreatic cancer, and a few years before that, his eldest cousin, Hamish, who had been like a brother to him, had died in a freak road accident. Like me, Kenny had experienced grief and loss, and, like me, he wanted to make every second count.

The Five Nations went very well for Scotland. Apart from a loss to England at Twickenham, they'd won every match. Their final match of the tournament was in Paris on a Saturday, and Scotland had a record points win to leave themselves top of the table.

England were playing Wales on the Sunday, and if they lost, Scotland would be champions. That day, I had to fly to Manchester to watch the quarter-final of the FA Cup – Newcastle were playing Spurs at Old Trafford. I was with my old mate from Sky, Mel Chappell, who was a Spurs fan.

Newcastle won, and as we dashed for the plane back to London, we had the radio on in the cab, listening to the end of the Wales v England match, which was played at Wembley that year. Incredibly, in the dying minutes of the match, with a chance to win the game, the England captain and teammate of Kenny's at Wasps, Lawrence Dallaglio, made a strange call, going for a line out and not the posts. It cost England the win, and ultimately the title. Wales' win that day gifted the championship to Scotland.

I rang Kenny to congratulate him. He had flown back from Paris and was watching the match unfold with his friend Simon Shaw in Chiswick. Kenny was ecstatic and busy throwing his clothes into a bag, ready to dash to Heathrow. The Scotland team were meeting up for drinks in Edinburgh, and then on the Monday there would be an official function and party at Murrayfield. We worked out we could be in Terminal 1 for an hour at the same time, so we planned to meet to raise a glass together after I'd landed. Then Kenny had a better idea.

'Why don't you just come up to Edinburgh?' he said.

'What? I only have a handbag and the outfit I'm wearing.'

'You can buy clothes up there, there's a Harvey Nichols near the hotel.' Kenny said. 'I have a room at The Balmoral, and you don't have any work for two days – you just told me.'

So I did. I got off one plane, went to the ticket desk in Terminal 1, and booked a seat on the next flight to Edinburgh. Just writing about something as spontaneous as that feels like another life.

Suffice to say, it was a superb couple of days.

Kenny was having a magnificent season. He was top points scorer in the league and often won man of the match for

Wasps. He was regularly the headline in the Monday morning newspapers.

He was spending more and more time at my house while looking for a place to buy of his own. One flat he viewed was about three minutes' walk from my place. It didn't make sense; we both knew we were going to be together.

He moved in after five months. By this point we'd met each other's families and liked what we'd found, and discovered we had many friends and acquaintances in common. We even supported the same charities. How had we not met before? Our hopes and dreams aligned. My new single life had lasted a grand total of twenty-two days.

A few months into our relationship, a national newspaper had written a double-page feature about me. I pushed it in front of Kenny's face one morning.

'What do you think of this? Is it OK?' I said.

His eyes darted all over the pages, and after about ninety seconds he muttered, 'It's, er . . . good? Are you happy with it?'

I don't know why, but I listened to my gut, and asked: 'Are you dyslexic?'

His face turned white and he gulped hard. There was silence for a moment. Then he looked me straight in the eye and said, 'Yes. Are you going to finish with me?'

I hugged him and said of course not. I could not comprehend what that meant to him at that moment. I had no idea of the pain that lay behind that admission, or even of what it really meant to be dyslexic. I couldn't imagine the challenges of trying to get through everyday life if you cannot read, and back then, Kenny barely could.

His eyes filled up with tears. Suddenly, this handsome, strong, brave, sporting hero I had fallen in love with was a small Scottish boy, vulnerable and afraid. School had been a largely unhappy experience for Kenny. He was labelled 'thick' early on and left to fester in the remedial sets. His desire to answer a question verbally when he knew the answer was scolded, and he was told he was being disruptive.

He regularly came home from another wretched day at school and punched his head in the hope he'd dislodge or engage the bit that didn't seem to be working. He missed months of school with stomach aches; he was anxious and afraid of going to a place that made him sad and low in self-esteem. But he was a farmer's son and had a family farm to work on, so the teachers decided he'd be OK for a job and left him to his own devices. He left school at sixteen years old without one GCSE, without even sitting one, and unable, as he puts it, 'to even read *Lassie*'. What he did have was an enormous sporting talent, and thank god there was a PE teacher, Norrie Berner, who saw that ability, and a local rugby club, along with a family of big rugby-loving cousins who nurtured his talent.

Over the following year, more of his dyslexic story and experiences dripped out; it was a torrent of sadness, subterfuge and missed opportunities. One day, after he got angry and teary as he was struggling to write down the telephone number for a cinema (people with dyslexia often have processing issues, and copying things down can be a major headache), I sat him down and said, 'We need to do something about this.'

I knew he'd never love reading like I did, and I wasn't trying to change him, but I refused to believe that there wasn't something out there that could help this resourceful, funny, entrepreneurial, wise human get through his day with a little less stress. What's more, I knew he wanted to find some peace with his educational experiences.

One evening, we found ourselves watching *Tonight with Trevor McDonald*, and the show featured children with dyslexia going through a physical literacy programme and seeing enormously positive outcomes. Within a week, Kenny was enrolled on a course that would change his life.

I guess you have to be ready to do something about the problem that is holding you back, and it's Kenny's story, so I am not going to go into all of the hours and months of hard work he did to get through it, but what I have learned through his experiences has been invaluable. I'm not just talking about the challenges of day-to-day life. We all know the list of famous high-achievers who are dyslexic, but for every Richard Branson, Walt Disney and Albert Einstein, there are hundreds and thousands of kids who don't get the breaks or support they need. They leave school with low self-esteem and even lower levels of ambition. Kenny has spent years going into schools, talking to kids and trying to encourage the dyslexic ones to expect as much from their lives as their more literate peers. Nearly half of young offenders are dyslexic, even though people with dyslexia make up just ten per cent of the population. This doesn't mean dyslexia makes them turn to crime; it's being disengaged and disenfranchised that does that. Sport gave Kenny his outlet, as it does for many kids on the spectrum of dyslexia. More recently, we have come to understand that the ways in which people with dyslexia think and solve problems is different, and now huge companies, like the global consultancy firm EY, actively seek to recruit dyslexic graduates.

Why have I spent so long talking about Kenny's dyslexia? Apart from the fact I find it fascinating how our brains can be wired so differently, and because I never used the word 'cerebellum' before I met him, it's because I think it kind of sums up why we are still married all these years later. His openness and honesty about his 'hidden secret' from the very start, and his ability to be vulnerable and exposed despite his physical stature, laid the foundations for a communication that can, at times, be searingly, brutally truthful.

And it's also another fine example of the power of sport: once again, a saviour and a beacon of hope.

23

Being Famous

In many ways, the Sky years, the pre-Kenny years, were more like typical university years than my actual time at uni. I was newly single, heading out on the town a few nights a week and getting off with inappropriate blokes. I didn't like myself very much, but I always seemed to forget that the next time I was drinking too much Chardonnay in a sweaty nightclub at 2am.

The anger, disappointment and self-doubt that such destructive behaviour brings was coming home to roost. I put on weight and I was getting spotty; I was not exactly the catch of the century. I had gone from being fastidious about diet and exercise to buying a box of white Magnums on my way home from work at 10.30pm from the Shell garage at the end of the road. I'd then finish them off in front of *The Late Show with David Letterman*.

I didn't eat breakfast because I rose late, and I often had freshly baked chocolate chip cookies from the Sky canteen for dinner, thanks to the casual nutritional advice from my new friend Mel, who'd warned me off grapes the previous year.

I don't remember who it was that subtly suggested I try getting a personal trainer, but all these years later, I thank you from the bottom of my very large bottom. If we are discussing metamorphosis, then I must also thank the wonderful Ed Percival, my mentor, because I started seeing a therapist, Wendy Mandy, on his recommendation. Wendy treated me with acupuncture, ostensibly for my bad skin, but there was a lot more to treat beneath the surface. I kept her needles busy for a good few years.

In spite of all of this urgent need for 'self-care', I managed to progress at work. One day, while busy prepping a bulletin, I took a call from a man called Gary Newbon. Gary was an ITV football stalwart, a reporter, presenter and editor. He said that his bosses at ITV wanted to talk to me about a new show they were launching. He also suggested that I might need an agent, and told me to speak to Jon Holmes, who was the man behind Gary Lineker's stellar broadcasting career. (There are lots of Garys in this book, aren't there?) Within a few months, I had an agent, the aforementioned Jon, who liked to meet me for lunch at 'his club', the Groucho. This was exactly how I had imagined my London life would look when I was a poor student living in the north of England: meetings with an old-school agent who lunched at the Groucho.

The only other time I had been to the Groucho was when I had won a writing competition to be a student ambassador for *Cosmopolitan* magazine. The renowned editor, Marcelle D'Argy Smith, gathered the eight winners from around the UK for lunch. Among the pearls of wisdom about journalism she dispensed that day, she told us all that being pretty wasn't enough anymore, because anyone could be pretty thanks to surgery and better clothes; we'd need to be tough, smart cookies to survive and thrive in the world of work. It was a strange sentiment for a speech, but I appreciated the free lunch.

It turned out ITV wanted me to be the new co-host of *On the Ball*. It was a revival of a long-running Saturday lunchtime football show that would, in its new guise, be going up against the iconic BBC show *Football Focus*. The slot had previously been filled by *Saint and Greavesie*, hosted by the Scottish football hero Ian St John and the Spurs, Chelsea and England legend that was Jimmy Greaves. The two men were, in the kindest way possible, the personification of 'old school'. It was clear their fans would not necessarily warm to the young, female me straight away.

ITV had a new boss called Brian Barwick, formerly of the BBC, and Barwick had big plans for me. They'd use me on Central TV in Birmingham to gain experience hosting live football, and then they'd get me on the network for the Champions League highlights shows. This was an enormous leap from the relative anonymity I had enjoyed at Sky, where I could get away with slipping up a couple of times a night in my bulletins and learning my trade in the dark. I would now be broadcasting into millions of homes on the nation's biggest independent network.

The first-ever episode of the new *On the Ball* was a minor television disaster. We had a young up-and-coming footballer named Rio Ferdinand as our only guest on the show, and we were supposed to have three chats of about three minutes each with him. But we were so inept that we ran over time on every item and didn't ask him a single question. He sat there looking bemused, no doubt wondering why he'd got up so early on a Saturday. When we got to the very end of the show, feeling guilty and fearing he'd never come back, I asked him: 'So ... will West Ham win today?'

'Yes,' said young Rio.

'Goodbye from us,' I garbled as the titles rolled.

I also wrote an opening link that even now makes me cringe: 'We've got more shocks for you than a hairdryer falling into a full bath.'

The wise commentator Clive Tyldesley rang me on the Monday morning. 'Did you write that opening link?' he asked. It's always ominous when someone asks this kind of question, as it invariably means they think it was crap.

'Yes,' I admitted.

'It wasn't great. Try to be a bit more careful and journalistic. The show wasn't bad, but stuff like that lets you down.' He spoke tactfully, with a metaphorical arm round me, and I appreciated it. Feedback from people you trust is hard to come by in our industry, and Clive has always been very good at feedback. Even years after I left ITV, he'd still drop me a nice text every now and again, for which I was always grateful.

The show did get better. I stopped writing links with awful metaphors, and Barry Venison and I developed a nice friendship and fun 'on-air' chemistry. Barry had been part of the Newcastle team I had fallen in love with a few years before and he was making his way into broadcasting after finishing his playing career.

Working for ITV was different. Very quickly, I found myself being recognised in the street and invited to big events like the GQ Men of the Year Awards and the National Television Awards. I started seeing my TV heroes close up at parties, and getting followed by paparazzi on the street. All of that can make your head go a bit funny; it can make you a bit of an arsehole if you aren't careful, and I walked quite close to the 'being an arsehole' line at times.

*

I started dipping my toe in the entertainment TV water. I launched the channel ITV2 on a show with Billie Piper and Vinnie Jones, and appeared on *Fort Boyard* with Frank Bruno and Dirty Den, where I was a total disaster. Please feel free to google it.

I was invited on to shows like *They Think It's All Over* as a guest, where the macho atmosphere in the studio was softened by the delight that is Jo Brand. Her bolshy TV demeanour at the time had made me think she'd hate me, but she was enormously generous, lending me gags and encouraging me. Comedy and sports TV were probably going through similar transitions at the time with regard to gender balance. Women like Jo were real trailblazers.

I didn't fully understand the position I was in, the opportunity I was being given. When you are twenty-four, you think that these things are going to go on forever. My boss Brian was nervous. 'Don't go and do too much telly outside of the sport, because they need to trust you,' he said. 'They' meant the viewers, and the 'trust' needed was implicitly because I was a woman. I deferred to Brian's wisdom and turned down some good shows and interesting opportunities. It may have frustrated me at the time but, with hindsight, he was right; I might not have seen myself as a woman in a man's world, but the viewers still did. Brian's advice to stick to the 'main' thing and earn their respect was worth heeding.

I am so grateful that I was able to go through my formative years in the industry without the added pressure of social media. If someone dislikes what I say or do on TV now, they just pick up their phone and they can tell me directly on Twitter. In 1999, they had to write a letter, and who can be bothered to do that?

I'll tell you who – people being kept at Her Majesty's pleasure, or people who seemed to be housed temporarily in B&Bs

in coastal towns for some unfortunate reason. I have received 'fan mail' that contained all kinds of odd stuff, including sachets of coffee, pairs of tights and even some half-eaten chocolates (not all with the same letter; that would be a mega fan). I didn't let the sachets of coffee go to my head. I did once receive an envelope containing some human excrement; sadly, I was out of my office at the time and my PA opened it, for which I am still truly sorry. It turned out Fiona Bruce, Huw Edwards and Jeremy Paxman had also received a 'gift' from the same person, so I was in very good company. I am assuming the sender didn't like us very much.

By the time social media was a 'thing' – I joined Twitter in 2010 – I was ready for the unkind messages that would appear from time to time. At the beginning of the internet, I once typed my name into the search bar (or 'Pandora's Box' as it should be known). I don't know what I was expecting to appear, but I wasn't ready for the physical descriptions of me that popped up: 'Yorath has hair like a lion and hands even more manly than Madonna's'; 'She'd be an expensive date, her nose is so big she would hoover up a lot of cocaine.' I didn't take cocaine, but that wasn't the point. I don't know where exactly I had landed in the wild west that is the world-wide web, but I was fairly stunned by what I saw.

I quickly shut the 'Pandora's box', went to the mirror and studied my face and my hair. I was twenty-four years old at the time. All I could see now were the flaws they'd described – a big nose, large hands, and frizzy, unruly hair – I couldn't see any of my positives. Was this how other people were seeing me? It was fairly devastating for my self-esteem. I preferred living in my head to this online universe of hate.

This was only the start, of course.

Social media is a minefield. For every man tweeting they'd

like to suck your toes, there are another four telling you that you are an idiot woman who needs to get back in the kitchen. Then there's one wondering where you got your dress from, as he would like to buy one for his wife, and another asking: 'What did you think of Newcastle United's left back at the weekend?'

If you ask someone a tough question in an interview, half the audience will think you are too harsh and the other half won't think you have gone far enough – and all of them will tell you very quickly, because all they have to do is tweet. They can just press 'send' and move on to their next target.

There was a time when I tried to engage and explain myself, but it's like trying to tango with an octopus; there is no point, and it looks awful, because what you must remember is that all your followers can see the unedifying exchanges. As my colleague Michael Johnson (the former world record-holder and winner of multiple Olympic gold medals) once said to me, 'Why are you replying to that guy? He has six followers, and you've just let your 400,000 followers see you fighting with him.'

Maybe Michael Johnson was born wise, but I wasn't, and it took one fairly huge episode on social media – with a massive fallout – for me to learn a really big life lesson.

It was a lovely early spring evening, and I was going for a facial in Chelsea. As I waited for the therapist to begin my appointment, I began scrolling through Twitter. At the time, there were a load of injunctions being slapped on tabloid newspapers, as very famous and wealthy people were trying to keep bad news out of the press. There was a rumour swirling about an ex-footballer trying to keep a story hidden, so of course people were speculating about who the ex-footballer was, and what he was trying to hide.

A message popped up on my timeline: 'I hear this

injunction concerns @gabbylogan who is having an affair with Alan Shearer.'

I laughed when I read it. Then I got angry. Then I panicked. I had a few minutes before my appointment, so I replied to the message in a hurry: 'I think you should be careful what you write on here. The publishing laws apply [sic] and you are guilty of defamation of character with that.'

I had obviously prodded the bear. The tweeter quickly replied: 'So @gabbylogan, are you saying that you haven't been having an affair with Alan Shearer?'

'No, of course not,' I replied, then went in for my facial.

I spent two hours blissed out on the therapist's bed, having my face massaged and unaware of the storm of nonsense I had just stirred up.

I didn't check my phone when I got out, because in 2011 people didn't do that all the time. I just got in the car and drove home. Later that evening, I saw the messages had received a lot more retweets and likes than usual, and that I had missed a few phone calls from unknown numbers.

The following morning, I was walking the kids to school, and I noticed a paparazzi jumping out of the bush every few hundred metres, then running on and hiding in another bush.

Why was my school run suddenly interesting? I was not regular tabloid fodder.

On the Sunday morning, I was called early by my agent and told to go and buy the *News of the World*.

The headline 'TV's Gabby Logan denies affair with Alan Shearer' ran across the top of pages four and five. Underneath ran a story of absolute nothingness, pictures of Kenny and I walking the kids to school, and an article about me being at the World Cup in 2010 with Alan Shearer. Which was not really correct; although we had both been at the 2010 World Cup for the BBC, I was nowhere near him, as the studio team, which Alan was on, were based in Cape Town, while I was based in Rustenberg with the England football team.

Kenny and I knew that there was not a grain of truth pertaining to anything this article suggested, but that didn't stop the gossiping. People Kenny had known for years rang him to 'lend support'. A few days after the article appeared, I was sitting in the kids' playroom with one of my best friends and her daughter. At around 6pm, the doorbell rang. I thought it was the dry cleaning, which usually arrived at that time. Reuben was six years old and more than capable of answering the door, so he ran off to get it. I expected to see him back in a few minutes with an armful of clothes, but after a few minutes had passed and he hadn't returned, I got up and walked into my hallway, expecting to see Reuben chatting to the dry-cleaning man outside. Instead, there was a young woman inside my house. She had dark shoulder-length hair and was wearing an ill-fitting suit. In her hand was a reporter's notepad.

'Hello?' I said, confused.

'Hello, Gabby. I'm from the *Daily Mail*, and I wanted to get your side of the Alan Shearer story. Surely you'd like to set the record straight on the affair.'

'Get out of my house, now.' I was surprised by how calm I was, but with three small children ambling about, I didn't want to lose the plot.

She didn't move, and I ended up escorting her to the door and then the gate.

That night when I had calmed down, I wondered what had made a young woman in her mid-twenties want to engage in a form of journalism that involved using a six-year-old boy to enter someone's home and accuse them of having an affair with a colleague. It seemed a strange way to exhibit your talents.

After a few days of back-and-forth conversations between agents and lawyers, the deputy editor ended up writing me an apology, but only after the journalist had tried to develop a defence that inferred I was a bad mother for allowing my 'toddler' to answer the door. She was worried for his safety, she claimed, which is why she had come into the house. The 'toddler' in question was actually a ginormous six-year-old, who most people assumed was about nine, and he had never been more than six metres away from me at any time during the incident.

But remember, this all came down to my insistence on replying to a goading tweet. If I hadn't replied to the tweet asking me about having an affair, then there would have been no headline. I realise now I was baited into it.

I have always been a little bit too proud for my own good. If someone wrote something cruel about me in a newspaper, I bit my lip and pretended it didn't hurt. Comments like 'horrible dress', 'dumb blonde' and 'she looks like a dentist's receptionist' would always sting, but I didn't want to give the perpetrator the satisfaction of seeing me upset. What hurt most was the fact that my peers, family and friends might read those comments and actually agree. You cannot please all the people all the time, and never has that been more apparent to me than when I took part in *Strictly Come Dancing*. It was 2007, and the internet was really taking off. A lot of people didn't have social media yet, but there were chat rooms and forums where *Strictly* fans loved to share their thoughts.

I loved learning to dance and applied myself in the usual 'Gabby' way, sure that simple hard work and determination would see me through. I'd go as far as my talent and tenacity would let me; I wanted to soak it all up. Wrong approach, Gabs. The viewers were not liking me.

'There's something I just don't like about her,' wrote one chat room user.

'Yeah, she's just too competitive,' another agreed.

Folks, let's be clear: I wasn't saying things like 'I want to beat Alesha Dixon to a pulp after her tango today,' or 'I am going to put grease on Kelly Brook's ballroom shoes before her foxtrot.' I was just training hard, and then perhaps looking a bit too disappointed if I got a low score. Essentially, I think I was showing all the signs of being a 'sportswoman', which until 2012 was a dirty word (2012 being the year of the London Olympics, when we finally woke up to the possibility in this country of women being respected for being good at sport, and saw major broadcasters making a commitment to broadcast more women's sport).

Kenny appeared on the same series of *Strictly* as me, and he was smashing it when it came to the public vote. People loved him; he was showing all the signs of being a 'sportsman' which was perfectly fine for him as he was a bloke and apparently being competitive and training hard was OK if you had a penis. Perhaps I should have been a bit more hapless or humble; displayed more of a 'thanks for giving me this opportunity' kind of demeanour, more what the audience at the time probably expected from a woman. James Jordan, my dance partner, talked to me about 'playing the game', but I was insistent that wasn't for me, even though I didn't really know what it meant. 'Be yourself,' people say. Well I was, perhaps, being 'too much' of myself.

This period was one of the best of my professional life, and simultaneously one of the most frustrating and sad. I adored every second of my time on the show; it is a total honour to get to dance with these otherworldly beings. It was also a little strange, as a married woman, to meet your dance partner at 10am, and by 10.30am find yourself crotch to crotch, practising a 'hold'. I get why 'things' happen and that people talk about the *Strictly* curse. But I don't think the show itself can be blamed for that. If you are happy in your relationship, you'll be fine; if there are some cracks, then the show might expose them. And if you're single, well go on and fill your boots with some of the fittest humans on the planet.

But the experience had made me examine who I was. I realised that the traits that had served me quite well so far in my sporting and professional life didn't necessarily translate to winning votes on a reality show. Which didn't matter per se, but it affected me more than I wanted it to.

'People really don't like me,' I cried into the sofa the day after I was knocked out. I had finished in the top half of the leader board for my samba, according to the judges, but came rock bottom with the public, before being ousted in the dance-off.

Not being liked is fairly tough to process. Maybe I needed to change myself? Surely, at thirty-four years old, I wasn't beyond a bit of 'personality tweaking'? Maybe I needed to be less competitive, to be more nurturing, to get more emotional when things go wrong, and to stop battling through the tough times.

My head was a mess. Did society need to catch up with powerful women and accept them in the way it did men, or did I need to change to fit in with the society I was working in? It was probably a bit of both.

To become the first woman to host a live football match on TV, I guess had to have the guts and determination to battle my way through a man's world, ignoring some of the gender-based criticism levelled at me, while at the same time trying to retain the essence of what made me a woman.

Who'd have predicted that a reality dancing show on TV would throw all of that up in the air for me?

21

When It All Goes a
Bit Pete Tong

There will always be people, in every area of life, who, no matter what you do or say, just don't want to be on your team. And that is OK.

Mark Sharman had been one of my bosses at Sky. When I left the station to go to ITV, I didn't think I'd ever see him again. Executives from Sky don't tend to leave and go to public service broadcasting or terrestrial TV. Mark and I had got on OK at Sky; he was the one who gave me the ice hockey job to stop me badgering him about my goal of becoming a football presenter. I always sensed that he felt I was OK at reading autocue, but didn't really want me to do anything with more responsibility. In hindsight, maybe employing me in the first place had been more about perception; it was 'good' to be seen to have women on the presenting rota.

In the autumn of 2004, my boss at ITV, Brian Barwick, was offered the role of Chief Executive of the FA. He had been an enormous support, a great boss and someone I called a friend. I was very sad to see him go.

He'd also just agreed a very big contract for me, which I had signed just a few months before. Financially, it was worth more than I have ever earned, before or since, and it gave me an incredible portfolio of sport at ITV. I was also newly pregnant with twins; we'd gone through IVF, and I didn't want to announce anything before the twelve-week scan, so barely anyone knew I was with 'children'. I was around ten weeks pregnant when ITV announced that Barwick's successor was to be Mark Sharman.

I had a very strong gut feeling that the 'old-school' producer Sharman would not be an enormous fan of a pregnant sports presenter hosting the Champions League Final to over twelve million people on his channel. Let alone one who was carrying two babies. I would be twenty-eight weeks pregnant at the time of that season's final in Istanbul. It turns out that a woman twenty-eight weeks pregnant with twins is almost exactly the size of Luxembourg.

I was irrationally petrified of what Sharman's reaction would be; I even rehearsed how our first meeting might go, with my mum playing the role of Sharman. Kenny, Mum and I had nipped off for a mid-season break to Barbados. Kenny had a few days off Wasps training and he was no longer playing for Scotland, so we took my mum with us so that I could have a full week there and Kenny had someone to enjoy a glass of wine with for the few nights of his stay.

As we bobbed about in the Caribbean sea one afternoon, me fretting about telling my boss I was pregnant, Mum suggested we did a role play. Mum was a great believer in manifestation and had probably just read *The Secret*. I reluctantly joined in.

'Mark, how are you?' I said.

'I am great! So excited about working with you again, Gabby, after all these years,' Mum said, pretending to be Sharman.

'He definitely won't say that!' I protested.

'Just go along with it.'

'I was really pleased when I heard you had got the job,' I said, back in character. 'I have some big news of my own. I'm pregnant.'

'That's fantastic news,' Mum replied.

'With twins!' I added.

'Well, how amazing. Well done you. When are you due?'

'Next August, so don't worry. I'll be fine for the Champions League season.'

'Well, you must take care of yourself, but I am delighted that you will be able to lead the season's coverage for me.'

Then out of character and back being Christine, Mum said, 'It'll be fine; he can use you as an asset. How brilliant to have a pregnant female sports presenter!'

I didn't share her optimism.

Two weeks later, I was waiting for the real Mark Sharman in a favourite restaurant in Chiswick called Annie's.

'I won't shake your hand, as I have a cold,' he said as he walked in, rubbing his face with his hand just to be sure we wouldn't touch. He sniffed into a tissue. His eyes were red and watery; it was a horrible, filthy, wet cold and he probably shouldn't have been out of bed.

I told him my news straight away.

'I knew you were going to say that,' he said, with not one trace of emotion.

The rest of the conversation is a blur. It can't have lasted more than fifteen minutes. He drank a glass of water and went on his way.

You know when someone is never ever pleased to see you?

Well, that's how the next two years were for me working under Mark Sharman at ITV. Granted, he wasn't an effusive type of guy, he'd never been one to waste smiles, but whenever I was in his vicinity, he looked like he'd just rather be anywhere else.

I don't think his plan to replace me with Steve Ryder, which he ultimately achieved, was a sexist one; sometimes you have to accept that someone just doesn't rate you. But getting to that point of acceptance is a tough old journey of introspection, and to emerge with any self-esteem intact is an even greater challenge.

Add to that the fact Sharman seemed to love telling me fairly regularly how beautiful my great friend Kirsty Gallacher was. She was working as a presenter at Sky Sports at the time. 'She's like a movie star,' he'd say, with little cartoon love hearts falling from his eyes. It was a very strange thing for him to do, and it was as if he said it to further undermine my already dwindling confidence. 'And you're almost thirty years older than her, so pipe down Grandad,' I wish I had said, but never did.

Indeed, Kirsty was and is a great beauty; any fool could see that. But I wondered did Mark follow the same train of thought in a conversation about work matters with Jim Rosenthal? Maybe he mentioned to him how sculpted Gary Lineker's thighs were?

I ploughed on. After heaving my huge, baby-filled belly around European capitals for five months, I eventually presented the final in Istanbul, then gave birth a few weeks later. Forty-two days later – and, I imagine, much to Mark's annoyance – I was back in the hot seat, ready for the start of the following Champions League season. I was determined that I could have babies, do my job well and win him over. Well, I managed the first one.

The following season was a fairly painful experience pro-
fessionally. Compared to the open dialogue and discussions
I had enjoyed with Brian Barwick, I was being ignored by
Mark Sharman.

Then little stories started appearing in some of the
industry-related gossip columns in national newspapers, none
of them very flattering or favourable towards me. There were
lots of apparent 'insider' quotes. One article reviewing ITV's
coverage of the Champions League Final in Paris that season
described my white fitted Calvin Klein jacket as looking like
that of 'a nurse', and noted that my eye make-up was 'too
vampish'. It was very odd; they'd never spent much time
dissecting my appearance before, but now it seemed to be
open season on me. I admit I cried at that one. I loved that
jacket. I've still got it.

On the morning I was due to host the Oxford and
Cambridge Boat Race, a story appeared saying I was being
dropped from England matches at the upcoming World Cup
in Germany. I was learning of my career's demise through the
tabloid papers. The source was obviously good, because I was
indeed dropped. Instead of the high-profile England games I
was due to be working on, I spent the World Cup on a joyful
'tour bus' hosting 'other' fixtures. Along with Ally McCoist,
Ruud Gullit and Andy Townsend, I travelled from Berlin to
Wiesbaden and then to Düsseldorf, presenting the 'B' games.
Then, after the group stages finished, I was expecting to get
my schedule for the knock-out matches, but I was told to
go home and not bother coming back. Steve Ryder and Jim
Rosenthal would be taking over my games. We had a massive night of beer, sweaty dancing and playing air guitar in a
basement nightclub in Düsseldorf, and that turned out to be
an early leaving do.

A few days later, when I was back home in west London,

the commentator and former Spurs boss David Pleat called me out of the blue.

'Hi, Gabby. I am so sorry to hear you're leaving ITV,' he said, with what sounded like genuine concern.

I was pacing up and down the garden of our rental house in Barnes, listening to David, a very kind, old-fashioned football man effectively deliver my P45. David had heard I was leaving when he was sitting in the bar with ITV colleagues in Germany. He had no idea that he was the first to tell me. I didn't want to make him feel uncomfortable, so I acted as if I already knew.

I was, however, reeling. I really didn't see how I could go on in the industry. I felt humiliated and shamed. *I'm thirty-four; I could just do something else. It's not too late to change careers,* I told myself.

'I'll buy and sell flats and do them up,' I told Kenny over dinner. We'd had a modicum of success in the property game, but I was no expert like my mum. 'I can go back to law school and do my conversion course. I'll become a shit-hot lawyer.'

I was angry. No, I was livid. I didn't want to do a job where my career hung so precariously in the balance of subjectivity, on the whim of someone else's opinion.

I'd had a good run, but I wasn't sure I could take much more of this nonsense. Unbeknown to me at the time, my phone was also being hacked by two national newspapers. There was a perfect storm of leaked stories and stolen ones, which were driving me a little bit potty. Later, I would be compensated by both newspapers, but I look back at that time and I am amazed that our marriage – and our sanity – survived.

'Sleep on it,' said Kenny.

'Sleep on it,' said my agent.

*

My plan to become the next Kevin McCloud was put on hold – and, as Kenny pointed out, becoming a 'shit-hot barrister' might take me ten years, and he wasn't sure I would like the long hours with two small babies.

Perhaps smelling a whiff of dissatisfaction (and maybe the potential for headline-grabbing gossip) the BBC had asked me to join the line-up for that season's *Strictly Come Dancing* (this was 2006, the year before I actually ended up joining the show). This invite was the tonic I needed. I could learn to dance, have fun, let my hair down and subtly reinvent myself – as what? Well, I had no idea, but it seemed like a fun thing to do.

I was still under contract with ITV until December, but I had been demoted from Champions League matches to the Europa League, and my schedule was more than capable of absorbing some *Strictly* rehearsals.

The day before I was due to take part in the official photography session for the show, Jon Holmes phoned me. 'Gabby, I have disappointing news. ITV say you can't do *Strictly*.'

'That's ridiculous. They've practically sacked me, and I have no other work on. What am I supposed to do?'

'*Dancing on Ice*, they said,' replied Jon.

'I don't want to dance on ice, Jon. I want to dance in the ballroom.' Even then, I remember thinking I sounded ridiculous.

I was just hours away from the sequins, within touching distance of the fake-tan booth. But ITV won, and I had to pull out.

Excellent, fine. More time to spend with my lovely babies. I was getting very good at finding the silver linings in my clouds.

And then Jon called me with some *good* news.

Nial Sloane, the boss of BBC Sport, had been in touch.

The BBC were launching a new show, which would be like *Newsnight* but for sport. They wanted to put some top journalists on it and have studio debates, as well as long-form interviews, which they always struggled to find time for in their other sports programming. The show would be broadcast live on Mondays on BBC One, straight after the main evening news, and they were interested in me hosting.

Before any contractual terms were discussed, they wanted me to take a screen test at TV Centre in Shepherds Bush – the same TV centre I had wandered into as a fifteen-year-old gymnast all those years before. It might even have been in the same studio where we'd recorded *Blue Peter*. The screen test was set up like a practice show; they had some stand-in guests and they were able to meet me, decide whether I was an ogre or not and take a look at me on camera. Thankfully, they weren't repulsed.

I would start the show in January 2007, and also host the FA Cup and other football programmes like *Match of the Day* occasionally. I would also be part of the team that went to Beijing to cover the 2008 Olympics. The Olympic dream was back on.

On the flipside I would also be taking a massive salary cut; I was to be paid about a third of what I had earned at ITV. Which is ironic, as when the story broke that I was going to the BBC, I received many texts from well-wishers who assumed I had essentially won the lottery. Despite the reduction in salary, I felt like I had won the lottery, because I was being given a second chance.

I wasn't so sad to leave Mark Sharman, but I was gutted to be leaving ITV. I had made some wonderful friends and worked with colleagues who had taught me so much and seen me through some tricky times: Nicky Moody, Rick Walmsley, Dickie Day, David Moss, Jamie Oakford, Gabriel

Clarke, Steve Tudgay, and John McKenna, to name a few. I've been lucky enough to cross paths with quite a few of them again while working for Prime Video during the last few football seasons (which is an excellent lesson in leaving on good terms). I had travelled the world and worked on some of the biggest sporting events on the planet. More importantly, I had met my husband and had my babies in my time there, and now I was stepping into the unknown.

The last year at ITV had been by far the most difficult and uncomfortable in my professional life, on top of which I was juggling young babies and the ever-emotional struggle of being a working mum. Add to that everything that was going on with my dad, and I think it's fair to say it was a 'character-building' phase of my life.

I now realise that Mark Sharman wasn't the enemy; he was actually my saviour. I had to leave the safety of ITV in order to grow and become better professionally and personally; I needed to feel uncomfortable in order to stretch myself. In life, there will always be a Sharman, someone we think is the problem, but it's a problem we will never solve if we keep looking to them for the answer. I hold no animosity towards him whatsoever.

You'll never please all of the people all of the time. Success is pleasing some of them most of the time.

25

Babies

You never see or hear a baby until you desperately want one – and then they are everywhere, and everyone is having them.

I was enjoying some tapas the night Will Young won *Pop Idol* in 2002. I appreciate you might not recall what you had for dinner that evening. Sitting in a tiny Spanish restaurant in Clapham, I voted for Will, which wasn't easy – his rival, Gareth Gates, comes from Yorkshire, so I should have been in his camp. After voting on my phone, I turned to my dining companions, Viva, Kerry and Mel, three of my closest girlfriends, and casually uttered: 'I'm going to stop using contraception.'

'What?!' exclaimed one with horror.

'You're only twenty-eight!' said another. 'You only got married a few months ago.'

It was clear that this was not a popular decision. Had I accidentally misspoken and said: 'I'm going to start using heroin'?

'I don't know how long it will take, and I don't want to be too old,' I said, in my defence.

'What about your career?' Kerry asked.

'What about it?' I replied.

And that was that.

We some drank more wine, and they forgot all about babies.

Because they didn't want one then.

Around a year later, I was staying with Kenny in Scotland while he was training with the national team ahead of the Six Nations. As he went off to Murrayfield to smash himself into men with cauliflower ears and thighs the size of wheelbarrows, I wandered into Edinburgh for a mooch. I found myself in Waterstones, in the wellbeing section, picking up a book about conception and pregnancy. When I stopped using contraception, I didn't start doing anything else. I just assumed, as we were young and healthy, that it would happen. But according to page ninety-eight of this book I was now reading with vigour, hunched in the corner of the store, hoping nobody I knew would see me, it appeared there was much more needed than just sex. Was I ovulating? I didn't know. Had I not peed on a stick? No. Was I taking folic acid? No. Did I travel a lot? Yes. Drink alcohol? Yes, sometimes. Did I fly a lot? Yes. Did I work hard and in a stressful environment? Yes. Oh dear. Apparently the only thing I had going for me was I was under thirty and I didn't smoke – and I would be thirty in a few months' time.

Soon, I was getting stressed about not getting pregnant – and page ninety-eight had already warned me that stress doesn't help. Silly me. But then another period arrived, and then another. How stressful. Every period was taking me further and further away from being a mum. Why did they keep on coming? I went to a wedding, and as we watched the happy couple emerge into the sunlight after the ceremony, the mother of the bride told me, 'You're a career girl, so I don't suppose you'll be having a family,' gesturing towards her adorable six-month-old granddaughter, who was cradled in the arms of her now-married daughter. I was crushed. I felt like screaming, 'I am trying really hard, you know!'

But I smiled and threw confetti instead. People had decided I wanted a career, not a baby. I wanted both, duh.

Before he proposed to me (at the top of the Wallace Monument in Stirling), Kenny went to see a urologist to check out his semen. Most men go to Tiffany's. After a lifetime of being kicked in the balls, he'd occasionally noticed blood in his semen. He had asked various club doctors about this, and they'd all assured him it was fine and shouldn't affect anything, but he wanted to be sure his sperm were still capable of making a baby. He didn't tell me, so I had no idea he was off ejaculating into a jar in Slough one afternoon and then popping back a week later to get the results.

'I didn't want to ask you to marry me and then find out I was sterile,' he explained later.

As he sat down to get his results, the doctor opened his file, a look of worry appearing on his face, his eyes darting all over the data as if in disbelief.

'I am terribly sorry,' he said, not even looking up at Kenny. 'Your sperm count is unfeasibly low, and the motility of the sperm you do have is almost unmeasurable; these are awful results.'

Kenny was devastated, almost brought to tears. He was trembling with shock.

All those studs in the testicles might have rendered him infertile after all.

'Oh, hang on ... are you Mr Milson?' the doctor said.

'No. Kenny Logan.'

'Ahhhh ... no, sorry ... oh dear. That was the wrong file.

You are absolutely fine, Mr Logan. Yes . . . let me see . . . very healthy sperm. All is good here. No problems at all.'

Kenny didn't tell me about this exchange with the hapless doctor until I had a ring on my finger a few months later. We both said a prayer for Mr Milson (not his real name) and hoped he was sixty-five years old and trying his luck with a third wife.

Kenny's sperm was fine, so I had to assume, two years after we had started trying to get pregnant, that I was the one stopping us becoming parents.

We tried so many things. We went through all the usual steps, going from our local GP to a specialist gynaecologist to a consultant. We even got ourselves a boxer puppy (Sydney, who you met earlier when she was being walked by my dad). She was an incredible addition to our lives, but couldn't directly make me pregnant. Apparently, having a puppy helps conception because it brings out the caring hormones and makes the woman more likely to stay pregnant. We had tests and investigations, and I had dye squirted in my tubes, only to be told after a few months: 'Well, you are in the twenty per cent of infertile people who have no explanation for their infertility. There's nothing to operate on, fix or change. Just keep trying.'

I had kind of known in my heart that this would be the outcome, as I had never once had any problems with periods or my menstrual cycle. I'd just paid a few thousand pounds for these tests, though, so I had hoped for more than 'just keep trying'.

As a proactive person, I wanted to have a plan: something that would change our circumstances. I finally got the consultant to admit that we might eventually need 'intervention'. Well, why were we waiting? All that was happening was my eggs were getting older. I wanted to get help now.

After the normal conversations and weighing up of issues, we eventually started IVF. The weeks of hormone injections were done in secret; I carried on travelling for work and exercising and trying to be as discreet about it as possible. I stayed at my mum's house one night and left them out in the cold on the window ledge, as I didn't want to alert her by using the fridge. If we were going to need five rounds of IVF, I didn't want it to be all people ever talked to us about. Kenny and I used our sporting backgrounds to good effect; we'd eat our best, be as fit as we could, and come the day of the competition (the embryo creation day), he'd give it his best shot! If we failed, we'd go again. Kenny was playing rugby in Glasgow – we had a lovely apartment there – so I was regularly flying up to see him, and he had to do emergency dashes home to London for appointments.

Everyone is different, and I know many women who hated the effect the hormones had on them, and even some whose relationships didn't last the test. But all I can tell you is I didn't feel too bad. I was a bit weepy at times, but that was probably the stress of the subterfuge as much as anything else. And the fact that my friends seemed to just pop kids out for fun. One of the three besties, Kerry, who had been shocked at my dropping contraception that night in the tapas restaurant had already had three kids by the time I started my IVF; the night we ate pil pil prawns in Clapham, she hadn't even met the father of her babies.

Eventually, we reached the Olympic final: better known as egg-collection day. The whole point of IVF is to create great eggs that are harvested and then fertilised in a dish or tube. After a few days, there will hopefully be a few that have turned into embryos, which are at first called blastocysts. Collecting the eggs is not painful, it's just quite nerve-wracking. We were scanned every few days in the build-up, which I thought of as being like the heats at the Olympics: we were hoping to make it through each test and get over each hurdle. It all looked good, so Kenny did his bit and the mix happened in the dish, somewhere in deepest Essex. After five days, we had seven good embryos to choose from. That part blows my mind when I look at my teenagers and imagine that if their embryo had been a bit slippery and tricky to handle, they might have been discarded. The body makes that natural selection in a normal pregnancy; here, we were reliant on human intervention to pick the embryos with the best chance of survival. We had already decided to put two embryos in my womb, as there was a very good chance neither would take. It was possible that my womb that was the problem, not the eggs. The other five embryos would be frozen for potential future use.

The embryos were implanted in mid-November 2004. Kenny had flown down from Glasgow late the night before, making an excuse to get out of training. A lovely man in Loughton with a long needle was responsible for making me pregnant while Heart FM played loudly in the background. It took all of two minutes; he was an expert.

When we got home later that day I felt a bit uncomfortable but wasn't sore. Kenny was fussing around me, making me sit down and relax when we got home, and then he had to dash off to Glasgow again. After a couple of hours, I decided I needed a shower, and wanted to get ready for bed. We were still living in the four-storey townhouse on the Thames, and our bedroom was on the top floor. As I got higher up the stairs, the smell of burning filled my nostrils. I went back to the kitchen and checked the oven. It was off. I set off up the stairs again, and realised the smell was coming from the top of the house. As I climbed, I was sure the air was becoming more acrid. I opened the bedroom door, and there was dark smoke and bits of blackened material falling from the ceiling. Then my eyes darted to a full-length mirror by my dressing table, which in the darkness appeared to have blood on it. There was black soot mixed in the with the blood. Was someone in the bathroom? My head was scrambled. Nobody could have got past me without me noticing, and Kenny had been up here just a few hours before; surely he'd have disturbed any intruder. Stupidly, as there was smoke, I turned on the lights. The 'blood' was in fact lipstick.

It was a message.

How sinister – the intruder had left a message. *Oh, god.* My heart was beating faster.

I walked closer to the mirror so I could read the message.

'Gabby, I love you so much and we are going to be great parents. Look after yourself and I will see you in a few days. Love Kenny xx.'

OK, so Kenny wrote a love letter on the mirror – lovely touch, but why did he set fire to the bedroom?

I nervously went into the bathroom. The fire had obviously started in there, as there was black soot everywhere. Bits of pink material were strewn all over the floor.

It didn't take this Hercule Poirot long to work it out.

Kenny had obviously turned on the radiator to warm my dressing gown. A sweet gesture, but the gown being a bit cheap and nasty had then caught fire. It turned out the radiator was faulty. We hadn't used it before, and the thermostat didn't have a top range – it just kept going up, getting hotter and hotter. Thank god the bathroom was fully tiled. The fire had burned itself out, as there was no other flammable material in there for it to catch hold of.

Disaster averted. I was so exhausted that I went to bed in a blackened room, my first sleep as a newly pregnant woman.

*

I carried on with the secrecy, because who shares a pregnancy after five days? I was for ever looking for signs my body was changing, but there was nothing apart from the lack of a period – which was, of course, the best 'nothing' of all.

Then, after eight weeks, came the all-important blood test. This would tell us if we were still pregnant. Kenny was training in Glasgow. I woke up at 4am on the morning of the test and went to the toilet. There was blood in my pyjama bottoms. Not a period exactly, but more than a few drops.

'We're not pregnant,' I sobbed down the phone to Kenny, waking him up in the middle of the night.

'We'll go again. We will get there,' he said.

I was advised to go for the test anyway, expecting the worst. The result would be phoned in the following day. I was doing a work shopping day with Charlotte Green, a stylist and one of my best friends, and we were in Prada on Regent Street when my phone rang. I saw the caller was Talha Shawaf, my obstetrician, so I went under the stairs for privacy.

'Congratulations,' he said.

I was pregnant.

(My daughter quite likes this bit of her birth story – that I found out in Prada. Of course, the irony is that once I had her, I couldn't afford to shop there any more.)

The pregnancy was strong, my numbers were high, the obstetrician said. I didn't realise he was trying to tell me that both embryos were probably still alive.

I just heard 'you're pregnant'.

Two weeks later we had a scan, and there they were: two beautiful beating hearts.

My pregnancy went like this: cinnamon swirls with the raisins taken out of them from Starbucks; food without sauce on it for four months; chronic headaches for five months; goat's milk with selected herbs heated up in the evening to help prepare the cervix for a natural birth (this became my replacement Sauvignon Blanc); acupuncture; exercise; a tar-like oil rubbed on my belly and breasts every night to prevent stretch marks; hundreds of new bras and then gallons of Gaviscon, until I realised it wasn't my boobs getting bigger or intolerable heartburn I was suffering from, but a displaced rib; dog-walking in Glasgow (where Sydney, our boxer, lived); and by six months, a bump so large a lorry driver one day stopped and asked if I need a lift to hospital as he thought I must already be in labour.

But, by god, I loved it all, even the terrible sleep and the pain from the displaced rib. (We've never worked out which baby kicked it, but my money is on Reuben.)

Having been through a fairly unnatural process to achieve pregnancy, I was desperate to give birth through the more natural route: to go into labour and pop them out the vagina. My obstetrician, a multiple-birth specialist, didn't laugh at me exactly, but he said, 'It is rarer to do that than have a C-birth for twins, that's for sure. You'd be one of a handful of women I have overseen give birth to twins vaginally, so let's do a deal. When you get to three or four centimetres' dilation, you have to agree to an epidural in case you need an emergency Caesarean. Deal?'

'OK. Deal.' You defer to the master in these situations.

My midwife, Jenny Smith, was on my side. 'We can do this,' she assured me, every step of the way.

We had a date set: 27 July.

'If you haven't gone into spontaneous labour by then, we'll induce you. That's thirty-eight weeks, and after that, twin mortality rate rises steeply.' The obstetrician gravely informed me.

On 20 July, we had our last meeting.

'You're so healthy and the babies are doing so well, I think you could wait another week,' said my obstetrician. 'We could push it back into August, get you closer to forty weeks?'

'No way.' I burst into tears. 'I can't fit in my car; I can't get up the stairs without taking a rest. You promised 27 July – and what happened to twin mortality?'

He didn't want to mess with me at that stage. 'OK, 27 July it is,' he agreed.

When you read baby books, you take in what you want to be true and don't really absorb the bad or sad bits. You'd never make it through the full nine months if you really computed all the things that could go wrong.

I hadn't read the bit about induction generally being unsuccessful first time; nor had I read that it is quite an aggressive way to head into labour. There's no slow build-up, just WHAM-OUCH-KAPOW-type contractions. I also entirely failed to absorb the chapter on twin pregnancy having potential for haemorrhaging.

Three hours after I was induced, there was nothing to report, not even a whimper. It was 11pm.

Kenny went home on the doctor's advice: 'We could be in for a long old haul here, go home and we'll see you tomorrow.'

I lay in bed, thinking this could be my last good sleep for a while, so I watched telly for a bit and tried to doze.

'Jesus Christ!' *What was that?*

Two minutes later, another one.

'Bloody hell!'

I did three hours like that on my own, having very regular contractions, and then, at 2am, I went to reception.

A tall midwife with a very stern expression glared over the top of her tiny glasses as I shuffled down the corridor in between my fairly violent contractions.

'I think I'm in labour,' I whispered.

'Yes, dear. It's why you came here.' She dropped the mic and turned to do some more filing.

I shuffled back. This was a tough school.

Time to ring the man who'd got me in this state. No, not the kind Heart FM fan in Loughton.

'Kenny, do you think you can come back? I'm in labour,' I asked kindly, as if he had the option of saying no.

Then, after another couple of hours of horrible labour with no pain relief, I rang my midwife Jenny, then the obstetrician. By 7am, we had got the whole squad together, and by 10am my mum and dad (who were now separated and heading for divorce) were on their way down the M1 from Leeds, along with my teenage brother Jordan.

How civilised of me, I thought. *These babies will be born by lunchtime, and then everyone can go to dinner together afterwards.*

Lunchtime came and went. Then dinnertime passed as well.

It was now 7.30pm, and I had been awake for thirty-six hours. I was four centimetres dilated, and had been given an epidural eight hours before. My contractions were so sparse, I could hardly tell when they were happening.

The obstetrician came in and gave me a stern look. 'We had a deal, Gabby, and there is a point at which these babies will start to become very stressed. They need to be born. You were induced twenty-four hours ago. We need to prepare for a Caesarean. I'll give you an hour or so to get your head round it and have some time alone, and then we need to go into theatre.' He knew I would be devastated, but he was right: we'd had a deal.

Sensing I needed headspace, Kenny went to the waiting room to watch TV, and everyone else left me alone. I lay on the bed and told myself this was the best outcome. The babies would come out with perfectly round heads, and I could have a nice intact vagina. Sure, I was sad; all that goat's milk I had boiled up every night that had made me smell like a sewer had been in vain, and I really had thought I was going to get to push them out on my own, by candlelight, listening to Sade.

After an hour, Jenny came in and asked to inspect me for the two-hundredth time that day.

Her face lit up. 'You're fully dilated, Gabby – ten centimetres at least. You're going to have to start pushing . . . you need to give birth.'

I'd gone from four to ten centimetres in an hour. The moment I'd released my expectations and stopped pressurising myself, it had happened.

What a lesson that was.

Soon, though, I was regretting my desire to be an earth mother.

The pain.

Let's not go right there; suffice to say, I remember thinking in the middle of one long 'push' that I would rather run a marathon than do this – and I am no long-distance runner.

Reuben was first out, coming into the world just after 11.30pm. He cried and looked suitably cone-headed, as any baby who had been engaged for months with a sister lying on top of him would. Kenny took a picture and ran to the waiting room to show the family.

One down, one to go.

I had hoped for a cup of tea and a slice of cake, at the very least a pat on the back. But there wasn't even a biscuit.

The overriding mood seemed to be: *Crack on, Gabby, let's keep this show on the road.* They'd all had a long day.

'You'd better keep pushing. This twin will need a separate birthday party if you don't deliver her in the next twenty minutes.'

Jesus, this is relentless, I thought.

Now the perceived wisdom was that Lois, who was breech,

would turn once she had space. That she'd kind of do a front somersault and swim out of the birth canal. But apparently she was getting stressed. *Try being me, love; I've just given birth and I have to do it again.* There wasn't time to wait for her to move into the orthodox head-first birthing position. The birth canal was open thanks to Reuben, so she'd have to come out breech.

Feet first.

I'd push in the normal way, and once her legs appeared, they'd guide her out carefully by her ankles and then her bottom.

She arrived that way just before midnight, for which I am always grateful when arranging their birthday parties every year. If she was a few minutes over midnight, I would probably have just lied to her and told her she was born the day before.

She had masses of dark hair and a perfect head, but took a few seconds to give us a cry. It must be a strange way to enter the world, after all.

The babies were wrapped in swaddling clothes and lain in a manger – well, it felt like that, but really it was a large, see-through washing-up bowl of a crib. Before Kenny had a chance to take another picture of Lois and run it outside to the waiting family, though, things took a turn for the worse.

The heparin that had been injected to help my distended womb contract wasn't working. I was losing blood.

Years later, Kenny tipped an open two-litre bottle of water on its side to show me just how fast the flow of blood was. Things went from serene to organised chaos in about three minutes. The 'crash' button was pressed and the noise in the room grew.

'Keep your eyes open, Gabby.'

'Keep looking at the babies.'

'Her skin's gone white.'

Kenny put some blue scrubs on.

The babies were silent and sleepy.

'She's closing her eyes.'

'Am I going to die?' I asked.

I am fairly sure my obstetrician said no.

'Get the oxygen mask on her.'

'No, that's uncomfortable,' I moaned, resisting.

'You need it.'

'You're going into theatre. We need to do a transfusion.'

'The babies?' I asked.

'They're fine here, they're doing well.'

'Are we going to weigh them?'

'Later,' someone replied.

The bed started to move away from my new babies. I had only known them a few minutes. The wheels of my bed had blood on them. As we sped down the corridor, we went past the waiting room where my family had sat patiently for ten hours.

My mum got up and followed the trail of blood from the wheels back to the room where I had given birth. Inside, she found the babies.

'There was nobody there apart from a nurse sweeping blood, so I stood with them,' she told me the next day.

In theatre, new people were joining my team.

'I'm Bill, I'm the porter. I'm going to move you on to a different bed.'

'I'm Sally the theatre nurse. Just open your mouth so I can insert this tube.'

It's too bright in here. I want to close my eyes.

'Don't,' said Sally.

My legs were lifted up and there appeared to be about three new people looking intently at my vagina. I'd stopped feeling

self-conscious about all the vagina peering a long time before.
They stuffed me with cotton wool to stop the flow, which
seemed very basic, but it helped.

Lots of hooks and needles were now in my arm and hand.
I saw the blood, the life-giving red liquid, previously belonging to some kind person who had walked into a blood bank
one day and given a pint of blood. In total, I had five pints of
kind people's blood pumped into me; the average adult has
ten pints of blood in their body.

The effect was almost immediate. I became more alert, and
apparently the colour was coming back to my face.

I felt like I was back in the room, not hovering above it.

The constant stream of information was brilliantly executed.

'I am replacing your cannula.'

'I'm just giving you some more oxygen.'

I'm sure it is intended to keep the patient awake
and involved.

Kenny, still dressed in his blue scrubs, was kneeling down,
stroking my head.

The obstetrician took a large needle and threaded it.

'Now it's time for your designer vagina,' Kenny whispered
into my ear in a mock-Australian accent.

I laughed hard. It hurt. My stomach felt like I had
been punched.

It was almost 2am when we emerged from theatre. By now,
I had been awake for forty-four hours.

I was taken to a ward and the curtain was pulled round me.
My mum and dad and brother appeared.

'Here, love.' My mum handed me some foil-wrapped
cheese sandwiches made with Marks and Spencer honey
seeded bread.

Nothing had ever tasted so good.

'You need to feed the babies,' a nurse said.

'I can't.' I just didn't have the energy.

'She's knackered!' my mum said. My mum had had four babies, all naturally and three of them at home, but she wasn't a breastfeeder.

'Try,' the nurse insisted.

It was 2.30am and I was being pumped full of drugs and peeing into a catheter. I wasn't in the mood to argue, but I didn't even have the energy to sit up, let alone pop a breast or two out.

'What are the babies' names?' another nurse asked.

'Reuben—' Kenny started to answer.

'Can this wait? I really want to have a think and sleep on the names. Please?'

'OK,' the nurse said, and wrote 'Twin A' and 'Twin B' on a whiteboard. Then she put little plastic bands on their wrists, with their birth date and weights, and the names Twin A and Twin B.

It was agreed that as I had been through a traumatic birth, the babies would sleep in the nursery and be fed from a bottle.

I would try to get a good sleep, and we would begin the process of being a mum – a more enthusiastic, breastfeeding mum – tomorrow.

I woke up in a private room about seven hours later.

I went to reach for my watch to see the time, but I was totally unable to move. I couldn't lift my arm. I panicked. I felt paralysed. I moved my toes and tried to bend my legs at the knee, but I couldn't. I attempted to call for help, but my voice was not penetrating the thick walls and steel doors.

After twenty minutes, I managed to lift my arm out of the bed and towards the emergency cord. But it wouldn't reach. I finally garnered enough strength to nudge my phone, which moved it within touching distance. If my nails had been any shorter, I wouldn't have been able to reach.

I pulled the phone on to me and dialled Kenny.

'Hi, it's me. Can you call Queen Charlotte's and ask them to come and see me?' I said.

'What?' Kenny thought I was on drugs. 'But you're *there*!'

'I know, but I can't get anyone's attention.'

Ten minutes later, a couple of midwives came in. They sat me up in bed and opened the curtains. It was 11.30am. I had slept for seven hours, which is possibly a new post-partum world record.

The babies were wheeled in from the nursery, and I was shown how to breastfeed. I hadn't even had proper cuddles with them yet. I hadn't changed a nappy.

Thankfully, my body started to come back to life and my mobility returned. I got out of bed, ever so carefully, wheeling my catheter to the bathroom. I looked in the mirror. My legs were grossly swollen, and I was covered in blood from the birth.

I looked like an extra from a Quentin Tarantino movie.

But I genuinely didn't give a shit.

I placed the babies on the bed and stared at them in awe: two marvellous creations, perfect little people who were totally and utterly reliant on us.

So I cried my eyes out.

I really didn't want to muck this up.

26

Being Wrong

Any sportsperson will tell you that the best time to learn is when things are going wrong. A bad game is a lesson. The sooner you learn that, the quicker you get better. I'm not great at admitting I am wrong. But when you have kids, it's important they hear you apologise – as Kenny tells me regularly.

The thing about being a parent is that you get stuff wrong every single day. The main aim is to not get the really big stuff wrong, the life and death stuff. I do believe that if you admit to your kids that you're wrong too often, they will lose faith in you. You have a small window of about eight to ten years when they think you are a magical genius capable of anything, but even in those wonder years occasionally you need to say, 'I don't know the answer to that question. Shall we find out together?'

I know it's hard, because for most of us, it is not until we have children that we meet people who think we are the most incredible thing on the planet.

We had an inauspicious start to parenting. We left the hospital around lunchtime, one week after we had arrived. I wasn't intending to stay that long, but the cheese and ham omelettes were great. No, in truth, I got a bad infection and wasn't well enough to be discharged. The infection had given me elephant-sized legs that had to be encased in pressure tights, but I didn't care about that, because I was madly in love with these two tiny babies.

By the time I had to say goodbye to the unbelievably brilliant midwives, nurses and doctors who had looked after me so well, I was properly institutionalised. I'd already made a sizeable donation to my midwife's charity; I would have given her my house if she'd asked. I was so scared of leaving this safe haven that the night before my departure, I practised walking down the hospital staircase and leaving the front door. Only I cried all the way and hung on to the banister so tightly that I didn't actually make it to the door.

Poor Kenny looked petrified, as if he'd come to collect a patient from an asylum, not his wife and new babies. I asked him to bring some bright yellow, high-heeled Prada shoes and a cool top for my 'leaving outfit'. I'd seen Victoria Beckham and her kind leaving the Portland with their babies, and I wanted a piece of that glamour. Babies weren't going to change me, no siree.

I squeezed my swollen pink feet into the shoes and walked all of two steps before I took them off in pain and popped on my trainers. Not fashionable designer trainers, but the ugly, practical running pair that I had arrived in seven days before. How had this happened? Was the old me gone for good? I sat down and cried again.

We put the car seats into the back of the car and slowly pulled away. After 100 metres travelling at twenty miles per hour, we realised we hadn't actually put the seat belts on them, so the car seats were just free to rock and roll. Any sudden braking movement, and they'd have been in the front with me. We pulled up and tried again, exchanging a look between us that I read as: *Jesus Christ! We're pretty shit at this, aren't we?!*

One thing I had done before having children, and which I recommend to anyone considering reproducing, was a lot of therapy. You might not need as much as I did.

Thanks to the combined efforts of acupuncturist Wendy Mandy, whom I had found in my early twenties, Ed Percival and his neurolinguistic processing at Sky Sports, and a brilliant physio I had met through Kenny called Kevin Lidlow, I was able to process a lot of what had happened to me as a kid, from the Bradford fire through to Daniel dying, and then the unravelling of my parents' marriage and the changing shape of our family.

How it manifested itself physically and emotionally, and how I could deal with some of the sadness and disappointment was a great learning curve. I grouped the three wizards together, with their partners and kids, at our wedding and called their table the 'Gurus'.

Asking for help was not weakness; it was the route to strength. This was something I had seen again and again in my sporting life. So it made sense to me that I should seek support from a coach in my efforts to get better and avoid repeating some of the patterns and mistakes from my family's past. Having a better understanding of my family and the decisions they'd made put me in quite a healthy position from which to start my own.

Kenny had a very clear philosophy about how important it was for us to be a couple as well as parents. 'These babies are only here because we love each other. If we don't look after that, then we are not going to be giving them the life that we want to.'

I remember him telling me how, when he was a boy, he'd cycle to the garage and buy flowers for his mum's birthday or special occasions; but he didn't give them to her himself. He'd give them to his dad to present to her, because he knew his dad would forget otherwise. He was so desperate for his parents to show romance to each other that he engineered it.

Retaining the romance and being a proper couple was easier said than done for me; my priority had undeniably shifted overnight. If the babies fell asleep and there was another adult in the house, a cleaner or a nanny or a granny, Kenny would seize the moment and force me to go for a coffee. I would duly gulp down a cappuccino in record time and stare at my watch until he said we could go back. I couldn't enjoy this moment of 'freedom', knowing in my heart I was in the wrong place. It was a lesson to me that the instincts of a mother are so hormonally and viscerally charged that you can't explain it fully to a man who loves them just as much as you do, but is also desperate for you to still love him.

I would soon have to wrestle with the logistics of going back to work and leaving them for days at a time, so the coffee 'dates' were minutes I didn't need to be away. But I also understood that actually this was as much about Kenny as it was 'us'. Kenny needed to know that he was still important in this new paradigm; my role was to keep him convinced of that. I was the manager of a team that had some talented new young players, but the experienced star striker still had a role. Maybe he was more of a ten than an out-and-out nine now.

Have I extended the football metaphor too far? He wasn't getting benched, but I couldn't play him every week.

OK, too far.

I also had to find a way to deal with the 'working mum guilt' that society kept telling me I had, or should have. If I didn't have it, then why not? All the women in my family have worked and raised kids, and none of them had ever mentioned this guilt to me. I realised very quickly that I actually didn't feel bad about working. I loved my job, and I loved a bit of time away from the tough days at the coalface of twin baby duty, which were long and often monotonous.

One scorching hot day, the three of us were naked for most of the afternoon (me and the babies, not Kenny) while I tried to breastfeed them. They were so hot and tired that they fell asleep after a few minutes of sucking, but would then wake up five minutes later for another feed. It was a day-long procession of sweaty boobs and slithering babies. 'I feel like a cow,' I moaned as another one slipped off my breast. Luckily, it was the summer of the 2005 Ashes, so I sat with the cricket on the telly and enjoyed a thrilling test match. I watched most of that test series naked.

Anyone who ever says test cricket is too long and boring for modern attention spans hasn't spent a day continuously feeding twins in thirty-degree heat.

I had a district midwife who was obsessed with seeing me feed them at the same time. Every time she 'popped by', they had just been fed or weren't awake. I was beginning to think she didn't believe me, so one day I made them wait for food, then when she arrived, I performed for her.

I popped the breastfeeding cushion (a V-shaped thing) under my boobs and put the twins into the rugby-ball hold, cradling each head with my hands so their feet were under my armpits. She seemed suitably impressed, and never asked to see it again.

I will admit it wasn't the comfiest thing, and it certainly wasn't practical in public. Can you imagine the stares and tuts you'd get if you got both your tits out in Starbucks? But people did seem genuinely interested in the process. And when I say people, I mean the Queen.

Yes that's right, Her Majesty Queen Elizabeth II of Great Britain and Northern Ireland, head of the Commonwealth – *that* Queen. It was ITV's fiftieth birthday in 2005, and I was invited to a huge gala dinner at the Guildhall in London, which was to be attended by the Queen. I was selected to be one of a few groups of ITV on-screen 'talent' whom the Queen would talk to. My group included best friend Kirsty Gallacher, who presented *Kirsty's Home Videos* at the time, which the Queen apparently loved, and Claire Sweeney, formerly of the TV show *Brookside*. As the Queen approached our group, she was briefed by her lady-in-waiting, as is the norm. It's a bit like being a TV presenter, with an earpiece feeding you information, but they do it with hundreds of people every week.

'So, you've just given birth to twins?' The Queen came to me first.

'That's right, six weeks ago.' It was my first night out, and I'd squeezed myself into an old Alaïa dress, complete with my milky boobs and free-flowing hormones.

'Gosh, six weeks. So I take it you're not feeding them, then?' she asked. A bit judgey, the Queen.

'I am breastfeeding them, actually, but I expressed the milk tonight. My husband will give them a bottle.'

'And how do you breastfeed twins at the same time?' She was not letting this topic go.

I proceeded to explain the rugby-ball hold in great detail to the Queen. Sadly for Claire and Kirsty, the Queen's time with our little group was up, and she was ushered on to Ant and Dec.

A few years after the Queen incident, I was at Clarence House (home of Prince Charles and Camilla Parker Bowles) for a tour of the gardens as part of my role as a Prince's Trust ambassador. After the tour, we were on a terrace having tea and biscuits, and Camilla was doing the conversational rounds. She was very easy-going and the conversation was not led by a lady-in-waiting; it was just general nattering. She let slip that her daughter was about to have twins at Queen Charlotte's, and we appeared to share the same specialist. My mum, who was my plus-one, was doing the 'granny to twins' chat and discussing prams. Then Camilla said, 'Can I ask you, how does one feed twins?'

'Oh, for god's sake, what is it with your family? Ask your mother-in-law!'

I didn't say that.

No, instead, with a strange sense of déjà vu, I proceeded to explain the mechanics of the rugby-ball hold to the future Queen of Great Britain.

When the babies were a few weeks old, we were photographed by paparazzi while out for a stroll with the giant double buggy and Sydney the dog. A female columnist from a national newspaper used the picture in her column, and decided to write a piece declaring that it was 'a shame' I felt the need to go power-walking to get my figure back instead of enjoying the babies that I had struggled to conceive and undergone IVF to have. The implication was that I was being neglectful of my motherly duties because I was on a walk with vain intentions, when I was in fact actually with said babies. I sat on my bed and cried. *Jesus Christ, if I can't go for a walk without being judged, what are the chances of me heading off to an Olympic Games or even out for dinner with friends?*

I am not suggesting that sisterhood has no limits and that every female columnist should support every single woman, come what may, but I never feel comfortable when women attack other women with regards to being a mother.

Maybe she was annoyed because I seemed to be trying

to have it all. I was under no illusions; it was not possible to have it all. I never really felt I fitted into the mother-and-baby scene very well. It wasn't that I was an outsider because someone else puréed my kids food; I was probably an outsider because I didn't *care* that it wasn't me doing the puréeing. I decided early on that I was going to work, and in my line of work, it wasn't practical to bring two babies with me to a studio, so something was going to have to give.

My closest relative was 180 miles away in Leeds. My sister Louise was living in Las Vegas, and my mum had a thriving property business – and she was only fifty-five when Reuben and Lois were born, so she had a lot of her own life still to live. I was always going to have to pay for help, so I had to make sure we brought good people into the twins' lives, and I had to be at peace with that decision. Our first nanny, Judite, came through my best friend Kerry, who had also had twins the year before. (Kerry also had a thirteen-month-old – I know, she's a superwoman – so I knew Judite would be more than capable of coping with my two.) She was Portuguese and had the softest, sweetest voice. And she adored babies.

To top up the help when I needed weekend cover or I had to stay away, my Aunty Jayne, my mum's younger sister, came down from Leeds and helped us. Everyone needs an Aunty Jayne. She is the most caring and selfless person you'll ever meet. She's also amazingly practical and has a brilliantly mad sense of humour and fun, which kept us entertained for hours. We'd fight to be the one to meet her off the train because she always had some incredible story to tell about a man in her carriage who'd started playing the banjo, or a woman who'd smuggled a live chicken onboard in her bag. As I mentioned earlier, the women in our family have always been grafters, and Jayne is definitely one of those.

Even though my mum was busy running her business,

she was still very practical and good at rolling up her sleeves when we needed her. She loved hanging out with us and was always silently doing some washing or folding towels in the background of the chaos, and she was always on hand to help when we moved house, which happened every year for a while. Kenny's family were even further away in Scotland, so Grandma Logan couldn't be there as often, but she knitted plenty of outfits for the twins. I felt that between all of these good, kind women, we had a real chance at succeeding; we had a good team. With my mum and dad divorced and Kenny's dad deceased, he was used to being the 'man' in the room, and all these women spoiled him rotten. My Grandma Sheila, who was in her late seventies, was wowed by his practical skills. 'Gosh, he is so good to change nappies – and look at him emptying the dishwasher,' she'd marvel. 'Kenny, let me make you a cup of tea after all that, you must need one.' No wonder he didn't mind the matriarchs hanging around.

With this brilliant support system in place, I was happy to get back to work, but what I couldn't control was a plague that seemed to have descended on the tabloid media: the fascination with a woman's body after she had given birth. It was almost like a sport: marks were awarded for how soon you made it back into a pair of jeans or a bikini, with extra points for a swimsuit photoshoot. A well-known weekly gossip magazine put two paparazzi pictures of me on its front cover, one where I was bursting with babies, the day before I was induced, looking like a human space hopper, and another where I was strolling along with the pram, looking quite normal two weeks later.

'HOW DID GABBY LOGAN SHIFT THREE STONE IN ELEVEN WEEKS?' it asked incredulously, as if I was about to announce I was a WeightWatchers ambassador.

Er . . . I gave birth? I answered meekly in my head when I saw the magazine in my local newsagent.

The inference that I had done something impossible, immoral or time-consumingly vain was hurtful – and plainly idiotic. There is already a lot to screw with your head after you give birth: the lack of sleep, the funny, gorging, leaky boobs, the stretch marks, the bleeding, the emotional roller-coaster of hormonal fluctuations and overwhelming love, so what the post-partum world of womanhood doesn't need is another celebrity being lauded or chastised for the speed – or lack of – with which she manages to get back into her size-ten jeans. Who or what can that possibly be helping? Apart from the pockets of the predominantly male owners of the huge media groups that own the magazines and newspapers.

Whether you get 'back into shape' too quickly or not quickly enough, whether you breastfeed for six weeks or six years or not at all, whether you go back to work or become a full-time mum, whether you opt for freestyle parenting or a strict Gina Ford regime – whatever you do, there is always someone in the child-rearing community or a national news-paper ready to tell you why you are wrong.

The one time you really do need to listen to your gut, it's buried under a few pounds of post-baby chub and drowned out by the cries of tiny babies. In the end, the only way I was ever going to feel I was doing anything right was to own it. If you are happy with the way you are doing it, then nobody else can affect you. If you're not happy, then change it.

What mattered to me was that my children were happy, healthy and confident, and if that meant paying people to help me get them there because I was at work sometimes, well, so be it. As the proverb goes, it takes a village to raise a baby; the only difference for me and Kenny was that we had to pay for some of our villagers.

I have a friend, let's call her Jane (because that's her name), and Jane has four children. She had two already when mine were born. One night, she offered to babysit with her husband, Simon, so we could go out, leaving her children at home with a babysitter – that's how kind Jane was.

When we came in from dinner, she nervously suggested that Lois needed a higher tog of sleeping bag, as she was cold. I thanked her profusely; after all, if it meant Lois slept longer and better, why would I resent that kind of intel?

I'd ring Jane if one of them hadn't pooed for two days; I'd call her about medicines for coughs or the best kind of potty. I called her so often asking for advice that I promised if I ever wrote a baby book, we'd call it *Just Ask Jane*. You've already noticed that this book is not called that, but I dedicate this chapter to Jane and Aunty Jayne – and if all goes well, we might yet get *Just Ask Jane* off the ground.

Apparently, the Royal family are also writing a book about breastfeeding called *Just Ask Gabby*.

27

Awards Day

Awards ceremonies are a huge industry; there are so many of them now, there should be an awards ceremony for the best awards. Every industry has their own, and I have hosted hundreds of corporate awards over the years: 'The Best HiFi Awards', the 'Builders' Merchants Awards', 'HGV Industry Awards'. They were all memorable in their own special way, and helped me to refurbish bathrooms and kitchens and pay for nice holidays. When it comes to my industry, TV, I have been part of award-winning shows, and I've been personally shortlisted or nominated for BAFTAs, Royal Television Society awards and National Television Awards, although I've never scooped the actual big prize. (But, as we all know, awards are rubbish and mean nothing – until you win one.)

In the spring of 2012, I was asked if I would like to take part in a challenge for Sport Relief. This wasn't your regular 'cycle in the driving sleet for 100 kilometres a day or until you fall off the bike with exhaustion' type of challenge – this

was a *comedy* challenge. I would be one of five contestants
from the world of sport who'd learn the art of stand-up and
then perform in front of a sold-out crowd at the Bloomsbury
Theatre in London. We would each be allocated a comedy
mentor who would help us hone our routines, and they'd
also perform on the night. I jumped at the chance. What an
amazing challenge. I would learn some of the dark arts of
comedy, and if it all went wrong, it would be for charity, so
nobody could give me too much stick.

I lucked out; I was given Patrick Kielty as a mentor. I had
always enjoyed his stand-up on TV, and he seemed a clever
and thoughtful bloke. A TV writer called Phil Kerr was
assigned to help me get my material on the page, and Paddy
would help with the actual performance. The writing was
fun, and watching Phil craft jokes out of innocuous stories I
told him was incredibly insightful. Then, with Paddy's help, I
had to bring it all to life. On one of our filming days, he took
me to a famous pub in Kingston called The Fighting Cocks,
where the Outside the Box comedy club is held. For years,
some of the greatest comedians have tried out new material
there. It seats just thirty people, so, as Paddy explained, if
Robin Williams could make half of this room laugh, that
would be 5,000 people at the O2 Arena or Wembley; but if
only five people laughed, it was a pretty dispiriting evening
and the material needed more work. It was a brutal way to
work out what was good and what was turgid rubbish.

We visited during the day, so I performed my routine for
just Paddy and the cameraman, which was excruciating. For
some reason, when I came on, I decided to do Irish dancing, as if I was one of the women in *Riverdance*. I was just
messing around, trying to make the Irishman Paddy laugh –
which he did.

'Can you do that on the night?' he said.

'Don't see why not,' I replied.

'Right, well, that's how you're coming on.' He scribbled in his notebook and called the producers to find some traditional Irish music.

Then he helped me hone every line, making me repeat them until the timing and delivery were absolutely perfect.

I had a few more weeks before the big night to rehearse and iron out any creases, and was of course still carrying on with my 'day job' as a sports presenter. With a couple of weeks to go, my agent called and informed me that I had won the Tesco Mum of the Year Award. Reuben and Lois were six at this point, and were invited to join me at the ceremony at the Café de Paris. The kids were really chuffed, and I told them the award was for all of us, as we are 'Team Logan'. I knew I wasn't the 'best' mum in Britain, as there is no such thing, we all try our best, but it was a good marketing campaign, and a wholesome one at that. I was so synonymous with a male audience for presenting sport that it was lovely to be given something for doing my favourite job, being a mum.

There was only one snag: the lunch was on the same Sunday as the Sport Relief Comedy event. There was just about enough time to do both, but it was tight. I was whisked out at the end of the lunch and driven to the Bloomsbury Theatre to rehearse while Kenny got the kids home, and then he came back with my friend Mel to watch the show. The excitement of the lunch was a good numbing agent, because the minute I left the Café de Paris, I was sick with nerves. What the hell was I doing? Why had I agreed to this?

When I arrived, I was introduced to my competitors. I was up against world champion heavyweight boxer Tyson Fury, footballer Neil 'Razor' Ruddock, cricketer Michael Vaughan and World Cup-winning rugby player Ben Cohen.

For all the testosterone in that group, I could still smell the strong stench of fear – apart from Razor, whose scent was a bit more Pinot Noir.

But it wasn't just the amateurs who were petrified. Kielty had also become a nervous wreck, and not just for me. He was pacing backstage like an expectant father, delivering his lines to himself over and over. Next to him were the other mentors, Jason Manford and Daniel Sloss, who were also mumbling their lines to themselves. It seemed it didn't matter how many times you'd done this before; you were still a nervous wreck each time. It's amazing any of them come back for more.

I was positioned last but one, which was even more sick-making as I had to watch the others. Some hit the mark, others didn't, but the audience was very kind. My Irish dancing entrance was still part of the routine, but that night I was wearing four-inch lace-up Yves Saint Laurent shoe boots, which, funnily enough, I hadn't danced in before. I might be about to literally fall flat on my face, and then stand up and do it again metaphorically.

Somehow, I made it onstage with the dancing, and that earned me a bit of a laugh and some goodwill before I had even opened my mouth. Then I was off. The routine landed well; every joke got a really good laugh, and I even started ad-libbing. I didn't want it to end.

I came off buzzing.

So *that's* why they come back for more.

Claudia Winkleman, the funniest of all of us in real life, was the host for the evening, and she brought us all back onstage with our mentors and lined us up to reveal the results of the audience vote. After drumming up the tension, she revealed the winner. Incredibly, it was me. Before I knew it, I was holding a golden microphone on a wooden plinth with 'Stand up for Sport Relief' written on it.

Kenny was, as always, incredibly proud. On the way home, armed with my two trophies, we stopped for fish and chips, and then sat on the kitchen worktop, reliving the day with a glass of champagne.

'Tesco Mum of the Year and Stand up for Sport Relief winner in one day – they don't get much better,' I said.

I went to bed, but couldn't sleep. I was thinking up new material, wondering how I could be a stand-up comedian *and* a sports presenter. I hadn't felt the adrenaline rush I had experienced onstage that night since I was an international gymnast.

'Go for it,' Kenny said when I told him. I am sure he meant it. He has always backed my wildest plans and dreams.

But I woke up the next day and real life hit me. We had a mortgage and bills to pay; I couldn't go gigging for £20 a night in Middlesbrough. That ship had sailed. So, I was back to being a sports presenter again, albeit one who tried to squeeze in a few more gags.

Later that next day, when I wouldn't let Lois leave the table without finishing her fruit and yoghurt, I wasn't even the Tesco Mum of the Year any more.

'You are the Tesco *Worst* Mum,' she told me with a glint in her eye and a half smile.

Throughout my time working on my comedy routine with Paddy, I had teased him about being single and said he should get back together with Cat Deeley, the TV presenter he had dated before she went to work in LA. He clearly adored her. After the event, I sent him a box of wine to thank him for all his help. On the note, I wrote: 'Thanks for all the help making me funny, now go marry Cat,' or something helpful and glib like that.

A few months later, the tabloids reported they were dating

again, and a decade later, I can tell you they are married and have two sons. Now, I like to feel I might have given him the nudge he needed, but I wasn't invited to their wedding and I am not a godmother to his kids, so maybe he doesn't quite see it that way.

Doing the comedy took me out of my safety zone and made me push myself somewhere I had never been. It might not have led to a career change, but it boosted my confidence and gave me an insight into another world. It also taught me that I needed to keep doing that throughout my life: to keep trying things I wasn't comfortable with.

It also set me up for what was about to be a game-changing summer.

28

The Greatest Show on Earth

'When a man is tired of the Olympics, he is tired of life.' I am sure Samuel Johnson meant to say that, but he wrote 'London' instead – always playing to the crowd, old Sam. I think it is probably apparent by now that I am an Olympic Games nut. From that awakening watching the 1984 LA Games in a hotel room in Slough, to my first visit to an actual Games in Barcelona in 1992, to 2008, when I finally got to work on an Olympic Games when I joined the BBC, it has never disappointed. One of the main attractions of taking a large pay cut to work for the BBC was the possibility of being part of their Olympic coverage. I joined in 2007, knowing that the 2012 Games were going to be held in London. They would be the pinnacle of many a broadcasting career.

I think my whole family knew what the Olympics meant to me. I had a great Uncle Eddie who was ninety-seven in 2007, and when I moved to the BBC, he said to my mum: 'I am glad she's gone there; I can't wait to watch her on the London Olympics.' And he did – at 103 years old.

I never made an Olympic Games as a competitor, I haven't got the five rings tattoo like my best pal Viva, who went in 1992, but I was close to the next-best job now.

First, though, came the Beijing Olympics in 2008. My role was to host the highlights on BBC One at 7pm UK time. The time difference meant that we'd be broadcasting at 2am in China. If I had been asked to design my dream job that day as an eleven-year-old in a Slough hotel room when I first caught the Olympics 'bug', it probably would have looked a lot like this. We'd have the best of the action, amazing music montages and reportage from the best BBC reporters. Our medal-winning GB Olympians would sit on the sofa and chat to me about their success, watched by kids sitting at home, wide-eyed in awe just as I had been.

My editor Ali McIntyre was a genius at this kind of show. We had already worked together on *Inside Sport* and had a great rapport. He's a native of St Helens, a fount of all sporting knowledge and a relentless man. He's also a bit of a maverick, and one of the kindest humans you will ever meet.

When your working day is 1pm to 3am, it's important to get along with your editor. You have to live in each other's pockets, exchanging ideas and often having them rejected. There's no room for moodiness or taking offence. Luckily, Ali and I have a similar sense of humour and, more importantly, share a real passion for the power of sport.

We'd have a quick debrief after the show, and then I'd head off to my hotel. But it takes a while for the mind to stop whirring after a show like an Olympics highlights. Little mistakes are tossed around for a few hours. I'd lie in bed, thinking, *What did I say that for? Should I have asked her that? Was that the best way to finish the show?* It was usually around 5am before I stopped torturing myself and found sleep.

Ali was in at 9am and left the office long after me. He

survived on handfuls of Haribo and chocolate (the TV diet) and was a fizzing ball of brilliant energy.

The show was a great success and even won an award at the International Olympic Committee Golden Rings.

Every day was joyous, yet a huge learning curve. For the first time since I had joined the BBC, I was sitting writing scripts in the same office as Sue Barker, Clare Balding and Hazel Irving, a trinity of truly iconic broadcasters. I am not that much younger than Balding, but it felt like I had moved in with the grown-ups.

The Bird's Nest Stadium, which hosted the athletics and the opening and closing ceremonies, was the jewel in the crown of the Beijing Olympic venues, most of which were neatly built around a very large square with the media and broadcast centre positioned at the back of the site. Our studio was on the top floor of the Ling Long Pagoda, which over-looked the stadium. We could see the Olympic flame burning from the windows, and we heard the roar of the crowd when Usain Bolt broke the 100-metre world record to claim gold.

During an Olympic Games, the athletes tend to be up for media commitments because they know their window of opportunity for exposure is short, but the really tricky part about the show was persuading Great Britain's top Olympians to stay until 2am local time to come on. If they had competed in the morning and won a medal, there was a good chance they might be a bit tipsy by the time they got to us – or they might be fast asleep and forget all about us. There were a few no-shows – most notably Bradley Wiggins didn't make it on air one night. The next morning, we heard that the night-clubs of China's capital city had proved just too compelling. In fairness, I can see how they might be a bigger draw than a cup of tea and a biscuit in the Ling Long Pagoda.

Beijing was the early part of the big turn-around in Team

GB's fortunes. In Athens in 2004, Great Britain had picked up thirty medals; in 2008, it was fifty-one, and in 2012, it was sixty-five. Thanks to the National Lottery, which started in 1994, there were more full-time Olympians than ever before. They were, in effect, behaving like professional sportsmen and women: training full-time, and resting and recovering properly, rather than working in a shop, at a school or in a hospital, as had been the case in the era of Ovett and Coe, and even the early Olympics of Redgrave. National Lottery funding has helped garner enormous success across a host of sports that Britain previously had little joy in. Take gymnastics, for example: when Louis Smith took bronze on the pommel horse in Beijing, he became the first British gymnast to win a medal at an Olympic Games since 1908. In London 2012, Great Britain won a team bronze for the men and three more individual medals, and then in Rio in 2016, Max Whitlock won two golds, while Nile Wilson and Amy Tinkler each took home a bronze. The floodgates had opened thanks to a full-time professional set-up that was properly resourced. Some people don't like that; they feel it flies in the face of the amateur notion of the Olympics. The problem is, Great Britain is competing against Russian, German and Chinese athletes who have operated in this way for decades. The Lottery simply levelled the playing field.

One thing I learned very quickly about doing the kind of highlights show I was hosting in 2008 was that you don't actually get a chance to see the city you are in. You travel the world, and see a hotel room and a TV studio. I had been to Beijing earlier in the year to record a documentary for the BBC, so although I spent my days stuck in a window-less office watching banks of screens, I was lucky in that I'd already walked part of the Great Wall of China and had tea in a traditional *chawu*. So, I just got my head down and cracked on.

The walk to and from the hotel to work was often the only fresh air I managed to get – and 'fresh' is a very loose term when it comes to the air quality in Beijing. Living in our hotel gave me a real insight into our hosts, however. At 5am one day, I looked out of the window to see tens of buses pulling up outside the Cube, the swimming venue where Rebecca Adlington won two golds. Smartly dressed tourists stepped off the buses like very obedient ants. They were marched towards some tents at the back of the park. They walked in single file and with great precision, which is when I surmised that our 'tourists' were probably from a military background. But what were they doing?

It turned out there had been complaints from the TV companies to the local organising committee that there was no atmosphere anywhere and that the Olympic Park was a bit, well, dead. So, overnight, an atmosphere was bused in, which is easy to do when you have a billion compliant people and a feared government. What I had just witnessed were the 'crowds' arriving.

Around our hotel, the staff seemed to be both highly suspicious of and incredibly interested in us BBC folk. A young man called Geoffrey always brought me my room service, whether it was 3am or 2pm. I had a feeling that Geoffrey was my 'special' waiter. He became so familiar that he'd sit on the stool in my room while he waited for me to find his tip. One day, he stayed chatting for twenty minutes, and even asked if I could get him water polo tickets. Instead, I gave him a big enough tip to buy his own. I learned that Geoffrey's name was actually Liu. Just a few weeks before the Olympics, the hotel had asked all of the staff to choose a 'British name', as lots of Western journalists would be staying there. Among

my favourite name choices were a beautiful young receptionist, who opted for Sharon, and a twenty-year-old barman
who went by Stanley. Travel broadens the mind, but it's not
taking an Instagram-worthy picture of Machu Picchu or the
Hanging Gardens of Babylon that's important; it's sitting
down with Geoffrey, Sharon or Stanley and finding out that
really, we all want similar things in life. In Geoffrey's case,
tickets to the water polo.

During the two and half weeks we were in Beijing, there was
a commonly heard refrain among us Brits: 'How the hell are
we going to match this?'

Beijing had been spectacular. From the opening and closing ceremonies to the iconic architecture, they had nailed it
when it came to putting on the biggest show on earth.

It's easy to forget just how negative people were about
London 2012, almost right up to the opening ceremony.

Nothing would be finished on time, London would be
gridlocked, nobody would watch it, the weather would spoil
everything . . . the list of reasons why it would be the worst
Olympics of modern times went on and on. I felt like an
unpaid spokesperson for the defence. I had a bit of a ding-
dong on the TV show *8 Out of 10 Cats* (of all places) with
the *EastEnders* actress Natalie Cassidy (of all people), who
was fairly scathing in her prediction of how the Games were
going to go down.

'It's not for us regular Londoners,' she complained with
comedy effect. 'I don't even like sports day.'

The sound of the audience laughing along with her as I
sulked still cuts through me. I was a sore loser on that one.

I was tired and fed up with the antipathy and negativity.
Of course, there would be positive drugs tests and accusations
from cynics that 'it's all become too corporate', but if you just

scratched at the surface, I knew all the great stories would still be there.

I kept banging the positivity drum, telling anyone who would listen that the Olympics truly is the greatest show on earth, and we all should try to get behind it. Two days before the start of the Games, I was inside the Olympic Park at the studios, which had been built out of shipping containers, doing technical rehearsals. My colleague Gary Lineker was leaving as I arrived. We exchanged small talk, and then I asked if his then-wife Danielle was going to come down and watch any of the action. After all, I had bought tickets to ten random sports for my family.

'Nah, she doesn't enjoy sport,' he said quietly.

It was the straw that broke this camel's back. I didn't even know Danielle, but I had taken this Olympic fight on, and I wasn't stopping now.

'But Gary, does she enjoy the human spirit rising through adversity to claim unexpected victories? Underdogs battling to achieve their dreams? The smallest nation in the world competing with the biggest superpowers on the planet on the same stage? The uncovering of household names and heroes in a heartbeat? Does she? Does she enjoy that?'

Gary looked a bit confused, shrugged his shoulders and walked off, suitably bemused. He must have thought I'd lost the plot.

In the second week of the Games, I saw Danielle in the BBC production office, picking up some tickets. Apparently, she did like all of that stuff – and she wasn't alone.

It's about not even knowing Greg Rutherford's name one day, and then calling 'Super Saturday' the greatest day of sport you ever saw the next. It's watching a young British heavyweight boxer called Anthony Joshua go through the rounds and win gold, then learning he had almost succumbed to a life of gangs and crime a few years before. It's crying your eyes out as you watch a judoka called Gemma Gibbons crash to her knees when she guarantees herself a medal and mouth the words 'I love you, Mum,' to the heavens, as the commentator explains that her mother recently died.

You don't have to be truly engrossed by the individual sports, or even know that much about them. If you have a beating heart, it's hard not to be drawn into the emotion. In a way, that's the point of the Olympics, right there.

The London Olympics was an even bigger triumph for the country than any of us dared hope. I loved the sport, of course, but the way the country came together and unified in entertaining the world over those weeks was thrilling.

After the success of our show *Games Today* in Beijing, Ali and I were reunited once more for the new and imaginatively entitled *The Games Tonight*. This round-up show would go on air at around 10.15pm, and because we were broadcasting in the same time zone as the Games, we were often covering live action while attempting to be a highlights show at the same time. There was no time for rehearsal on the day, as I was taking over the seat Gary had broadcast from moments before.

The studio was in almost continuous use until 3am, with *BBC Breakfast* starting again at 6am.

The working day was much like Beijing. We'd sit in the bustling offices, watch copious hours of sport, write scripts, prep interviews and plan. All of which was punctuated by the odd crisis, such as a guest pulling out without warning, or Paul McCartney's management team not getting back to us with permission to use 'Live and Let Die' until the last minute.

The BBC was streaming up to twenty-two events at any one time, so I couldn't just go off and watch the diving all day, because the show I hosted would be covering up to fifteen different sports with four or five superb guests. We're talking proper living legends of Olympic history: Daley Thompson, Olga Korbut, Carl Lewis, Amir Khan and John McEnroe, to name a few. The heroes I had grown up drooling over were now sitting on the sofa next to me. At the end of the show, I'd wander back through the office and debrief with Ali, often being handed another stats pack for the following day as we chatted, and then I'd head off to bed. I think people imagine that you all go to a wine bar and Michael Johnson and Denise Lewis crack open the vintage Bollinger. That literally never happens.

Not that Denise doesn't open champagne – she would if we could, I am sure – it's just we never have time to party. The only TV show I have ever hosted that had a proper green room after the show was called *The Premiership Parliament*. It was on ITV on Monday nights and my co-host was the former Scotland international Ali McCoist, a man responsible for inadvertently damaging many a human liver. One night we left the green room so late it was technically the next morning, and our guest, the football manager Sam Allardyce, was hurried on to the back of a motorbike and whizzed to Heathrow for the 6.50am flight to Manchester to make sure he'd get to training at Bolton Wanderers on time. Unfortunately, he fell asleep in the airport lounge and missed his flight. McCoist is one of the greatest people you could ever work with, but there will always be a cheeky hint of chaos in his wake.

London has some of the greatest hotels in the world. In 2012, we were staying at the Ilford Holiday Inn, situated on a dual carriageway by a Shell garage. By the time I returned to the hotel from work each night, the bar was shut. Reception was manned by a lone night porter and there was no room service. I stocked up on Pringles from the garage and ate them on my bed. I was living the dream. No, I really was – I loved every second.

For our final show, we had an A-list line-up on the sofa: the sailor Ben Ainslee (now Sir Ben), who had just won his fifth gold; Kath Grainger (now Dame Katherine), who had won a gold in the rowing after three previous silvers; the great American sprinter, gold-medal winner and world record-holder Michael Johnson; Tom Daley, who had won a bronze that night in the diving, and was so fresh out of the pool that you could still smell the chlorine; and finally David Beckham. Beckham had been a kind of unofficial Team GB mascot. He was popping up all over – the velodrome, the beach volleyball, the gymnastics, the athletics – he was loving it all. And when you are offered David Beckham for a TV show, you don't turn him down.

We stuck to our regular format of highlights and chat, and flipped from sport to sport with ease, as we did every night. There were a few boxing matches to cover, but as we had no boxing guest, we were intending to move straight on from those to other topics. During the gold-medal match in the men's bantamweight division, I leaned over and shared some information with David about the boxer who would go on to take gold, Luke Campbell of Hull.

'This guy is phenomenal,' I said to David in hushed tones. 'He lost his mum and his sister in a car crash earlier this year.'

David looked genuinely saddened by this, but incredibly impressed by the young boxer and his ability to bounce back from such terrible tragedy. When we came back to the studio, I was intending to move on to diving, but David cut in.

'It's all the more incredible what this guy has done after his terrible year; he lost his mum and sister in a car accident,' he said.

I won't lie, it lowered the mood a little, but we cracked on.

The last thing we did every night of the show was to throw the magnets of the faces of medal winners on to the appropriately coloured giant medals that we kept on a balcony off the studio. It was a visual reminder of just how successful this Games had been. By now, the giant medals were jam-packed with faces, as Great Britain's haul smashed all previous records. We squeezed all of our guests on to the balcony and asked them to do the honours, placing the faces, and then for the final time, I said: 'Thanks for watching, and goodnight.' I was elated and desperate for a celebratory glass of wine.

As soon as the words had left my lips, however, I was asked to go back into the studio by Ali.

'Gabby, can you come back onset?'

How lovely, I thought. *They have bought me a cake.* I know, I know. I am an egomaniac TV presenter, what can I say?

'Don't speak. Your mic is going live. We haven't gone off air.'

But I'd said goodnight – I'd seen the titles roll.

As I walked back in, I saw on the monitor that the Olympic flame was in shot and the title music was playing softly.

'Gabby. Luke Campbell's mum and sister are not dead.' This wasn't Ali; that was the voice of Philip Bernie, the joint head of sport.

'It was Anthony Ogogo,' said another voice, one I recognised as one of the top producers in the department.

'No, it was Anthony Joshua.' Yet another of the big bosses. This was bad.

All the important head honchos were in the gallery, throwing their hats in the ring.

I couldn't risk saying a different boxer's family had died and get it wrong again, so I ignored the noise and the suggestions of various bereaved people, and simply said what I now knew to be true: 'Ladies and gentlemen, I am afraid some erroneous information made it to air tonight. Luke Campbell's mum and sister are alive and well. Goodnight.'

And after all the sweat and toil and joy and hard work, and the incredible success of that show, those would be the final words I spoke to the BBC audience at the 2012 Olympic Games.

I was utterly devastated.

I walked back to the make-up room with my head bowed in shame.

The stats guy on the show was a young man called Chris Birch. He saw me straight away.

'How? What? Why?' he asked, taking the error gravely and personally. His face was ashen. At every Olympic Games, dedicated stats experts like Chris produce a veritable bible full of facts and stats about the competitors and the events. It takes them months.

'I was watching Luke Campbell fight earlier this evening in the office, and you said, "This guy lost his mum and sister in a car crash this year,"' I explained.

At the time, Chris had indeed been sitting opposite me in the office watching boxing. He had a monitor and was observing a gold-medal fight – but, it transpired, he wasn't watching the same fight as me. We all had headphones on, so I hadn't realised. What he had said was true, but it pertained to another boxer.

Meanwhile, David Beckham was wandering down the corridor, looking confused.

'What's happened . . . ? Has anyone actually died in a car crash?' I don't think David and I have worked together since. He probably doesn't believe a word I say now.

As he was whisked off in a limo, I was left pondering just how badly damaged my career was.

I rang Kenny for reassurance. He was laughing. *Too soon, Kenny.*

Twitter was already on to it.

'Gabby Logan just killed off the Campbell family LOL,' tweeted Amir Khan.

Well cheers, big ears – we'd worked together just a few days before, a bit of solidarity might be nice.

I took my time heading back to the office.

Ali was waiting. He handed me a brown envelope, looking glum.

'What's this, a P45?' I said, only half joking.

'No, a death certificate!' There was a hint of a smirk. I hated letting Ali down.

It was, in fact, the International Olympic Committee's official certificate of broadcast, which is given to all the Olympic broadcasters at the end of their shows.

Ali then handed me Mrs Campbell's phone number, which I had asked him to find. Steve Bunce, our commentator in the boxing department, knows everyone in the world of boxing. If I phoned Mrs Campbell and apologised, I thought I would feel a tiny bit better, as if I had atoned for my sins.

After a night of tossing and turning and feeling sick with regret, I rang Mrs Campbell at 8am.

'Hello, it's Gabby Logan here from the BBC.'

'Oh yes, dear, I know all about you,' she said in a wonderful Hull accent.

'I am so sorry for the mistake.'

'I was out partying, celebrating our Luke's gold. So I didn't see it on the telly. But I when I got in and checked my phone, I had about 200 missed calls. People wanting to know if I was OK.'

'Oh, I am so sorry.' I tried to explain how the mistake had come about.

'Don't worry, pet. I came down to breakfast today and everyone in the restaurant in the hotel stood up, sang "Thriller" and did zombie impressions.'

I don't think she was joking.

Brian Barwick, my old boss at ITV, once said to me: 'Don't worry about the odd mistake. The viewers like it when a presenter isn't perfect.'

Maybe I took it a bit far that night.

The 2012 Olympic Games was an important milestone for women's sport in this country, and the best thing I have ever been part of professionally. Over half of the broadcasters on the BBC's coverage were female; it really felt like we had taken a giant leap forwards. The young girl who sat watching the 1984 Olympics in a hotel room in Slough, presented by four middle-aged men, would have been very impressed with the 2012 Olympic and Paralympic coverage.

There are many commercial and historical reasons why women's sport had previously been so under-represented, but it was clear from that summer that if it projected the personalities in the right way, the audience enjoyed women's sport every bit as much as they enjoyed men's. Jessica Ennis-Hill, Helen Glover, Rebecca Adlington, Lucy Bronze, Beth Tweddle, Katherine Grainger, Victoria Pendleton, Hannah Cockroft, Laura Kenny (née Trott) and so many others weaved their way into the nation's consciousness and have stayed there ever since.

The legacy is real. I interview professional sportswomen now who were young kids when they watched those Games. Those women and many others inspired them to achieve greatness. Alex Scott was part of the Great Britain football team who played in front of a sold-out Wembley Stadium against Brazil, a first for the women's game. Now Alex is one of the lead presenters on BBC Sport. I don't think those two facts are unlinked.

If you see it, you can be it.

Professionally, the 2012 Olympics took me on something of a journey. In spite of my killing off Luke Campbell's family, I had emerged with credit within the industry. I was in demand and asked to host a much wider range of shows, including entertainment, which had always seemed a very attractive genre of TV to me. The contracts were better than sport, and you had a wardrobe budget, stylists and 'runners': all the trappings that could render you a bit of a 'diva' if you weren't careful.

The one I enjoyed working on the most was *Splash*, which I hosted with Vernon Kay and Tom Daley. We only did two series, but it helped me itch the 'shiny floor' TV scratch.

The premise of the show was that a group of celebrities would learn to do what Tom Daley did – you know, that sport that had taken him more than a decade and thousands of hours to master? Well, the likes of Gemma Collins, Joey Essex and Eddie 'the Eagle' Edwards were hoping they would pull it off in just six weeks. In reality, most of them ended up bruised and battered, and only a few even made it up to the ten-metre board, from which they swan-dived at best and belly-flopped at worst.

The entertainment came from their 'journeys', and around the live show we had spectacular divers and dancers with great routines. It was never going to be the new *Strictly*, but it gave me a taste of the 'other side'. It clashed with the Rugby Six Nations, which I presented for the BBC, so I had to miss a few matches and I got a feeling that there were a few people at the BBC questioning my commitment to sport.

I never wanted to jump over lock, stock and barrel to entertainment, and I realised that I really did love hosting live sport above all else. However, that didn't stop me saying yes to one of the strangest shows I have ever presented, *Flockstars*, which saw celebrities learning to be shepherds. I genuinely thought that it might be the new *Bake Off*.

It wasn't.

I would still love to host my own chat show one day, but sadly the genre of long-form interviewing has all but died out, and by the time we learn to appreciate things like *Parkinson* again, I might be dead too. So, hurrah for podcasting, which is a perfect release; I get to chat with interesting people, letting conversations take us where they will, and I can still host big live sport on the telly.

Saying yes to some of those post-2012 offers might not have been entirely wise, but I don't regret them. The industry is fickle, and it can chew you up and spit you out as quickly as it draws you in. One day you are flavour of the month, the next you are yesterday's news. There's no point moaning or being bitter if someone else is chosen over you for a job you fancied.

I decided a while ago to roll with it, to not take offence and to keep working hard. Be on time (early), do your prep and try to leave the show in a better state than if you hadn't been hired – and if you can have a laugh along the way, all the better. When I finish work, I am the luckiest person in the world, because I go home to my family – to Kenny, Reuben and Lois – and they are truly my motivation, my reason to push on and be the best example I can.

29

Frozen and Eventually Fearless

Over the years, I have been asked to have a 'chat' with TV producers about appearing on various well-known reality shows, but as much as I loved my *Strictly Come Dancing* experience, I wasn't sure my ego could take being voted off in week one.

Also, I was always busy with sport and kids, and never overly excited about the premise of the shows. But in the autumn of 2021, an email dropped in my inbox that piqued my interest. My agents Holly and Emily seemed keen for me to chat with the producers, so I hopped on a Zoom call.

The show was based around the teachings and experiences of the breathing and cold-water therapy practised by the Dutch 'Iceman' Wim Hof. Among other things, Hof is known for holding world records for sitting in ice, swimming under ice and running a barefoot half-marathon over ice. He also has a globally used app based around his powerful breathing technique.

A group of eight celebrities would be holed up in a tent on

top of a mountain for a few weeks, with all digital devices removed, and subjected to a series of cold water, ice and heights-based challenges, which they'd be expected to conquer with Wim's guidance and using his breathing practices. It would be a physically and mentally demanding show, and of course, living together with seven strangers would be a challenging experience on its own. For some reason, it grabbed me.

I took the information to the Logan family dinner table. Kenny, having watched too many romances blossom on *Strictly* over the years, was mainly worried I would run off with Wim Hof. Lois googled sixty-three-year-old Wim and reassured Kenny that this was unlikely. Reuben couldn't understand how someone who wore heated electric vests and socks to present sport was even considering swimming in an iced lake, and then Lois pointed out that my fear of heights was so bad I couldn't go near the window when we had a family day trip to the top of the tallest building in London, the Shard.

They all made valid points, but overall they seemed to think it would be a good thing for me to do. Reuben, who thinks I am a human handbrake on his fun, was mainly salivating at the prospect of me being out of the country and off a phone for three weeks. Lois and Kenny said they'd miss me, but the pay-off in terms of life experience and enrichment would be worth it. At forty-eight years old, it did seem like a good time to take myself out of my comfort zone and find out if I had any hidden depths. So I said yes.

A few months later, when filming was supposed to start, there was an upsurge of Covid-19. This meant we had to isolate for five days in a hotel in a remote part of northern Italy before we could begin filming, staying in our hotel rooms for twenty-three hours a day. For the remaining hour, we could exercise, which for me usually involved running the couple of kilometres to the gates of the hotel and back again. The producers were obviously keen that we didn't catch Covid and ruin the show, but also that we didn't get the chance to mingle too much before it started, because the relationships between the eight of us would be a key ingredient to the series, and they wanted those early conversations as we got to know each other to be captured on camera.

But we were all very nosy and inquisitive humans, so hanging out of our hotel windows to socialise with each other became the norm. By the time we arrived at the TV 'camp-site', bonds had been formed and friendships were already blossoming. We met the hosts, Holly Willoughby and Lee Mack, when we arrived on site, and Lee asked me how we were getting on.

'Well, there are no dickheads,' I said, optimistically.

'It's usually the one who says that who is the dickhead,' he joked. I think.

The other seven in the tent were Professor Green, the Hackney-born rapper; scouser Chelcee Grimes, a song-writer, performer and footballer; Alfie Boe, the opera singer from Fleetwood; Dianne Buswell, the Australian flame-haired dancer from *Strictly Come Dancing*; Owain Wyn Evans, a young Welsh weatherman and presenter whose twenty-four-hour drumming session for Children in Need had recently earned him a status close to that of national treasure; Tamzin Outhwaite, the London-born actress who had shot to fame playing Mel in *EastEnders* in the late nineties, and who had been acting in big TV and stage shows ever since; and Patrice Evra, the French World Cup-winning footballer, who had spent seven enormously successful years at Manchester United. We were a diverse

and very well-selected group. I had met Chelcee briefly at
the 2019 Women's World Cup, and I had interviewed Patrice
a couple of times, but that was the extent of my previous
encounters with any of the others.

They were all people who had excelled in their chosen
fields; everyone had worked hard to get to where they were,
and there was a mutual appreciation of the others' talents and
dedication. Through our conversations over the weeks, there
seemed to be a common recognition that the hours we had
all put into our careers were a large part of our collective
success, but we also knew that chance and luck have a part
to play. Overall, I'd say we were a grateful bunch, and that
helped us to bond.

The narrative of the show was based on Wim's personal story. When he was in his early thirties, his wife had
kissed their four children goodbye, then jumped out of the
window of their eighth-floor flat. She had struggled with
depression and had tried taking antidepressants, but nothing had worked for her and now it was too late for Wim
to save her. Wim, a self-described school dropout, had a
lot on his plate with four children to look after, but he
wanted to try to understand more about his wife's mental
illness. So he went on a journey to understand the mind
and mental health.

For the opening episode, we sat around a campfire as
Wim told us about his wife. The next morning, we were
driven almost three hours to the Ponte Colossus bridge,
a 500-foot-high construction spanning a large canyon at
the top of the Italian Alps. We walked to the middle of
the bridge, where we found Wim hanging off the side. He
told us that during his journey towards understanding his
wife's mental anguish, he had decided he needed to jump
from something very high in order to connect to her pain.

At first, when he tried to jump, the fear had crippled him with anxiety and he couldn't do it. So, using cold water and breathing to release the trauma, he eventually managed to jump off a bridge (while harnessed), and in doing so released some of the pain he was holding. That process took him over a year.

After he'd told us this, he leaned back and said: 'In a few weeks, you will do this.' Then released his hands and jumped off. He fell about 100 feet, and then started to swing under the bridge, still 400 feet off the ground. I would like to tell you that I saw all of this.

I did not.

I was so petrified that I couldn't even look over the side. Worse, I couldn't even stand next to the handrail of the bridge. Voices in my head told me that I would topple over and die if I moved any closer.

I stared at the hosts of the show, Holly and Lee, and willed them to tell us he was joking. I don't actually know what they said next, because all I could think was how much I was regretting saying yes to the show.

I walked back towards our vehicle, known as the Ice Bus, and told Tamzin, 'Well, this is a waste of time for me, because I am *never* doing that.'

'Me neither,' she agreed.

As we walked across the bridge, we saw flowers attached to the railings where a twenty-two-year-old man had taken his life. The bridge is a well-known suicide spot. None of this helped.

There was definitely a division of opinion in the bus on the way home. Half of us couldn't imagine doing the bungee jump, and half were really up for it. For the first time on the trip, the atmosphere became a little fractious. We agreed that this shouldn't cause us to fall out, though, and that we'd try

not to think or talk too much about what was clearly meant
to be a dramatic denouement to the show. Instead, we agreed,
we'd face each challenge as they came.

I am a self-confessed control freak, so the hardest part of
the show at first was not having an agenda. We'd be given a
set of clothes and appropriate footwear, and told to be ready
for a certain time. The producers wanted us to be surprised –
ambushed, even – by the challenges. I hated this feeling,
and consequently spent a lot of time trying to ascertain
information from young runners and junior producers who
I thought might be looser of lip. I'll use this opportunity
to apologise to them and say I hope I haven't put you off
working in TV.

A few days before I had been traumatised by witnessing
the bridge jump, we had entered the campsite by forward-
abseiling down a fifty-foot cliff. I had seen the forward abseil
on shows like *SAS Who Dares Wins* and sitting in the comfort of my own home I had sworn it was something I would
never be able to do. The idea of looking over the edge of a
cliff and seeing the bottom as you descend made my stomach
somersault.

But when actually faced with this challenge, and seeing
how much my new teammates wanted me to do it, I somehow willed myself over. I was so thrilled that I had managed
to achieve the abseil, I naively assumed that the height 'challenges' were finished. *I mean, what could be worse than that?* I
calmly told myself.

A lot, it turned out.

The next day, we were driven a couple of hours to a frozen
lake and asked to jump through a small hole in the ice. I did
it, but struggled to get my breath when I came up. I was
clearly panicking, and felt like a newborn baby finding that
first breath in a most ungainly manner. I realised if I were

to have any hope of getting through the challenges, I would need to focus on the breathing.

Our first breathing session was led by Wim in a cold tent.

Each round of breathing is about sixty to eighty breaths long, followed by a hold of one to three minutes. Wim's style of breathing is deep but continuous, breathing in and out through the mouth, as opposed to yogic breathing, which uses the nose. After two rounds of breathing, I felt myself physically moving with the breath as if my body was coming off the ground. I knew we were being filmed, but I couldn't stop what was happening and I didn't care how it looked. By the fourth round, all of the images in my brain had turned red. I could *see* the blood pumping through me; it was as if I had a view of the inside of my body. My thoughts were dominated by my brother Daniel, my dad and my son Reuben. I couldn't make sense of it, but it was very emotional and I started to cry. It was an incredibly powerful experience, yet I was the most relaxed I have ever been without being asleep.

What happened next was one of the most extraordinary things that has ever happened to me. As the session finished, we sat up and mentally came back into the room. I stood up and looked at Tamzin, and felt an overwhelming rush of love that I knew I had to give her; but it wasn't from me, it was from her mum. I had known Tamzin all of a week at this point. I knew from our chats that her mum had died suddenly in her sixties of an aneurism, but that was all. I had to hug her.

'I am so sorry,' I whispered into her ear, 'but I have to hug you, because I have all this love to give you from your mum.'

Even writing it feels a bit ridiculous. I can't describe to you how powerful it was; I felt euphoric.

Tamzin started to cry. 'I know. She's here,' she said.

I hugged her tightly for ages until the outpouring of love started to slow down.

The rest of the day was a bit of a blur, but I felt strong and calm. Later in the day, Wim called me into his tent to chat. He talked to me about being a powerful woman who had lots on her plate; about letting things go and not always having to be in control. He talked about the trauma that was still inside me from Daniel's death. He really looked into my eyes, and I felt an honest connection with a man who, although he's a bit 'out there', clearly only wants to do good for the world.

Wim's focus is on mental health, and he has worked with scientists to prove that the breathing techniques and ice-cold showers he employs can reduce inflammation in the brain and the body. Inflammation-related diseases (including depression) kill 60–70 million people globally every year, so Wim is a man on a mission.

The TV show had to be entertaining as well as educational, however, as it was due to air prime-time on BBC One, so the challenges were designed to build up in intensity and excitement. In the next height-based challenge, we were asked to perform a yoga pose on top of a 150-foot-high platform.

Just walking out on to the platform would have been a big enough ask for me a few weeks before, but it's incredible how quickly the brain starts to adjust what is normal. Here I was, walking out without hesitation to the end of the board, where I got into my assigned yoga pose, 150 feet above a frozen waterfall.

The ice challenges were also increasing in intensity. Whether it was spending time in an iced barrel, sitting in a frozen lake for nearly seven minutes or daily ice-cold showers, we were obviously building up to something spectacular.

The breathing continued to have a profound effect on me. One day, after I finished, I opened my eyes and said to

Chelcee, who was in the bed across from me, 'Well, that was tremendous,' which made her laugh. But it was, almost like a gentle all-over body orgasm, if such a thing exists. I have never done hallucinogenic drugs, but I can't imagine they'd make you feel any better than breathing with Wim Hof – which is also cheaper, not to mention safer.

On the day of the final ice challenge, which was to swim for four metres under the ice of a frozen lake, I had another powerful experience during the morning breathing session. An image of my dad when he was around twenty-six years old came into my mind. He was pushing me on a swing; I must have been about four. He was laughing and looked so happy and handsome as we played together. The words 'let him go' kept being played in my mind, almost in time with the rhythm of the swing moving forwards and back.

I chatted to Chelcee and Tamzin afterwards. It wasn't difficult to interpret what I had seen in my mind during the breathing. It had been such a long time since I had known that happy, carefree man I saw pushing the swing, and it was an enormous relief to remember that he had once been free of the demons that now seemed to plague his mind. I had known for a while that getting that old smiling Dad back is not my job, nor am I capable of doing it, but after the breathing, I had a sense of lightness and felt reassured that we had done the right thing by him.

Wim had warned us that things can happen under the ice; it is a mirror for many people. And so it proved to be. It was by far the most emotional day we'd experienced as a group.

The weather had turned quite nasty, and after a week of big blue skies and sunshine, we suddenly had snow, wind and a drop in temperature. As we each waited for our turn, standing in our skimpy swimsuits on the ice, we shivered with nerves and the biting wind. For me, the experience was incredibly freeing, and I didn't panic apart from when I first jumped in and couldn't find the guide rope, but once it was in my hand, I swam the full length of four metres. I could see the light from the other hole in the ice the whole time I was under, and I felt safe. It was so cold, however, that when I got out I thought I had hit my head, I assumed I must be concussed, because I couldn't see anything for about thirty seconds. One of the symptoms of insidious hypothermia is a loss of consciousness. I was shaking and my teeth chattered; I was ushered into position to be interviewed, and Holly Willoughby kindly told me that I had a bogey dangling from my right nostril. Although I was more concerned about getting my eyesight back, I thanked her. Nobody needed to see that.

For my Hof campmates, the experiences were not uniformly positive. Chelcee described seeing her five-year-old self under the water, and told us how being with her younger self had made her feel more alone and vulnerable than she ever had in her life. As a four-year-old, she told us, she had been in the passenger seat of her father's car when he was shot through the window. He had died a year later. The swim seemed to leave her traumatised for quite a while. The beautiful, confident young woman I had got to know over the past few weeks was temporarily broken.

Patrice was the alpha male of the group, yet he was so immobilised with fear that he couldn't attempt the swim, and he got out of the water in tears without having gone under the ice. Just a few days before, he had sat in the same lake for sixteen minutes while most of us got out in under ten, but for Patrice, deciding not to do the swim was a freeing experience. It was the first time in his life that he had said no, that he hadn't felt the need to push himself beyond what his mind wanted to do. He valued that more than any of the other more obvious heroics he'd performed on the show.

Tamzin smashed her head on the ice and was disorientated and shocked for a while afterwards, with a massive egg on her forehead. Dianne was gripped by fear and close to a panic attack; she didn't feel good enough, she said, which was something that had plagued her through her younger dancing years. Stephen (Professor Green) said he saw only darkness under the ice. Owain and Alfie completed the challenge with less drama, but were still profoundly affected by it.

The journey home was a quiet and contemplative one. The following day was the grand finale to the show: the bridge jump. It seemed we all still had a lot to work through. Could we do it? Did we want to do it? Did we have a reason to do it?

Chelcee turned her negative day under the ice around quite quickly. She was determined that the little girl she had met under there should be freed, and that the bridge jump would be her way of showing that little girl that she was brave and not alone. I had no doubt she would complete the challenge, and although I was inspired by her, I was still struggling to commit to the jump myself. I wanted to find a reason to want to do it. Tamzin, Owain and Dianne were in a similar boat to me. I felt confident the other three blokes would jump. Alfie and Patrice had smashed all the height challenges, and Stephen was one of those men who quietly went about his business, ticking off experiences and pushing himself in an understated way.

A night's sleep had not helped me to make a decision, and as we made the long bus journey to the Ponte Colossus, I still didn't feel I could do it. We walked across, and as we approached the jump-off point, I didn't fancy my chances of even making it over the side to get into position. If I couldn't climb over, then I definitely couldn't jump.

Eventually, we were positioned 500 feet below the jump with the show's hosts, Holly and Lee, the tension mounting as we were told, one by one, who would jump next. When your name was called out, you were driven back to the bridge, which was about a ten-minute car ride up the winding mountain road. At the top, Wim and the safety team were waiting to set you on your way.

Chelcee was chosen to go first and had no hesitation. She was determined, clear and jumped, seemingly with ease, holding on to a clear reason why she was tackling this enormous challenge. When she came down, her elation was tangible. She was a different woman from the one we had seen emerge from the ice twenty-four hours before.

Dianne followed her up. By contrast, she was nervous and unsure, and spent about twenty minutes procrastinating. She threatened to give up, and almost climbed back over a few times; I was pretty sure she'd back out. Then suddenly, her mind shifted and from the vantage point below, we looked up and saw her turquoise costume and flame-red hair flying through the sky 500 feet above us as she let out a delighted scream.

It was such an inspiring sight; Dianne was even more petrified of heights than me, and there she was, swinging from a bridge. I felt braver and bolder just watching her. As I watched my new friends grappling with their fears and emotions, I felt a swell of pride and love.

Suddenly, I had my reason. I felt I had let go of many things over the weeks we had been in Italy, so I didn't need to release anything as I jumped. Instead, I was motivated by the incredible love I have for my family. They had supported my trip and been at the centre of my thoughts the whole time, and so it seemed fitting that I would do this for them. I knew they'd be so proud at how far I had come in tackling my fear of heights, along with what I had subjected myself to in the cold water, and how much work I had done to process and understand the challenges that had affected my life and the trauma that had lain buried.

Once I had decided to do it, I was desperate to hear my name called out – I just wanted to get on with it – but I had a long, nervous wait. Eventually, my name was called; I was to be the penultimate jumper. I got up on the bridge just in time to see my new buddy Tamzin calmly jumping off, looking almost regal, and then I was rigged up in my own harness. The bridge looked like a film set, with expensive cameras everywhere, a drone flying overhead and lots of crew on walkie-talkies.

The brilliant team from Remote Trauma talked me through the safety aspects and, in their no-nonsense way, told me what would happen when it was my turn. The harness could withstand the weight of a Range Rover, so it could easily withstand my 62kg frame. I took some deep Wim-inspired breaths and walked to the start position. Wim was waiting for me, decked out in his famous colourful kaftan and headband, on hand to help with the mental preparation. We chatted all sorts of nonsense – on my part, anyway.

I really don't know what I said. I think I told him that I loved him.

I felt calm and ready. I went to climb over the bridge and heard a clinking metal sound. The lovely bloke from Doncaster who had fitted my harness, pulled me back over.

'What's that noise?' I asked.

'It's the safety carabiner . . . you opened it with your foot. Don't worry, we'll put it back together.'

Jesus Christ, how the hell did I manage that?

I am so clumsy that this will come as no surprise to my friends and family. It meant at that moment, I only had one carabiner between me and the 500-foot drop.

When everything was ready, I climbed over the edge, moving carefully, placing one foot at a time on the other side of the very narrow pebble-dashed ledge, which was just three inches wide. I listened to the instructions; I had to lean back and let the rope hold my weight, so that the only part of me that was still touching the bridge were the tips of my toes. After a few minutes of chatting a bit more nonsense to Wim and the safety guy, I tucked my head so my chin was on my chest, and I jumped.

It seemed to take for ever.

I had counted three seconds with the others I had watched from down below.

Oh god.

It's me.

I'm the one who got the broken cord.

I mean, there was bound to be one, right?

My eyes were shut, so I was totally disorientated, but I was sure this was taking way too long.

Surely the next thing would be me hitting the ground in the cold, icy stream 500 feet below.

Then the cord jolted, ever so slightly, and I changed direction.

Thank god. I wasn't dead.

I was swinging under the bridge, back and forth, a bit like the child I had seen being pushed by her dad when I did the breathing session.

I smiled for the cameraman above me, who was nestled on the underside of the bridge, and sang the Tom Petty song 'Free Fallin'', which had become a camp anthem over the previous week.

I shut my eyes again and enjoyed the ride.

Then, once the swinging slowed down, it was time to be hoisted back up. Like a net full of cod being pulled out of the North Sea, they wound me up until I was able to grab hold of and climb up a flimsy-looking plastic ladder for the last twenty feet or so.

That was the worst bit.

Then I was bundled over the bridge and back on to the safety of the road.

It was over.

I haven't experienced relief and joy like that for a very long time. I was ecstatic, and I couldn't stop smiling.

I knew my little gang would be proud of me, but more importantly, perhaps, I was proud of me.

In the end, seven of the eight of us jumped. Professor Green got to the other side and into the jump position, but decided at the last second that he wouldn't do it. His father had taken his own life by jumping and for the Prof, who was himself a new dad to a little boy, not jumping was a more profound message for his own son.

I was really moved by him and his decision.

What happened in such a short period of time in Italy with regard to our fears, inhibitions and decision-making was something quite extraordinary to witness. For me, the best part about how we all managed to shift our mindsets and become open to change was that it was largely achieved through the use of breathing and cold showers. Simple things, that can be done by anyone, anytime, anywhere.

It cost nothing, but changed a lot.

I don't need to tell you about the rise in depression and mental illness in the Western world. We are living in a time when teenagers are displaying anxiety levels as high as the average patient in a 1950s mental asylum. If learning about breathing and the benefits of cold-water therapy can help us deal with the mental stresses of modern life, then I am proud to espouse it. On top of that, in doing the show, I met seven awesome people who made me laugh loads and taught me a lot.

And if this is 'half-time' in my life, then I reckon those three weeks in Italy were the perfect preparation for the second half.

Epilogue

You are so lovely to have read this book. Or maybe you have just swung straight to the 'up-sum' so you can pretend that you have.

I have tried to make a bit of sense of my life, and I'm sure a few of the things that have happened to me might also have happened to you (perhaps not the Rose of Tralee bit; I appreciate that's quite niche). Maybe you handled them differently, or maybe you are still figuring them out. One of the best things about getting older is the realisation that getting things wrong is OK; in fact, being wrong can lead to a better version of getting it right. One of the worst things, no matter what anyone tells you, is getting crepey skin on your knees and elbows, even though you regularly moisturise.

We all know, but don't always remember, that the things that really matter are your family, friends and your health. Never take that last one for granted – ever.

People come and go in our lives. We all have friends we lose contact with and extended family we don't talk to very often, but each of us is a product of all of those moments and influences, and even the most fleeting of conversations with a stranger can have an impact. Being open to change and new experiences keeps our minds agile and renews hope.

And for all the sadness and grief that we experienced when Daniel died, it was through my mum's example that we never lost hope.

I am blessed to have a mum with enormous positivity. This gave us kids a deep well of self-belief, backed up by her 'go get 'em' attitude – which she still holds in buckets at the age of seventy-two. She also gave me 'difficult' hair, which makes me look like a frizzy-tired poodle when I get caught in the rain or humidity, so it isn't all great.

You know I'd have loved to have had a fuller relationship with my dad. When he was shown the chapter about him, he didn't talk to me for a bit, which highlights that this continues to be a complicated relationship. But one I won't give up on. Of course, our parents won't always be the ones we think we deserve at times, that's the deal, but ninety-nine per cent of the time, they will be doing the very best they can. (That one goes out to Reuben and Lois Logan of Buckinghamshire.)

My kids have enjoyed a lot of great perks through my job (mainly tickets to major sporting events), but they have also had to deal with some pretty unusual situations, such as press intrusion in their home, being followed to school by a paparazzi photographer and watching people on social media giving their mum a rough ride.

I don't think my being in the public eye is the most challenging thing for my kids, though; I think the fact that I am (apparently) 'old-fashioned' and 'out of touch' is more annoying.

'You'd never survive as a teenager in 2022,' Reuben tells me regularly, with a look of bewildering sorrow. I have an uncanny ability to make them cringe that comes only marginally behind Kenny's, who once accidentally wolf-whistled Reuben's girlfriend when she came downstairs looking stunning in a pretty party dress.

'That was a compliment,' Kenny tried to explain to the poor girl.

'In 1998, maybe,' Reuben schooled him, rolling his eyes for the 2,657th time that week.

Navigating the life of teenagers is one of the biggest and best challenges I have ever experienced, and in a few more years, I will know how it went. I'm holding on tight that the ROI (return on investment) will be positive. By that, I mean that they will still want to spend one week on holiday with us each year; that's Kenny's measure of success. I'll take happy, healthy, kind people who might also choose to use napkins in their own homes. Suffice to say, those three humans are my greatest inspiration and biggest loves. Thank god I walked into the K Bar in Chelsea that Saturday night in 1999.

Sport has taught me so much over the course of my life, and as much as I love winning (I still can't seem to get rid of my competitive streak, even as I approach fifty), I think I have always preferred the journey to the destination. On that journey, I have been given guidance by some fantastic teachers and coaches – not just in sport, but also in school, work and life. There are many mentors and wise folk who have been there for me when I needed another lesson or a push to get back on track. They have also helped me realise the power and joy of paying it forward and helping others. I try to reply to young people who ask for help on social media or those who write asking for tips on how to get into the broadcasting industry. Maybe this book will help them see that there is no perfect way to forge a career, or even a life, but if you keep working hard, turn up on time and complete your tasks with a smile you have a chance of catching a break.

Acknowledgements

Earlier in this book, when I was talking about losing touch with Basia, my friend from middle school, I said that maybe I was scared of really committing to friendships because we were for ever on the move as children.

Somewhere along the way I changed because when I look at the great women I keep close now, they have come from many different periods of my life: Kerry N, Kirsty G, Mel C, Charlotte G, Viva S, Jane S, Kate S, Billie S, Katie D, and my gorgeous sister Louise, whose love and support is boundless. Even though I don't see all of you, all of the time, when we meet we click, and your influence on me goes on, so thank you for being wise, funny and caring friends.

To my sailing sisters, how lucky was I to be pulled into your coven when I was floundering in new surroundings? The friendship gods smiled on me that day, proof that we are never too old to make friends for life.

My twenty-three-year-old mum pushed me out as her first born and I weighed more than nine pounds, so apologies for that, Mum. Thanks for being fabulous, glamorous you and for always believing in us, which is the greatest gift you could ever give a child.

My super-agent, Holly B: you are fam. Liz B, you'll keep my

career going another ten years, you are an artist. Amanda H at YM&U, you made me carry on writing when I was crying and thought I was done, and nobody ever looked better in a black polo-neck on our Zoom meetings.

It takes a village to get me on TV. If you have ever given me a facial, I love you. Zoe and Maxine, you deserve medals for long service – twenty-five years and counting. Charlotte, as well as appearing in the funny and wise women list, you are also the best at what you do.

I am fortunate enough to have some absolutely cracking men in my life: you are more than husbands of mates or men I happened to have worked with – I think you know who you are so thanks for being the best allies. I want women to thrive in every area of life, but we need each other to grow for that to happen and I have been lucky or maybe subliminally sought out some of the best men as friends and colleagues.

Thank you Kevin L (body), Ed P (mind) and Wendy M (soul), you helped to fix me.

Jordan, my little brother, I think you had it toughest of all of us, but you are a fighter. I love you loads and you have taught me more than you'll ever know.

This writing journey started with Zoe and ended with Gina and Jillian, and along the way some super women from Little, Brown have whipped me into shape – thank you for the lessons and your patience with my technical ineptitude. Nicky Johnston, you captured me brilliantly for the cover, you are a master.

If you have given me help along the way and I didn't name-check you directly, it's not because I don't value you. It's because I am holding you back for *The Second Half*.

And Kenny, this book would not have happened without your incredible energy and belief in me and the endless cups of tea, even though I am a coffee drinker. Thank you.